The Congressional Experience

TRANSFORMING AMERICAN POLITICS
Lawrence C. Dodd, Series Editor

Dramatic changes in political institutions and behavior over the past three decades have underscored the dynamic nature of American politics, confronting political scientists with a new and pressing intellectual agenda. The pioneering work of early postwar scholars, while laying a firm empirical foundation for contemporary scholarship, failed to consider how American politics might change or to recognize the forces that would make fundamental change inevitable. In reassessing the static interpretations fostered by these classic studies, political scientists are now examining the underlying dynamics that generate transformational change.

Transforming American Politics brings together texts and monographs that address four closely related aspects of change. A first concern is documenting and explaining recent changes in American politics—in institutions, processes, behavior, and policymaking. A second is reinterpreting classic studies and theories to provide a more accurate perspective on postwar politics. The series looks at historical change to identify recurring patterns of political transformation within and across the distinctive eras of American politics. Last and perhaps most importantly, the series presents new theories and interpretations that explain the dynamic processes at work and thus clarify the direction of contemporary politics. All of the books focus on the central theme of transformation—transformation in both the conduct of American politics and in the way we study and understand its many aspects.

TITLES IN THIS SERIES

The Congressional Experience

A VIEW FROM THE HILL

David E. Price

Westview Press

BOULDER • SAN FRANCISCO • OXFORD

Transforming American Politics

Cover photo by Chuck Liddy, Durham *Herald-Sun*. Used by permission.

Copyright © 1992 by Westview Press, Inc.

Published in 1992 in the United States of America by Westview Press, Inc., 5500 Central Avenue, Boulder, Colorado 80301-2877, and in the United Kingdom by Westview Press, 36 Lonsdale Road, Summertown, Oxford OX2 7EW

Library of Congress Cataloging-in-Publication Data
Price, David Eugene.
  The congressional experience : a view from the hill / David E. Price.
    p. cm.—(Transforming American politics)
  Includes bibliographical references and index.
  ISBN 0-8133-1157-8. — ISBN 0-8133-1156-X (pbk.)
  1. Price, David Eugene. 2. Legislators—United States—Biography.
3. United States. Congress. House—Biography. 4. Politics,
Practical—North Carolina. 5. Politics, Practical—United States.
I. Title. II. Series.
E840.8.P65A3 1992
328.73′092—dc20
[B]   92-13949
                                                                   CIP

Printed and bound in the United States of America

The paper used in this publication meets the requirements
of the American National Standard for Permanence of Paper
for Printed Library Materials Z39.48-1984.

10   9   8   7   6   5   4   3   2   1

FOR LISA, KAREN, AND MICHAEL

Contents

Tables and Figures

Acknowledgments

To write a book in the midst of congressional service is an improbable undertaking, and I am indebted to many people for their help and encouragement. I would never have considered such a project without the urging of series editor Larry Dodd, and the many hours that he subsequently spent critiquing the manuscript helped me immensely. Gene Conti, Don DeArmon, Paul Feldman, Ferrel Guillory, and Mac McCorkle each read all or most of the manuscript and offered valuable suggestions for improvements. For help with specific chapters, I am indebted to Saul Shorr, Mark Mellman, and Ed Lazarus (Chapter 2); Gay Eddy, Joan Ewing, John Maron, and Rachel Perry (Chapter 8); and Robert Seymour (Chapter 9).

An earlier version of Chapter 6 appeared in *Challenges to Party Government* (Carbondale: Southern Illinois University Press, 1992); I am grateful to the editors of that volume, John White and Jerome Mileur, and to David Rohde for their suggestions. Chapter 10 is adapted from my Sorenson Lecture of February 13, 1990, at the Yale University Divinity School. I wish to thank Andrew Sorenson for his sponsorship of this annual lecture and Dennis Thompson for his helpful comments. I am also indebted to Don DeArmon, Paul Feldman, and Michael Malbin, who encouraged and helped me to pause and record my early impressions of the House of Representatives. Bill Keech and Barbara Sinclair made certain I saw relevant current work in political science. For help in tracking down and assembling data, I thank Roger Davidson, Walter Oleszek, David Beck, Maria McIntyre, and Kevin Levy.

Sally Maddison has been the keeper of the manuscript, producing endless revisions with extraordinary competence and good humor. It has also been a pleasure to work with the staff at Westview Press: Senior Production Editor Libby Barstow, Copy Editor Joan Sherman, Editorial Assistant Rachel Quenk, and Acquisitions Editor Jennifer Knerr, who saw the potential of this project at an early point and offered encouragement throughout.

Finally, I owe far more than the usual acknowledgment to my wife, Lisa, and our children, Karen and Michael. I am thinking not merely of their patience with the diversion and preoccupation this book occasioned but also of their role in the story it tells. Their efforts have made my "congressional experience" possible, and their attitudes have made it a positive experience for our family. The dedication of this volume is only a token of my indebtedness and gratitude to them.

David E. Price

1

Introduction

On November 4, 1986, I was elected to the U.S. House of Representatives from the Fourth District of North Carolina, a five-county area that includes the cities of Raleigh, Chapel Hill, and Asheboro. Many thoughts crowded in on me on election night, but one of the most vivid was of that spring evening in 1959 when I had first set foot in the part of North Carolina I was now to represent. At the time, I was a student at Mars Hill, a junior college in the North Carolina mountains a few miles from my home in the small town of Erwin, Tennessee. I had taken an eight-hour bus ride from Mars Hill to Chapel Hill to be interviewed for a Morehead Scholarship, a generous award that subsequently made it possible for me to attend the University of North Carolina (UNC). I was awed by the university and nervous about the interview; thinking back on some of the answers I gave the next morning ("Would you say Cecil Rhodes was an imperialist?" "I believe so"), I still marvel that I won the scholarship. But I did, and the next two years were among the most formative and exciting of my life.

I went north in 1961 to divinity school and eventually to graduate school and a faculty appointment in political science at Yale University. But the idea of returning to the Raleigh–Durham–Chapel Hill area of North Carolina exerted a continuing tug on me, particularly as I decided on a teaching career and thought about where I would like to put down personal and academic roots. Fortunately, my wife, Lisa, also found the idea agreeable, despite her budding political career as a member of New Haven's Board of Aldermen. Therefore, when I received an offer to join the political science faculty at Duke University and also to help launch the university's Institute of Policy Sciences and Public Affairs, I jumped at the opportunity. In mid-1973, we moved with our two children—Karen, three, and Michael, one—to Chapel Hill. Though we were delighted with the community and the job and saw the move as a long-term one, I would have been incredulous at the suggestion that within fourteen years I would represent the district in Congress.

The Fourth District is relatively compact by North Carolina standards (see Fig. 1.1), yet it displays an extraordinary economic, social, and political diversity. Some 61 percent of the population lives in Raleigh, the state

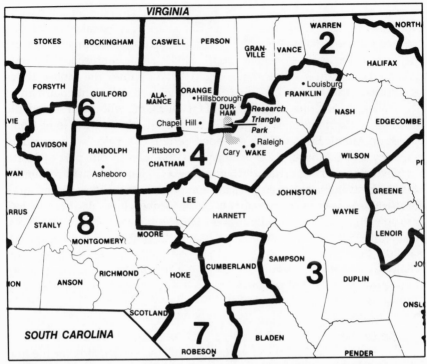

FIGURE 1.1   Map of North Carolina's Fourth Congressional District.

capital, and surrounding Wake County. Wake still ranks fourth among North Carolina counties in tobacco grown, and many of its small towns, like those of neighboring Franklin and Chatham counties, are rural and agricultural in outlook. Textiles and other traditional industries are still important, especially in the western part of the district. Nonetheless, the area has experienced rapid and diverse economic growth, most notably in the high-tech Research Triangle Park (which the Fourth District shares with the Second) and also in a variety of small businesses and midsized manufacturing firms. Raleigh, Cary, and Chapel Hill have become highly suburbanized, with an influx of Research Triangle employees, young professionals, and upscale retirees. Blacks comprise 19 percent of the district's population, and economic growth and diversification have brought small but increasing numbers of citizens of Chinese, Indian, Latin American, and other ethnic backgrounds to the area. Politically, the district is 60 percent Democratic by registration, but with a solidly Republican enclave in Randolph County and widespread split-ticket voting elsewhere, it has frequently gone both ways in national and statewide elections.

Several of the district's counties were represented in the distant past by Nathaniel Macon (1791–1815), North Carolina's only Speaker of the U.S. House of Representatives. For the first two-thirds of the twentieth century, the eastern part of the present Fourth District was represented by only two men: Edward W. Pou (1901–1934), who chaired the House Rules Committee, and Harold D. Cooley (1934–1967), flamboyant chairman of the House Agriculture Committee. Carl Durham, who represented the district's western counties from 1939 until 1961, chaired the Joint Committee on Atomic Energy. Such extended periods of service, with attendant seniority in the House, have become less common in our part of North Carolina since the departure of Durham and Cooley. The main reason for this has been the heightened partisan competition that has produced more frequent turnovers in congressional seats. Members have also become less intent on House careers, sometimes resigning to seek other political offices. And the drawing and redrawing of district lines following the Supreme Court's reapportionment decisions have destabilized traditional electoral coalitions and rendered elections less predictable.[1] When I was sworn in on January 6, 1987, I became the Fourth District's third representative in as many terms.

By the time I ran for Congress, I had amassed a good deal of political experience. Sen. E. L. ("Bob") Bartlett (D.-Alaska) hired me as a summer intern in 1963, and I returned to his staff as a legislative aide for the four succeeding summers, eventually doing interviews out of his office for a doctoral dissertation on the Senate. After moving back to North Carolina, I worked actively in local politics, managed a couple of congressional districts (including the Fourth) in Jimmy Carter's 1976 presidential campaign, and took leaves from Duke in 1980 and 1984 to serve as executive director and then chairman of the North Carolina Democratic Party. But these were diversions, albeit increasingly serious ones, from a primary career in teaching and research. By 1986, I had studied and taught and written about Congress, among other subjects, for some twenty years.

Among some voters—and occasionally among congressional colleagues—my academic background has represented a barrier to be overcome. But usually it has not. My district, it is claimed, has the highest number of Ph.D.'s per capita of any comparable area in the country. Certainly, with eleven institutions of higher education and the kind of people who work in the Research Triangle Park, I have some remarkably literate constituents. I sometimes reflect ambivalently on this as I contemplate the piles of well-reasoned letters on every conceivable issue that come into my office. Yet the electoral advantages are considerable. During my first campaign, we polled to test public reactions to my academic affiliation and background, expecting to downplay them in the campaign.

Instead, we found highly positive associations and ended up running a television ad that featured me in the classroom!

It was, I suppose, in light of my dual background as an academic and a political practitioner that I was asked to contribute some reflections on my first term in office to the 1989 edition of *Congress Reconsidered*.[2] I was reluctant at first, pressed for time and uncertain of the value of the exercise, but I ended up being challenged by the idea of giving an account of congressional operations that would combine personal experience with at least a modest effort at the sort of generalization and analysis characteristic of political science. My own story and the stories of other people and events would be told not mainly for their own sake but as a way of showing how the U.S. Congress works. The article that I produced, greatly expanded and supplemented, forms the core of the present book, which includes chapters on getting elected and reelected, adjusting to life in Congress and finding a niche in the House, policy entrepreneurship, party operations, the budget process, and serving the district.

Certain additional topics that were familiar to me in their academic incarnation—the place of religion in politics, governmental ethics, and the critique of Congress as an institution—have taken on particular interest during my years in office, and I will, in later chapters, offer some reflections on them. Unfortunately, in much of what now passes for discussion on these themes, ideas are used more as weaponry than as a means to enlightenment. I cannot begin to take all that on here, but I will try to nudge these discussions in a more productive direction.

The period covered here—from my election in 1986 through early 1992, midway in my third term—was a contentious and challenging time for Congress and for the country. It spanned the waning of Ronald Reagan's presidency, weakened by the Iran-contra affair, and the advent of George Bush's administration. It saw a new House Speaker, Jim Wright, put his distinct imprint on the 100th Congress (1987–1988) and then resign in 1989 amid ethics charges. It was a time of phenomenal change and great hopefulness in world politics, from the collapse of international communism, the reunification of Germany, and the dissolution of the Soviet Union to the allied military victory in the Persian Gulf and the advent of Middle East peace talks. But at home, it was a period of tepid economic performance and, in 1990 and 1991, a deepening recession. The financial collapse of the savings and loan (S & L) industry and the indictment of numerous high-fliers from the financial world signaled that the excesses of the 1980s were coming home to roost. It was a period when Republicans controlled the executive branch and Democrats the legislative—a time of repeated veto battles and other confrontations and of a deepening federal budget crisis.

It was also a period when the reputation of Congress, never Americans' favorite political institution, reached alarming levels of public disapproval. Media portrayals were often harsh, and politicians ranging from the president to House members themselves often ran for office by running against the institution. Much of the criticism, unfortunately, took the form of indiscriminate and highly partisan "Congress-bashing."[3] And this, in turn, often discouraged genuine accountability by crowding out more reasoned and relevant judgments about individual and institutional performance. My hope in this book is to encourage and facilitate more useful assessments, by conveying a realistic sense of how Congress works and by beginning to raise some of the right evaluative questions.

But first things first. Remembering the dictum of former House Speaker Tip O'Neill that "all politics is local,"[4] I will begin with an account of how I came to run for Congress and managed, with the help of many, many people, to get elected.

2

Getting Elected

The University of North Carolina at Chapel Hill has an elaborate student government and a tradition of lively campus politics. The years I was there, 1959–1961, were particularly active ones because of the civil rights movement. The sit-ins that began at a Greensboro lunch counter in February 1960 rapidly spread across the state, and many students became involved in efforts to desegregate restaurants, theaters, and other public accommodations. The movement awakened my political consciousness and channeled my campus involvement. I was president of the Baptist Student Union at a time when campus religious groups were perhaps the most active proponents of change, and my main achievement as a member of the student legislature was the narrow passage of a resolution urging Chapel Hill merchants to desegregate their businesses.

I knew a number of campus politicians who were reasonably certain that they would someday be governor, senator, or, at the very least, a member of Congress. I did not regard such expectations as realistic for myself, and, in any case, I had other career interests I wanted to pursue. But those years were politically formative in a number of respects. I began to realize that, by conviction, I was a Democrat, despite an East Tennessee background that had predisposed me in the opposite direction. I came to admire political leaders like Adlai Stevenson, John F. Kennedy, and North Carolina's young governor, Terry Sanford. Most of the new ideas and responses to social problems seemed to be coming from Democrats; the Eisenhower-era Republican Party, by contrast, seemed cautious and complacent. Like others in my student generation, I discovered that communities and political institutions could respond positively to pressures for change—a far different experience from those of the Vietnam and Watergate generations to follow. A spark was lit that later led me, whatever else I was doing, to involve myself in local politics and community affairs.

During my years of graduate study and teaching in New Haven, those involvements ranged from canvassing for the Johnson-Humphrey ticket in 1964 to returning to Tennessee in 1970 in order to organize campus groups and get-out-the-vote operations in Sen. Albert Gore's last reelection campaign to helping my wife win a seat on the New Haven Board of

7

Aldermen.[1] On returning to North Carolina in 1973, she and I immediately became active with the Democratic Party. Today, when someone gives me the line about how closed and conspiratorial politics is, I sometimes tell them about our first party precinct meeting, less than a month after arriving in Chapel Hill. My wife emerged from that meeting as precinct chairwoman and I as a member of the precinct committee—an outcome that said more about the state of local party organization than about anything we said or did.

I had already ventured into North Carolina politics from afar the year before, working with a friend from the Gore campaign to lay the groundwork for a "Muskie for President" primary effort in the state. I still regard the faltering of Sen. Edmund Muskie's campaign in 1972 as an especially unfortunate and fateful failure, considering the directions in which George McGovern's nomination took the Democratic Party and Richard Nixon's subsequent election took the country. In any event, it was collaborators from the Muskie campaign who recruited me in 1976, after I had permanently returned to North Carolina, to manage two congressional districts (including the one I now represent) in Jimmy Carter's bid for the presidency. That, in turn, led to my being asked to take a year's leave from my teaching position at Duke University in 1980 to serve as the North Carolina Democratic Party's executive director. This tour of duty put me in the thick of statewide politics; it was also the beginning of a close relationship with state senator Russell Walker of Asheboro, who was serving as state party chairman and who has been my most valued mentor and role model in politics.

During these years, I also became a friend and political ally of North Carolina's governor, Jim Hunt, a young progressive whose main causes were education and economic development. Hunt also took an active hand in party affairs and, in 1981, was named by the Democratic national chairman to head the party's Commission on Presidential Nomination— a body charged with undertaking a "complete review" of the nomination process and devising needed changes in party rules.[2] Hunt recruited me as his staff director. The assignment struck me as both politically important and academically interesting, offering an opportunity—realized only in part—to alter the "reformed" Democratic presidential nomination process in ways that might restore some of the strength lost by the organized party and its convention. What was far less clear at the time was how this stint in Washington and the acquaintances struck up with party leaders might prove useful should I someday decide to run for office myself.

Such possibilities were still far from my mind when Hunt asked me to take another leave in 1984 to return to the state Democratic Party as a full-time professional chairman. I was in no mood to resist for this was the event we had all been waiting for. This was the year of the marathon

Senate race between Hunt and incumbent Sen. Jesse Helms, the television commentator–turned–politician who had become the Senate's most visible champion of right-wing causes. Many had thought, quite justifiably, of the 1970 race between Gore and William Brock as a momentous one with national implications, but it paled in comparison to the Hunt-Helms contest. The 1984 race produced expenditures of $26.4 million—Senator Helms's $16.9-million campaign was the most expensive Senate campaign in American history until he broke his own record in 1990—and focused national and international attention on North Carolina. Our state party spent an unprecedented $2 million and organized a massive voter-contact and mobilization effort.

The results were bitterly disappointing. Helms, aided by Ronald Reagan's national landslide, won with 52 percent of the vote. This "sent a signal throughout the world," the senator told his supporters on election night, "that North Carolina is a God-fearing, conservative state."[3] Behind these code words, I saw a devastating setback for the hopes and aspirations that had first brought me into politics and for the progress we had begun to make in North Carolina.

Our Senate loss was accompanied by the loss of the governorship and of three Democratic House seats as well. One of these was in the Fourth District, where six-term Democratic incumbent Ike Andrews was defeated by Bill Cobey, a former athletic director at the University of North Carolina who had close ties to Helms's organization, the National Congressional Club. I was deeply stung by these defeats and, in the weeks that followed, thought a great deal about how they might be reversed. And for the first time, I seriously entertained the prospect that I might myself be a candidate. By the time spring arrived, I had made my decision: I was running for Congress.

THE FIRST CAMPAIGN

It was my work as state party chairman that first led others to think seriously of me—and led me to think of myself—as a potential candidate. The job's traditional elements (organizational work in the counties, fundraising, voter-contact and turnout operations) reached a new level of intensity and put me in touch with hundreds of party activists. And the position attained a new level of public visibility as I held dozens of press conferences and otherwise took the lead in challenging and refuting the opposition. It was no longer a behind-the-scenes job, and the kind of experience and exposure it offered were an ideal preparation for a congressional candidacy.

Still, I had not expected the Fourth District seat to turn over, and it took a while to get comfortable with the idea that I might run myself, rather than assume a supporting role for others, or that politics might become my full-time vocation, rather than a sporadic engagement. Of immense help was the fact that my wife, Lisa, became more and more enthused at the idea. Her political interests had always been strong: She grew up in a family of New Deal Democrats in the Washington suburbs; her college experience with civil rights was similar to my own; and she was a social worker in a War-on-Poverty job training agency when I met her during one of my Washington summers. She had been elected to the Board of Aldermen in New Haven and had shared my political interests in North Carolina.

To run for Congress in what was certain to be an expensive and difficult race gave us both pause, and I had seen enough political families to know that I would never run without my wife's full support. We had searching conversations with friends and family and two congressional couples whom we respected. The decision was made easier by the fact that our children were now teenagers and increasingly independent and that I had earned a sabbatical year at Duke; this would let me draw half my salary and (barely) get by financially. But the basic question was whether we *wanted* to do this, knowing how much work and sacrifice it would require but also sensing how exciting and rewarding it could be. Without too much agonizing, we decided that the answer was yes. It was a commitment my wife took very seriously, and, indeed, she has been intensely active, both behind the scenes and in public, in each of my three campaigns.

Our discussions also involved a group of friends who, once the decision to run was made, became the "Wednesday night group"—an inner circle without whom the effort would never have gotten off the ground. We met weekly to discuss campaign strategy, parcel out key contacts and tasks, and bolster one another's morale. This group was a fertile source of campaign ideas, good and bad. (One scheme for bringing attention to my race, mercifully abandoned, would have had me staging a Lawton Chiles–style "walk" from Liberty in the western part of the district to Justice, a community in the east!) Our group included several young attorneys with whom I had been associated in politics, a government affairs official from Duke, and an old college friend and his wife, who was an active local realtor. The campaign manager was Randolph Cloud, a veteran of several local campaigns who had worked with me as get-out-the-vote coordinator for the state party in 1984. We later added a deputy manager, Michelle Smith, who, despite limited political experience, proved to be an exceptionally quick study. This was fortunate for the leadership of the campaign was thrust on her when Cloud left after the primary.

My decision to run was prompted, in part, by the realization that 1986 represented a window of opportunity that might not open again. I knew quite well what the odds were nationally of defeating an incumbent; the general election success rate for incumbents seeking reelection had fallen below 92 percent only once since 1966. But North Carolina had been something of an exception to this pattern: Close contests and incumbent defeats had become fairly common since the 1960s, particularly in those western districts where both parties historically had strong bases and in Piedmont and urban-suburban districts where split-ticket voting was on the increase, with GOP candidates often benefiting from national trends. My district, the Fourth, had displayed considerable volatility—voting for Governor Hunt over Senator Helms by 14,282 votes in 1984, for example, but at the same time giving President Reagan a 46,552-vote margin in his victory over Walter Mondale. Congressman Andrews had lost to Bill Cobey by fewer than 3,000 votes.

The district's volatility and the narrowness of Cobey's win suggested that he could be beaten in 1986. I felt that he had won because of factors peculiar to 1984—the presidential landslide and Andrews's personal vulnerabilities—and that Cobey's beliefs and background put him considerably to the right of modal opinion in our part of the state. The Fourth District was by no means "Helms country," despite the fact that the senator lived in Raleigh. Yet Cobey stood out, even in comparison to the other North Carolina Republican members, in his ties to the Helms organization and in his decision to firmly align himself with the most conservative group of House Republicans, the so-called Conservative Opportunity Society, once he got to Washington. He seemed an uneasy fit for the district and was likely to be especially vulnerable in 1986, his first try for reelection—before he had a chance to fully reap the advantages of incumbency and in a year when there would be no Republican presidential coattails.

In firming up my decision to run, I talked with a number of elected officials and other political leaders in the district, including several who, I thought, might consider running themselves. Some of these had advantages that I lacked, such as living in Wake County (the district's largest), enjoying greater name recognition, having stronger financial ties, and so forth. I learned that a race was out of the question for most of those who came to mind as possible contenders, but I saw few advantages in deferring or holding back and decided to make an early, firm announcement of my intent to run. This I did at the time of the county Democratic conventions in April, over a year before the May 1986 primary. Although this probably helped limit the proliferation of candidates, the primary field still eventually expanded to four. Wilma Woodard, a well-known state senator from Wake County, was generally considered to be the front-runner.

Most members of our Wednesday night group had worked together in the Hunt campaign and had taken from that experience the idea of blending the "old" politics and the "new." We believed strongly in the politics of personal contact; I began to steadily call on people who could be helpful and to attend every party gathering or community function I could find. But we knew that even traditional voter-contact and fundraising functions now required high-tech backup, and we moved early to establish a computer capability and to contract for direct mail services. We also assumed from the beginning—long before we had the money to pay for it—that we would have an extensive media campaign. Hardhitting television ads had come early to North Carolina, thanks largely to Senator Helms and the National Congressional Club, and had reached saturation levels in 1984. Television had been a major factor in Cobey's unseating of Andrews, and we assumed more of the same would be necessary if we were to shake loose the new incumbent.

We decided to seek outside professional assistance in three areas: media, polling, and out-of-district fund-raising. My status as a challenger, with no money and three primary opponents, made me a less than lucrative target for the better-known Washington consultants. But I had some decided prejudices against these operators in any case, stemming from my experience with the Hunt campaign. I had heard far too much pontification from media and polling experts based, it seemed to me, on thin survey data and on a deficient "feel" for the state. If I were ever to run myself, I said at the time, I would want consultants who were "young and lean and hungry and who wanted to win as badly as I did." So we looked to smaller, independent operators who seemed personally compatible and who we thought would give my campaign a great deal of personal attention. Fortunately, we found a team that filled the bill and that was willing to work with us during the lean times with some confidence that better-funded campaigns might follow.

As media consultant we chose Saul Shorr of Philadelphia, whose use of humor and instinct for the clever counterpunch especially appealed to me. For polling we engaged Mark Mellman and Ed Lazarus, who had gotten their start in 1982 as Yale graduate students helping elect Bruce Morrison to Congress and who, by 1985, were well on their way to being established nationally. For fund-raising we chose Linda Davis, a North Carolinian who was successfully free-lancing in Washington as head of her own small consulting firm. This proved to be a compatible team and a durable one as well, holding together through 1986 and subsequent elections.

I maintained my full teaching schedule through the end of 1985 but nonetheless managed to campaign extensively. I scheduled dozens of meetings with political and community leaders, as attested to by two notebooks full of notations from these personal conversations. I rightly considered it a major breakthrough when people such as the preeminent Democratic fund-raiser in my district and a respected black city council member in Raleigh agreed to help me. I also attended countless community functions and visited the small-town business districts and suburban malls, ideally with a local supporter making certain I was introduced around. But a rude awakening came when, in February of 1986, we could finally afford to take our first poll. Despite a year of personal campaigning and considerable prior exposure as state party chairman, my name recognition among Democrats had reached only 11 percent. I was headed for a second-place primary finish.

What changed all that was television. The kind of campaigning one does in small towns and rural areas is not sufficient to reach many people in a growing district like mine—people who may be new to the area, whose community roots do not go deep, whose political contacts are few, and who receive most of their political information through television. Fortunately, four out of my five counties were in a single media market, but the market was the second-most expensive in the state, and my campaign was struggling financially.

By April 1986, we had raised $155,000, a sum that, though quite respectable for a challenger running in a contested primary, is hardly enough to permit an extensive television campaign. I did, however, have some fund-raising advantages. I had more contacts and more credibility in Washington circles than would have been true for most challengers, and I cultivated potential donors carefully, calling on them personally and sending them a steady flow of information about the campaign—particularly any coverage that suggested I might win. Yet these efforts would not pay off with many groups until I had proved myself in the primary. I did receive early endorsements and contributions from a number of labor organizations, which had reasons to oppose both the incumbent and my major primary opponent. An endorsement by Raleigh's major black political organization was critical organizationally but less so financially. Other groups, like doctors and teachers, contributed to my main primary opponent, to whom they felt obligated because of help she had given them in the state legislature. Mainly, the organized groups and political action committees (PACs) simply stayed out of the primary. Their rule of thumb is generally to support incumbents if they have been reasonably receptive to the group's concerns—after all, playing the percentages, it is reasonable for them to expect that the incumbents will survive and that their organization will need to deal with these incumbents in the future. But even those issue-oriented, Democratic-leaning PACs that had good reason to like me and to oppose the incumbent were usually unwilling to help me until I had survived the primary and could show that I had a good chance to win in November.

I have undertaken few ventures as difficult and discouraging as raising money for the primary campaign. Our trademark became "low-dollar" fund-raisers, to which a host or group of sponsors would invite their circle of friends and associates. These events were profitable politically as well as financially, but with net receipts per event of $500 to $2,500, the dollars added up only slowly. (I seldom had the heart to tell sponsors of such events that their labors would underwrite the purchase of *one* prime-time, thirty-second television spot.) We sent mail appeals to party activists and to lists of donors from the 1984 Senate campaign and then periodically resolicited all who had given to that point. I also spent a great amount of time personally approaching potential large contributors, with mixed success. My wife and I shed our inhibitions and contacted our Christmas card lists from years past, our professional colleagues at home and across the country, and far-flung family members. Finally, we did what we had said we would never do—we took out a $45,000 second mortgage on our home.

With all of this, the campaign was able to buy $75,000 worth of television time during the three weeks before the May primary, going some $80,000 in debt. We also spent $20,000 on radio spots, an often underestimated medium that is especially useful for boosting name familiarity (especially when one can play on a name like Price!). Our sixty-second "name familiarity" radio ad mentioned my name no less than fifteen times:

Background: Marching band music throughout.

WOMAN: What's the cheering about?
MAN: Oh . . . Price for Congress.
WOMAN: There's a Price for Congress?
MAN: (Laughing) No . . . not *a* price for Congress—David Price for Congress.
WOMAN: Oh . . . David Price.
MAN: Yeah, David Price. He's putting some real decency back into North Carolina politics.
WOMAN: No mud-slinging or name-calling?
MAN: Uh-uh, not David Price. Just straight talk about the issues . . . like improving education, reducing the federal deficit.
WOMAN: Hey, this Price is going up in my book.
MAN: Come on! Listen to David Price's background. He's been an educator most of his life, like his parents; he was a Morehead Scholar at Carolina, earned a divinity degree and later his Ph.D. in political science.
WOMAN: Sounds priceless.
MAN: David Price teaches government at Duke University. He's a nationally known expert on how Congress works. Price was chairman of North Carolina's Democratic Party and Jim Hunt chose him to direct a national committee to reform the presidential nominating process. He's really experienced!

WOMAN: Hmm? That's quite a Price.
MAN: An honest Price.
WOMAN: David Price . . .
MAN: for Congress.

With limited resources and a need to make a forceful impression in a fluid primary situation, we decided to produce three low-budget television ads. One featured quotes from my recent endorsement by the Raleigh *News and Observer*, the district's most prominent newspaper. The two ads that we ran most heavily showed me talking about one major theme: the need to straighten out North Carolina politics, stop mudslinging, and deal with the real issues again. We knew from polling and from campaign experience that this was a powerful theme, drawing on people's negative memories of the 1984 Senate race and their reactions to the nasty 1986 Senate Republican primary then under way. But it wasn't until the primary results came in that we realized just how right we had been. I received 48 percent of the vote, and Senator Woodard, who polled 32 percent, elected not to call for a runoff.

Fund-raising for the general election was a continuing struggle but one that paid richer dividends. We spent $550,000 in the fall campaign, including $300,000 for television airtime. This permitted a more diversified ad campaign—"soft" biographical spots in September and more forceful, issue-oriented spots in October. Some of these latter ads dealt with the incumbent's record: I knew that I had to take him on directly to give voters sufficient grounds for distinguishing between the two of us, but I also knew that this had to be done very carefully, lest I appear to be violating my own injunctions about getting North Carolina politics on a more positive, issue-based footing. The ads therefore focused on three areas—Social Security, African famine relief, and farm credit—that illustrated the incumbent's isolation from mainstream members of both parties in terms of his roll-call voting and featured me looking into the camera and saying simply that I would have voted differently.

We also could afford more polling after the primary. The most important message the polls conveyed concerned the incumbent's vulnerability: Although he enjoyed considerable personal popularity, there was a sizable gap between the number of voters who recognized his name and those who gave him a high job performance rating or were firmly committed to vote for him. The early "horse race" numbers were inconclusive, primarily measuring the gap in name familiarity, but they did document a narrowing of that gap over the months of the campaign; the incumbent's lead dropped from 21 percentage points in July to 10 points on October 4 and 1 point on October 26. But the only poll that actually showed me ahead was the election itself, when I received 56 percent of the vote—the highest

FIGURE 2.1 Editorial cartoon in September 17, 1986, Raleigh *News and Observer* after Bill Cobey sent his "Dear Christian Friend" letter. Reprinted by permission of *News and Observer.*

percentage by which any challenger in the nation defeated an incumbent in 1986.

Television was, no doubt, the major factor producing this result, but other campaign efforts played a part as well: organizing and personal campaigning in small towns and rural areas, voter-contact and turnout operations undertaken in conjunction with party and other organizations, canvassing and literature drops that utilized hundreds of volunteers and helped raise the campaign's visibility. Cobey was damaged when the press headlined a "Dear Christian Friend" letter he had sent to individuals on a mailing list compiled by the religious Right, encouraging the faithful to support him lest he be replaced by "someone who is not willing to take a strong stand for the principles outlined in the Word of God." Although our polling did not detect any measurable impact from this letter, my surmise is that it helped both by generally raising the visibility of the race (see Fig. 2.1) and by framing a key issue for some groups (for example, white-collar suburbanites) that I very much needed to reach. Finally, of course, we were helped by the year's electoral trends—the absence of presidential coattails and a return to the fold by enough Democrats to produce senatorial victories across the South, including former Governor Terry Sanford's win in North Carolina.

FIGURE 2.2   Election night, 1986. To my right is my nephew, Bob Shepherd, and concealed behind me are my sister, Mary Anne Combs, and her other son, Steven Shepherd. To my left are my wife, Lisa; my brother-in-law, Sam Combs; our son, Michael; our daughter, Karen; my father, Albert Price; Nell Benson, wife of our finance chairman; campaign manager Michelle Smith; and finance chairman Cliff Benson.

I will never forget the exhilaration of election night 1986, and neither will my family and the friends who had lived and breathed the campaign for almost two years (see Fig. 2.2). My father, who had been featured in one of Saul Shorr's best spots, came over from Tennessee to help work the polls and was shocked to be greeted on election night as a television celebrity. We had talked a great deal during the campaign about "recapturing our politics" and "turning North Carolina around," and on that night, it seemed to have happened, dispelling the dark clouds of 1984. We also felt we had succeeded in our announced strategy of combining the old and new politics, integrating traditional organizing techniques and lots of personal campaigning into an effort that was also well financed, professionally managed, and media smart. We felt confident about the future, but if we thought it would be ours without a fight, we had the election night comments of the state Republican chairman to ponder: The Fourth District, he opined, had just elected another one-term congressman!

GETTING REELECTED

I knew that the Republicans were likely to see my seat as a promising target in 1988—my first reelection try, when the presence on the ballot of the presidential and gubernatorial races might be expected to give them an advantage. It became clear by mid-1987 that the most likely challenger was Tom Fetzer, a thirty-three-year-old protégé of senators John East and Jesse Helms who had spent virtually his entire working life as a political operative, including several positions with the National Congressional Club. The more moderate wing of the GOP had apparently agreed not to challenge his nomination. I had mixed feelings about this. My district was relatively unsympathetic to Senator Helms, and a Congressional Club affiliation could, in fact, be used effectively against an opponent. At the same time, I knew what having an opponent from that quarter was likely to mean in terms of the money he could raise and the negative tone of the campaign. As it turned out, I was not to be disappointed on either count.

In the early months of 1987, we retired the $80,000 debt from the previous year and began planning the 1988 effort. Fund-raising was certainly easier as an incumbent, but it was still a struggle, both because of the amounts required—my 1988 campaign eventually cost over $900,000—and because of my district's history of modest giving and the weakness of my ties to potentially large donors. Knowing that the campaign would be long and demanding and not wanting to divert my congressional staff, I recruited as campaign manager an outside professional, Mike Davis, whom I had come to know well when he was deputy manager of Hunt's 1984 campaign. I escaped primary opposition and kept most of my personal appearances in a congressional mode, officially kicking off the campaign only after Labor Day 1988. But, by then, we had held dozens of organizational meetings and fund-raisers, both in the district and in Washington, and campaign headquarters had been open for four months, eventually accommodating a paid staff of seven, in addition to numerous volunteers.

Blessed for the first time with an adequate campaign budget, we produced a series of television spots touting my work on consumer protection, education, home ownership, agriculture, and cutting bureaucratic red tape for constituents. We ran the ads fairly heavily throughout September and October, while carefully planning ways to counter the opposition attack that was sure to come. Fetzer ran rather generic anti-Congress material in September, but we got some clues as to what would follow when the firm conducting his early September poll had the misfortune to call one of our campaign workers, thus providing us a list of the various negative messages that were being tested.

On September 30, we got our answer as to what the thrust of Fetzer's message would be: taxes. The ad he first aired that day went as follows:

ANNOUNCER: Liberal politicians. False promises.

[audio clips from Price appearances in 1986, identified by script on screen]

QUESTIONER: Mr. Price, under what circumstances would you support a federal tax increase?

DAVID PRICE: [1.] I would not support a federal tax increase, and I've said repeatedly that I would not . . .
[2.] I do oppose a tax increase . . .
[3.] We're not going to reduce that deficit by tax increases . . .

ANNOUNCER: False promises. In his first year David Price voted to increase taxes four different times.

[visual: newspaper headline, "Democrats Seek Billions in New Taxes"]

David Price: False Promises. Liberal Votes.

Viewers attentive to past North Carolina campaigns could note certain Congressional Club trademarks in the ad, such as the pseudodocumentary use of snippets, generally out of context, purporting to show not only that the opponent differed on the issue but that he was dissembling and opportunistic.

Our counterpunch was already taped, and within a day, we had it on the air:

ANNOUNCER: In recent days, we've seen TV ads that distort the record of our Congressman, David Price. We know the ads are paid for by the Tom Fetzer Campaign . . .

But *who* is Tom Fetzer?

[script on screen, synchronized with audio]

Tom Fetzer has spent most of his adult life working for Jesse Helms's Congressional Club, or its candidates.
In fact, Fetzer actually *headed* the Club's operations.
We've seen Congressional Club tactics before . . .

The distortions . . .
The negative campaigning . . .
The mudslinging.

[audible stamp of universal "NO" symbol (circle and slash) on these words]

Will we allow ourselves to be "Clubbed" again?

The result: Although my negative ratings went from 9 percent to 15 percent between our early September and early October polls, Fetzer's negatives increased far more, from 12 percent to 31 percent. This pointed up one of Fetzer's strategic mistakes, his failure to give the voters any positive information about himself. By running mainly negative material, first against Congress and then against the incumbent congressman, he failed to identify himself positively and thus left himself vulnerable to my definition. Moreover, his ads served to validate his identification with the Congressional Club and the campaign tactics for which that organization was notorious. Our ads "framed" his ads, so that when viewers saw the latter, they got not only a negative message about me but also a negative impression of him, his associations, and his tactics.

Fetzer aired several variations of his message on taxes in the early weeks of October, a message reinforced by the "no new taxes" pledge featured in George Bush's presidential campaign. As far as I could tell, the allegation that I had voted to "increase taxes four different times" was based on a strained interpretation of a series of budget resolution and "reconciliation" votes (see Chapter 7). By mid-October, Fetzer was relying heavily on ten-second "zingers" that simplified the message even further:

ANNOUNCER: [script on screen synchronized with audio]
How *liberal* is David Price?
He voted to *increase taxes* an average of $700 per family.

Too liberal—that's David Price.

Naturally, I found all this highly frustrating, and my first impulse was to run an ad that set the record straight. We therefore cut a spot that featured me looking into the camera and saying:

I'm David Price. My opponent, Tom Fetzer, is distorting my record.

But the facts are clear. I have never voted to raise your tax rates.

Tom Fetzer is actually criticizing me for supporting a bipartisan deficit reduction agreement that closed tax loopholes and cut spending by more than 36 billion dollars.

President Reagan asked me to vote for it.

Tom Fetzer is assuming voters won't know the difference between increasing taxes and tightening loopholes.

Let's stop the distortion and stick to the facts.

As it turned out, we never ran this ad or any other like it. Despite my impulse and the urgings of supporters to answer my opponent's charges, I became convinced that to run such an ad would be to play into his hands. We would then be debating *his* issue. He might excerpt a clip from my ad and do a response to the response, appearing to refute it. Viewers might then perceive a bewildering array of charges and countercharges that nonetheless seemed somehow to implicate me. And in the meantime, my own positive message would have been lost.

Consequently, we settled on a second "framing" ad, one that rolled a long list of issues down the screen; it reminded viewers that Fetzer had run an almost totally negative campaign, distorting my record, and had not told them where he stood on much of anything. This kept the focus on his campaign tactics while reinforcing the Congressional Club association, without moving the campaign to his chosen turf—taxes. Meanwhile, all through October, we continued to mix in my positive ads on education, housing, and so forth. The strategy worked very well; our late October polls showed my favorability ratings again picking up, and I finished with a 58 percent win.

It was reassuring to me and to those directing my campaign to be able to effectively neutralize the well-financed attack ads that we had known were coming. Our confidence had been shaken by the failure of the Hunt campaign to mount an effective defense in 1984 and by Michael Dukakis's stunning helplessness against George Bush's prison furlough/pledge of allegiance campaign in 1988. But we prepared carefully and developed a strategy that, I think, holds a great deal of promise for such situations: (1) Lay out a compelling positive message, focusing on issues or character traits that voters care about, and never let yourself get more than temporarily diverted from that message; (2) make campaigning itself an issue, tapping into the negative feelings that most people have about distortions and personal attacks (regardless of the fact that those same people may also be influenced by such ads); (3) frame the opposition's ads, so that when viewers see them they are drawing as many conclusions about your opponent as about you; and (4) do all this, of course, in a straightforward and truthful manner, so that you are not and do not appear to be descending to your opponent's level.

Despite my successful experience in 1988 (and an even more difficult but equally successful campaign in 1990), I am not sanguine about the state of television campaign advertising. We need to consider ways of curbing the worst abuses; some have proposed, for example, that candidates running negative ads be required to assume more responsibility for them, either by appearing personally in the ad or by including a disclaimer. As candidates and as parties, we also need to restore the vitality of pretelevision modes of communicating—targeted mail, tabloids, voter-contact activities—and to encourage television and radio formats that go beyond the thirty-second ad. But these short, forceful ads are uniquely effective in reaching voters, and the First Amendment precludes the sorts of limits on them that have been imposed in some other countries. Ultimately, then, we are going to have to live with them. This will place a burden of ethical responsibility on candidates and their consultants. And it will require successful politicians to work at anticipating attacks and countering them effectively.

THE THIRD CAMPAIGN

Some expected 1990 to be an easier year. After all, they reasoned, the presidential race would not be on the ballot, another two years in office would have enhanced my standing in the district, and my solid 1988 win would likely discourage potential challengers. These factors did, in fact, help; I went into the 1990 race, for example, with favorability ratings and vote-to-reelect numbers some 10 points above what they had been in 1988. But there was one potential challenger who was not to be deterred: John Carrington, a wealthy, self-made businessman who, immediately after his second unsuccessful try for statewide office in 1988, immediately announced that he might bid for Congress next.

Carrington's electoral career provides an extreme example of the sorts of outcomes moneyed candidates coupled with weak parties can produce. He moved from New Jersey to North Carolina in 1976 but never even registered to vote in the state until he decided to run for lieutenant governor eight years later. In both that race and his 1988 run for secretary of state, he dominated a weak Republican primary field and captured the nomination solely on the basis of a television campaign financed out of his own pocket. Carrington then came remarkably close to winning in the general election (46 percent in 1984, 48 percent in 1988), aided by strong Republican showings at the top of the ticket. But the first time he was actively embraced by the Republican party organization was in 1990: They had no one else to run against me, and in Carrington they saw a candidate who would pay his own way and who, by concentrating his considerable resources in one media market, might win or at least do considerable damage to me. In contrast to Fetzer's 1988 challenge, the Congressional Club played little part in this campaign; Senator Helms had his own race to contend with, and although Carrington's positions and tactics were often indistinguishable from the Club's, he was not close to the organization.

Although we had known throughout my first term what we were likely to face in 1988, we were unsure of Carrington's intentions until he actually filed in early 1990. Even then, it was hard to know what we were up against. Normally, an opponent's Federal Election Commission (FEC) reports give an indication of the candidate's breadth of support and of the scale of the campaign he or she is likely to mount. In Carrington's case, the FEC reports were useless—they revealed very little support, but his campaign potential was nonetheless immense, limited only by his willingness to spend. As it turned out, the $500,000 he had given to each of his previous campaigns was not a very reliable guide to what he was willing to do in 1990, for he would contribute over $800,000 toward total campaign expenditures of $891,000.

We hoped to run a less elaborate and less expensive campaign than we had in 1988. We opened headquarters later and cut back the size of the paid staff. We also made greater use of resources at hand: My administrative assistant, Gene Conti, took a leave of absence to manage the campaign, and my press secretary and two other staff members also took leaves at appropriate times to gear up the campaign operation. But it was not to be a low-key political year. Carrington's willingness to spend and the harshness of his television attacks helped ensure that, and so did the overall political climate, with Congress and the president mired in a highly visible budget battle until late in October and Congress-bashing reaching a fever pitch. We therefore invested as much in polling as we had in the previous two campaigns combined. It was a good investment for it let us spot trouble early and step up our campaign efforts accordingly. In the end, we spent a total of $698,000 and bought as much television time as we had in 1988. So much for the scaled-back campaign!

Early in the summer, Carrington began to run ads on radio and cable television attacking Congress as an institution, adding over-the-air television after Labor Day. But he repeated Fetzer's mistake of failing to use any material introducing or defining himself. His early ads consequently did little to boost his favorability numbers or to dispel the relatively high unfavorability ratings he brought from his previous campaigns. Nor did his early ads do any discernible damage to me. This changed when, in late September, he switched from generic anticongressional ads to spots attacking me personally. But even then, he was in a poor position to pick up the slack; although he could make some people think less of me, he had given them no reason to vote for him.

The damage inflicted by his ads nonetheless concerned us a great deal. Carrington threw various accusations my way, but his most persistent theme was that I was in the pocket of the savings and loan industry and was to blame for a debacle that was going to cost every American taxpayer thousands of dollars. My 1987 vote in the Banking Committee for one short-term recapitalization plan for the S & L insurance fund rather than another—a question on which the two main S & L industry associations were divided—was portrayed by Carrington as a capitulation to the industry that brought about the entire disaster. My overnight trip to address the southeastern S & L trade association on a consumer protection bill that I was pushing through the Banking Committee was presented as a reward for my vote—a "paid vacation on Captiva Island." One ad even featured an unflattering picture of me with dollar signs superimposed over my eyes.

There was so much error and distortion in all of this that it was hard to know where to begin a counterattack. Drawing on our 1988 experience, our first response ad attempted to frame Carrington's message, reminding viewers of the kind of tactics he had used in his past failed campaigns:

ANNOUNCER: John Carrington has a track record.

[copy on screen tracks audio, with newspaper editorials in background]
When John Carrington ran for Secretary of State, and lost, an editorial said, "John Carrington's campaign has spent a fortune on mean-spirited commercials."
When John Carrington ran for Lieutenant Governor, and lost, an editorial said, "John Carrington's campaign has consisted largely of negative commercials that unfairly distort the record of his opponent."
Now against David Price, John Carrington is at it again with the same negative campaign tactics.

[on screen: "The Carrington record speaks for itself."]

You'd have thought that John Carrington would have learned by now.

But 1990 was not 1988: The political climate was far more hostile to incumbents, and negative attacks were harder to discredit. Carrington's unfavorability numbers, already relatively high, continued to rise in early October, but my vote-to-reelect and job performance numbers were eroding more rapidly. Clearly, we needed to fight back with something more potent. In particular, we needed to deal with the savings and loan accusations, and my impulse to rush out and set the record straight was even stronger than in 1988. However, we still understood the pitfalls of a point-for-point response and instead decided on an ad that, drawing on a local newspaper editorial, showed that I did have answers to the charges. More importantly, it let me tell of the initiatives I had taken to address the S & L problem:

ANNOUNCER: [copy of editorial on screen] John Carrington is distorting David Price's record on Savings and Loans. A recent editorial called Carrington's charges "ill-founded."

DAVID PRICE [into camera]: Let's get to the facts. I wrote the law that prevents corrupt Savings and Loan executives from writing themselves big bonus checks and I sponsored legislation to require the Attorney General to go after the Savings and Loan crooks.

ANNOUNCER: A clean campaign. A Congressman fighting for you. Re-elect David Price.[4]

This more direct and forceful ad helped stop the slippage our October 17 poll had revealed. Within a week, the horse-race numbers had leveled off at around 43 percent for me and 25 percent for Carrington. But my favorability and job performance ratings continued to slip. Though we knew this was as much the function of the negative media coverage Congress was then getting as of Carrington's ads, we also recognized the continuing need to frame his message. He gave us an unexpected assist as we were preparing copy for our late October ads, acknowledging to a reporter that his attack ads were "a garbage way of running a campaign."[5] We were on the air within three days, first with an ad documenting via newspaper copy what Carrington had said about his own campaign and then with an ad that featured me looking at one of *his* ads on a television monitor and turning to comment on it:

Clip from Carrington ad [on TV monitor]: "David Price voted to let them keep gambling with your money."

ANNOUNCER: Here's what John Carrington says about the TV ads he's running: "This is a garbage way of running a campaign, but it's the only way." [Quote superimposed on screen, with monitor still showing.]

DAVID PRICE [pointing to monitor, then looking into camera]: Mr. Carrington calls his own ads garbage, but he's wrong to think this is the only way to run a campaign. For four years now we've shown that a positive, clean campaign can address real issues.

Please join me in saying no to John Carrington's distortions.

Our successive efforts to neutralize Carrington's attacks represented a continuation of our 1988 strategy but with modifications necessitated by the huge quantity of his ads, the sharply personal nature of his attacks, and the stormy political climate that threatened damage to all incumbents. The same was true of the positive ads with which we opened our television campaign in early September and that we continued to run throughout the two-month campaign. We again stressed my work on middle-class issues like education and housing, but gone were the pictures of me bustling around Washington. Although I have steadfastly refused to run for Congress by running against Congress (see Chapter 10), 1990 was not a good year to stress one's credentials as an "insider," no matter how essential those skills might be to producing the results that voters cared about. Consequently, we hearkened back to my first campaign when, as a challenger, I set out to "turn North Carolina politics around," even using a clip from an early 1986 spot in my first ad for 1990. And in discussing education, we reminded viewers that I was not a career politician. I had taught for seventeen years before coming to Congress, we stressed, and that had given me a fresh perspective on the issues.

The 1990 campaign was by far the most frustrating of the three for me. I felt under siege, both personally and as an incumbent; Congress was taking a beating in the media; and the ads being run against me went far beyond anything I had experienced before. Meanwhile, I felt helpless as I watched from afar, stuck in Washington as the budget battles dragged on. But my wife, my campaign manager, and others filled in for me very well. Our volunteers put in long hours on the phones, in the neighborhoods and headquarters; our contributors came through with the funds for stepped-up media buys; and our polling and media consultants monitored the situation daily and kept us on the offensive.

Our October 27 poll confirmed that the turnaround we had detected on October 22 was genuine; my vote-to-reelect numbers were on the way back up, and Carrington's unfavorable numbers had actually overtaken his favorables. I finished with a 58 percent win. This closely replicated the 1988 result, defying a national trend that saw the average victory margin of incumbents decline by almost 5 points.[6] Our team felt hugely relieved and vindicated on election night, although the occasion was marred by the failure of Harvey Gantt's spirited challenge to Senator Helms.

INCUMBENTS, CHALLENGERS, AND CAMPAIGN FINANCE

Having raised and spent $2.5 million to gain and hold a congressional seat against opponents who spent a like amount, I naturally have some thoughts about two matters that are much discussed these days: the relative strengths of incumbents and challengers and the state of campaign finance. I share the misgivings that others have expressed about how much money a serious race for Congress requires, the good people that this eliminates, and the constant preoccupation with fund-raising it requires. I do not, however, have an easy solution to suggest. Spending limits per se are not an adequate answer. In a general election, a limit of about $600,000 (with an additional $300,000 for a candidate with a contested primary) would help control some of the excesses and should be part of any serious reform proposal. But to set the limits much lower than this would place an unfair disadvantage on challengers and would make it difficult, in many districts, to mount an effective media campaign. I *needed* to spend at least $500,000 in the 1986 general election because television, with its high cost, is critical to political communication in a district like mine and because the incumbent I faced had many advantages.

Although spending limits must be high enough to permit full and effective campaigns, there is still much that might be done to relieve fund-raising pressures, to encourage a healthy diversity of funding sources, and to level the playing field for incumbents and challengers alike. Solutions might include the provision of a "floor" of public funds, which would match small individual contributions and be financed by an expansion of the tax checkoff system (or perhaps by a fee on PACs and large contributors); tax incentives for small contributors; limits on the percentage or cumulative amount of contributions that could come from PACs; requirements that television time be offered free or at reduced rates; and the encouragement of an expanded role for parties in political finance (see Chapter 6).

Such reforms would mean little if they were not accompanied by the closing of gaping loopholes that exist in present law, such as the "right" of candidates to pump unlimited amounts of their own wealth into their campaigns or of a group unaffiliated with a campaign to make unlimited "independent expenditures" on the candidate's behalf or against his or her opponent. The best solution would be to limit such contributions and expenditures outright, although the courts have thrown up formidable obstacles to such efforts. The next best course would be to create disincentives for these types of contributions and expenditures or to give their victims ways of compensating for them. A candidate's spending limits might be raised, for example, by the amount the opponent contributes to his or her own race. Or public funding for a candidate might be increased by an amount equal to the independent expenditures made against his or her candidacy. What is certain is that the loopholes must be dealt with, for they will otherwise make a shambles of carefully constructed spending limits or of efforts to ensure a balance of funding sources.

I will never forget how difficult it was to raise the first dollars in 1986. And I understand quite well why many potentially strong challengers and potentially able representatives simply cannot or will not do what it takes to establish financial viability and why so many who do reach that point can do so only on the basis of personal wealth. The modus operandi of most large contributors, PACs, and even party committees often makes their calculations of an incumbent's "safety" a self-fulfilling prophecy. I was one of only 6 challengers to defeat incumbent House members in the

TABLE 2.1   Congressional Challengers: Funding Levels and Outcomes,
1984–1990 (general elections only)

Year	Well-funded Challengers (>$300,000) Rep	Dem	Total	Well-funded Challengers Polling at Least 45%	Well-funded Challengers Winning	Other Challengers (<$300,000) Winning
1984	41	11	52	29 (56%)	13 (25%)	2
1986	20	27	47	23 (49%)	6 (13%)	0
1988	15	28	43	21 (49%)	6 (14%)	0
1990	22	15	38ᵃ	23 (61%)	10 (26%)	5

ªIncludes one Independent.

Source: Compiled from data in relevant numbers of The Almanac of American Politics (Washington, D.C.: National Journal).

general election in 1986. This was an unusually small number, but as Table 2.1 indicates, the number of successful general election challengers has not exceeded 15 in the last four elections.

These figures warrant closer examination. The 42 successful general election challengers in the 1984–1990 election cycles spent an average of $500,000 each, and only 7 spent less than $300,000. Yet few challengers' campaigns are funded at even this level: Only 52 challengers spent $300,000 or more in 1984, and by 1990, that number had dwindled to 38. Many of these challengers did rather well, all things considered. Half of them polled at least 45 percent of the vote even in 1986 and 1988, bad years for challengers, and in 1984 and 1990 they did considerably better. Had more money been available earlier in the campaigns, the balance in many of these cases might have been tipped. In several dozen other potentially promising districts, challenger races never reached a viable financing threshold or strong candidates could not be recruited because of the daunting financial prospect.

There are many reasons for the advantages congressional incumbents enjoy, but the status quo orientation of political finance surely ranks high on the list. The parties have considerable potential to serve as a counterweight. Gary Jacobson credited the GOP with undertaking recruitment and financing efforts that enabled them to take full advantage of favorable national trends in 1980 (picking up 33 House seats) and to avoid disaster when the political tides turned in 1982 (losing only 26 seats).[7] The Democrats, by contrast, did not recruit or finance the field of candidates they needed to capitalize fully on the opportunities of 1982. Then, in 1984, Democrats concentrated their limited resources on protecting vulnerable incumbents; of the 52 challengers spending $300,000 or more, 41 were Republicans. Two years later, the balance shifted considerably; 27 of the 47 well-financed challengers were Democrats, which indicated that the efforts of the Democratic Congressional Campaign Committee (DCCC) to improve its performance were having some effect. But Table 2.1 suggests that the efforts of both parties have declined in more recent years.

The evidence of missed opportunities is especially strong for 1990, a year when anti-incumbent sentiment ran high but did not heat up early enough to measurably effect candidate recruitment. (In Chapter 7, I will discuss whether Congress fully deserved the black eye it got from the 1990 budget conflicts.) Well-financed challengers did unusually well, and several others came from nowhere to defeat well-established incumbents. Members generally saw their reelection margins slip—53 House incumbents were reelected in 1990 with their lowest margin ever, and another 57 won with their lowest margin since their first election—but neither party had a team of viable challengers in place to take advantage of the situation.[8]

House membership is not as stagnant as the incumbent reelection rate (96 percent) suggests. When deaths, resignations, and retirements are added to incumbent defeats, the result is a turnover of from 10 to 20 percent of the House's membership per Congress. Over half of the members from each party have served less than ten years. It is also striking to realize, amid all the talk of a "permanent" Democratic majority, that if the Republicans had held on to all the seats they won at some point during the 1980s, they would control the House today.[9] Still, too many members are free of even occasional electoral challenges, and too many able people are prevented from running well—or deterred from running at all—by financial obstacles. This is a major reason for key campaign finance reforms such as a floor of public funding and an enforced balance between PAC and individual contributors. It is also a major challenge to the political parties and an important reason for strengthening their role in the recruitment and support of candidates.

3

Getting Adjusted

"It was like being dropped into the jungle and having to learn to survive," a freshman senator told Richard Fenno after his first year in office. "Gradually, you cut out a little place for yourself, a clearing in which you can live."[1] I would not have given quite as dramatic a description of my first year, perhaps because my staff work in the Senate, my years of studying congressional policymaking, and my previous work in national politics had taught me what to expect. Still, the adjustments confronting any new member are profound: from campaigning to organizing legislative and constituent services offices, from the expectations and demands of one job or profession to those of another, from hometown family life to the bifurcated existence of an airborne commuter. I will describe some of these transitions in the present chapter and then turn, in Chapter 4, to the further task described by Fenno's senator: finding a niche within the institution, cutting out "a clearing in which you can live." Though every senator or representative must make these adjustments in some fashion, members vary a great deal in how they handle them and in how happy, confident, and productive they are as they "move from involvement in running for office to involvement in running the country."[2]

GETTING STARTED

Veteran House members can recall numerous horror stories of the trial-and-error process by which they first became "oriented" to the institution. That process has now been eased considerably, although not completely, by the sessions set up for new members before the Congress formally convenes. Both party caucuses organize several days of orientation in early December in conjunction with the party sessions that elect leaders and adopt rules for the new Congress. My first trip to Washington as a member-elect and my first encounter with my future colleagues came on December 1, 1986. We plunged immediately into a series of briefings on everything from ethics to setting up an office to survival techniques for families, as well as the receptions and dinners at which the leaders and prospective leaders of the House welcomed us to Washington.

"The orientation process has emotional ups and downs that compare fully with the campaign," I wrote in a journal I kept during the early weeks of the 100th Congress. "Most new members seem to come in with euphoria from election night still lingering, full of campaign stories. But a sense of relief and satisfaction at simply being here quickly becomes mixed with anxiety about all there is to be done and about one's own status in the unfolding order of things." Indeed, the new member comes from the electoral arena into an arena that is equally political and equally challenging, though not identical in the skills it requires or the behavior it rewards—the arena of House politics.

After the party-sponsored sessions, most freshmen members from both parties then travel to the Kennedy School of Government at Harvard University for a valuable week of lectures and discussion focused on major issues. Many in my class also took advantage of a supplementary orientation, held in Williamsburg in January, that was organized by the Brookings Institution, the American Enterprise Institute, and the Congressional Research Service of the Library of Congress. Most members find these sessions rewarding, not only in furnishing a common background on various issues but also in providing an introduction to the workings of Congress—far preferable to just sinking or swimming after the formal session begins. The orientation weeks also help establish a strong bond among members of the entering class, an identity that stays with them throughout their legislative careers.

The class of 1986 was relatively small, comprising 26 Democrats and 23 Republicans. There were a few well-known personalities among us: John Lewis (D.-Georgia), hero of the civil rights movement; Tom McMillen (D.-Maryland), basketball star from the University of Maryland and the Atlanta Hawks; Fred Grandy (R.-Iowa), who played Gopher on television's "Love Boat"; and Joseph Kennedy (D.-Massachusetts), son of Sen. Robert Kennedy and nephew of the late president. It did not take the rest of our class long to figure out, whenever TV cameras or reporters approached us during orientation week, that some of us were less newsworthy than others!

The new class was politically diverse and did not reflect any identifiable national electoral trend. I was one of the few who had defeated an incumbent; most had been elected to "open" seats (that is, seats without incumbents) on the basis of factors peculiar to their districts. We were often reminded of how different our situation was from that of some classes of the previous decade, especially the large post-Watergate class of 1974, where the incoming members were critically important in reforming the House—changing party and chamber rules, deposing aging and unpopular committee chairmen, and so forth. Our relative conventionality probably said less about us than about the circumstances of our election and the political temper of the times. Nevertheless, an effective bonding took place during these early weeks, and an easy accessibility and familiarity was established among class members that would be replicated more slowly and more irregularly as we took our places among our seniors in the House.

The 100th Congress represented a changing of the guard in House leadership but not one attended by a great deal of conflict or controversy. Majority Leader Jim Wright of Texas was unchallenged in his race for the speakership, as was Tom Foley of Washington in his move from majority whip to majority leader. In the only contested leadership race, Tony Coelho (D.-California), to whom many members felt indebted by virtue of his energetic chairmanship of the Democratic Congressional Campaign Committee, defeated two other contenders for the post of majority whip. Coelho was beginning his fifth term; his selection, like the reelection of sixth-termer Dick Gephardt to head the Democratic Caucus, showed how accessible the leadership ranks had become to aggressive younger members. It also reflected the fact that, despite the high reelection rate for incumbents, increased rates of voluntary retirement had produced a younger and more junior House membership; well over half of the Democratic members seated in the 100th Congress had first been elected within the last decade.

Voting procedures in the Democratic Caucus for committee chairs are designed to favor incumbent chairmen. The caucus simply votes yes or no on a given name and does not consider alternative names unless the sitting chairman is voted down. Only one chairman was rejected in this fashion at the beginning of the 100th Congress, although some others received enough negative votes to alert them to brewing discontent. Armed Services Chairman Les Aspin (D.-Wisconsin) was on the short end of a 124–130 vote on January 7, 1987. This meant that the caucus would have to choose between him and his main challenger, Marvin Leath of Texas, who was backed by an incongruous (and probably unstable) coalition of some of the committee's and the House's most liberal and conservative members, united only by their dissatisfaction with Aspin's leadership. Also in the running were Nicholas Mavroules (Massachusetts) and Charles Bennett (Florida), the Armed Services Committee's second-ranking member who had been passed over two years before when Aspin had defied seniority to unseat the aging and infirm committee chairman at that time, Melvin Price of Illinois.

We members encountering the Armed Services battle, I noted then, felt like we "had walked into a blood feud," the background of which we barely understood. Like most freshmen, I was sought out for lengthy conversations by Aspin, Leath, Mavroules, and Bennett and subjected to repeated pleas and pressures by their various allies. One Steering and

Policy Committee member went so far as to tie his willingness to help me obtain my preferred committee assignments to a vote for Leath. Such heavy-handedness was exceptional, but the closeness of the race put the incoming freshmen in a critical position. I chose to keep my own counsel on the race, seeing little to be gained by declaring for one candidate or the other. In the end, Aspin narrowly retained his chair; although a majority of the caucus had been willing to vote against him, that majority was not available to any one of the challengers. Moreover, some members, having delivered a reprimand to Aspin on the first vote, were willing to let it go at that.

SETTING UP SHOP

My experience in Senator Bartlett's office, where the needs of Alaskans were attended to very carefully, impressed on me the importance of having a competent, energetic staff and a well-managed office.[3] I learned the same lesson in a less positive way through campaign experiences with a couple of senators who had gotten reputations for poor constituent services and slack staff operations—reputations that proved hard to shake and very damaging politically. I therefore devoted a great deal of time to staffing decisions in the three months following my election.

I decided to ask my campaign manager, Michelle Smith, who also had some Hill experience, to come to Washington as my administrative assistant. She and I were given a tiny cubicle in which to interview prospective aides and to handle calls and letters until permanent office space could be assigned. We immediately confronted thousands of pieces of mail that had accumulated since the election, with no possible way of responding until mid-January. But two items—requests for me to back American Airlines's application for a London "gateway" from Raleigh-Durham Airport and letters opposing the startup of a nuclear power plant in my district—had arrived in such volume that we decided to use an outside mail house to send these responses before we set up our office. Unfortunately, the mail house confused the two lists, sending several hundred power plant responses to people who had written about the airport! So we were more than ready to get our own house in order when the day to move into my assigned office finally came.

Freshmen are at the bottom of the list when it comes to selecting offices, but I didn't do too badly in the drawing to determine the order in which we new members would choose. I ended up in the Longworth House Office Building, the middle of the three House office buildings in both location and age. My office's main drawback was that its three rooms were not adjacent; the third room was an annex on another floor. I was finally able to remedy this deficiency by choosing another office at the beginning of my third term.

I deployed my staff in a fashion that has become rather common in the House, setting up several district offices and locating most constituent service functions there. The main district office in Raleigh included a district manager, two field representatives, two casework specialists, and two persons who alternated between receptionist and clerical duties. We also established one-person constituent service offices in Asheboro and Chapel Hill.

In Washington, I recruited Gene Conti, a longtime friend who had worked for eight years at the Office of Management and Budget and the Treasury Department, as legislative director. He became administrative assistant after Michelle Smith left to attend law school. I also named an office manager, who oversaw everything from computer operations to my personal schedule; an assistant legislative director, who helped me handle committee work; a press secretary; a computer operator; a receptionist; and three legislative assistants, who covered specific projects but mainly helped us cope with the flood of mail on pending issues.

My allowance for staff salaries was just over $400,000, which sounds larger than it is. I was well aware of the need to hire relatively senior people with Washington experience for the top positions. Then, like most members, I hired younger people, who were hoping to gain in experience and exposure what I couldn't pay them in dollars, for most other staff positions. Some came to the congressional staff from the campaign staff, and most had helped in some fashion with the campaign. And although I did not make it an absolute condition, every staff member, as it developed, had some past or present North Carolina connection.

We modified the definitions of these staff positions only slightly and experienced very little turnover during my first two terms. When I was appointed to the Appropriations Committee in 1991, I moved two of my senior aides into the additional staff slots to which Appropriations members are entitled. This necessitated some shifts in other staff members' responsibilities and eventually the hiring of an additional person. But the staff welcomed the change, both because of the new areas of initiative it opened up and because it enabled us, for the first time in four years, to give the staff decent raises in pay.

FAMILY AND CAREER

The two couples my wife and I talked with as we weighed the decision to run told us of the quite different ways they had chosen to cope with the demands congressional life placed on their families. One family lived in Washington, and the member made sporadic weekend trips back to the district; the other family lived in the district, to which the member returned every weekend. Although each couple claimed that their arrangement worked satisfactorily and though we knew that roughly equal numbers of members chose each pattern, we never doubted what would be best for us: To keep our main residence in Chapel Hill. This decision spared us the rigors of the Washington real estate market and the family upheavals attendant on moving. I rented an apartment on Capitol Hill, found myself able once again to walk to work, and settled into a pattern of heading for the airport after the final vote was taken on the House floor each week, usually late on Thursday afternoon.

We chose this option partly because of the ease of the commute—two hours door to door, with several nonstop flights each day—and because my political situation required maximizing my presence in the district. But it also suited our family situation. We knew that a move would be difficult for our teenage children. And though relocating to the Washington area would have been relatively comfortable for my wife, who grew up there, she preferred the idea of frequent visits to the capital rather than moving our primary residence there. As it turned out, the visits were not to be as frequent as we thought, thanks to the soaring cost of airline tickets and to her taking a demanding job in 1989 as assistant to the mayor of Chapel Hill.

The fact that we already were familiar with Washington and had a number of friends in the area actually made our decision easier, for we had less to lose by not electing to live there. We have missed out on a certain amount of social and family contact with my colleagues, but because even those members who live in Washington so frequently travel to their districts, there is far less of this weekend socializing than there used to be. And the wear and tear of weekly commuting is not as severe as one might imagine, once a routine is established. In fact, I have found that the resulting compartmentalizing of my life works rather well. When I am in Washington, usually on Tuesday through Thursday, I generally work fifteen-hour days, staying at my office into the night. But when I head for home, I am able to put much of that behind me, concentrating on district matters and on our family life. I can't imagine that it would work as well in reverse: dragging home late when Congress is in session and then heading for North Carolina on the weekends, leaving the family behind. But these are highly personal decisions, and if our children had been at a different stage or if my commute had required multiple connecting flights, the options would probably have looked very different to us.

Becoming a member of the House shakes up not only family life but also the roles and routines associated with one's previous career. I took a special interest, naturally, in Fenno's interview with a freshman senator who had been a college professor. "Life in the Senate," he said, "is the antithesis of academic life."[4] I would not put it quite that way: Such a view seems both to exaggerate the orderliness and tranquility of modern academic life and to underestimate the extent to which one can impose a modicum of order on life in the Congress. Still, few jobs present as many diverse and competing demands as does service in Congress.

Consider, for example, my schedule for two rather typical days in the spring of 1991, reprinted here without change except for the deletion of some personal names and the addition of a few explanatory notes (Table 3.1). By this time, I had moved to the Appropriations Committee from the three committees on which I sat during my first term, so the hearing schedule was less demanding; nonetheless, the Agriculture Appropriations Subcommittee held hearings on each of these two days. I also testified on a North Carolina environmental matter before a subcommittee of which I was not a member. The Budget Study Group and the Mainstream Forum, two of the informal organizations with which I am affiliated (see Chapter 4), held meetings, and the Prayer Breakfast, an informal fellowship group, met, as usual, on Thursday morning. I had several scheduled media interviews and probably a number of unscheduled press calls as well. There were a number of party meetings and activities (see Chapter 6): The Democratic Caucus met to discuss the pending budget resolution; a whip's task force was organized to mobilize Democrats behind the resolution; the caucus held a "party effectiveness" luncheon open to all members to discuss a major pending issue; and I participated in a caucus-organized set of one-minute speeches at the beginning of the House session. The other items are self-explanatory—meetings with North Carolina groups on issues of concern, talks to student groups, and various receptions that substituted for dinner or at least provided enough sustenance to take me through the evening of editing letters and reading in my office. And of course, the schedule does not capture the numerous trips to the House floor for votes, the phone calls, and the staff conferences scattered throughout every day.

These schedules list only events I actually attended; they also reflect the rules of thumb by which my staff and I keep life from getting even more hectic. In general, I talk with groups about pending legislation only when there is a North Carolina connection; most Washington groups are well aware that their delegations need to include at least one representative from the district. I also generally skip receptions at the end of the day unless constituents are to be there or a colleague has asked me to attend.

This sheer busyness in Washington and at home as well (see Chapter 8) surpasses what almost all members have experienced in their previous careers and requires specific survival techniques. Most important, you must set priorities—separate those matters in which you want to invest

38

TABLE 3.1 Typical Member's Daily Schedule in Washington

Wednesday, April 10, 1991	
8:00 A.M.	Budget Study Group—Chairman Leon Panetta, Budget Committee, room 340 Cannon Building
8:45 A.M.	Mainstream Forum Meeting, room 2344 Rayburn Building
9:15 A.M.	Meeting with Consulting Engineers Council of N.C. from Raleigh about various issues of concern
9:45 A.M.	Meet with N.C. Soybean Assn. representatives re: agriculture appropriations projects
10:15 A.M.	WCHL radio interview (by phone)
10:30 A.M.	Tape weekly radio show—budget
11:00 A.M.	Meet with former student, now an author, about intellectual property issue
1:00 P.M.	Agriculture Subcommittee Hearing—Budget Overview and General Agriculture Outlook, room 2362 Rayburn Building
2:30 P.M.	Meeting with Chairman Bill Ford and southern Democrats re: HR-5, Striker Replacement Bill, possible amendments
3:15 P.M.	Meet with Close-Up students from district on steps of Capitol for photo and discussions
3:45 P.M.	Meet with Duke professor re: energy research programs
4:30 P.M.	Meet with constituent of Kurdish background re: situation in Iraq
5:30–7:00 P.M.	Reception—Sponsored by National Assn. of Home Builders, honoring new president Mark Tipton from Raleigh, H-328 Capitol
6:00–8:00 P.M.	Reception—Honoring retiring Rep. Bill Gray, Washington Court Hotel
6:00–8:00 P.M.	Reception—Sponsored by Firefighters Assn., room B-339 Rayburn Building
6:00–8:00 P.M.	Reception—American Financial Services Assn., Gold Room

Thursday, April 11, 1991	
8:00 A.M.	Prayer Breakfast—Rep. Charles Taylor to speak, room H-130 Capitol
9:00 A.M.	Whip meeting, room H-324 Capitol
10:00 A.M.	Democratic Caucus Meeting, Hall of the House, re: budget
10:25 A.M.	UNISYS reps. in office (staff, DP meets briefly)
10:30 A.M.	Firefighters from Raleigh re: Hatch Act Reform, Manufacturer's Presumptive Liability, etc.
11:00 A.M.	American Business Council of the Gulf Countries re: rebuilding the Gulf, improving competitiveness in Gulf market
11:15 A.M.	Whip Task Force meeting re: Budget Resolution, room H-114 Capitol
12:00 P.M.	Speech—One minute on House floor re: budget
12:30 P.M.	Party Effectiveness Lunch—re: banking reform, room H-324 Capitol
1:00 P.M.	Agriculture Subcommittee Hearing—Inspector General Overview and the Office of the General Counsel, room 2362 Rayburn Building
3:00 P.M.	Testify at Oceanography Subcommittee Hearing re: naval vessel waste disposal on N.C. Outer Banks, room 1334 Longworth Building
3:30 P.M.	Speak to Duke public policy students re: operations of Congress, room 188 Russell Building
5:00 P.M.	Interview with Mathew Cross, WUNC stringer re: offshore drilling
6:45 P.M.	Depart National Airport for Raleigh-Durham

considerable time and energy from those you wish to handle perfunctorily or not deal with personally at all.[5] Confronted with three simultaneous subcommittee hearings, a member often has a choice: pop in on each of the three for fifteen minutes or choose one and remain long enough to learn and contribute something. It is also essential to delegate a great deal to staff and to develop a good mutual understanding within the office as to when the member's personal direction and attention are required. But there are no management techniques on earth that could make a representative's life totally predictable or controllable or that could convert a congressional office into a tidy bureaucracy. A member (or aide) who requires that kind of control—who cannot tolerate, for example, being diverted to talk to a visiting school class or to hear out a visiting delegation of homebuilders or social workers—is simply in the wrong line of work.[6]

There are, no doubt, numerous ways in which my previous career has influenced my adaptation as a member of Congress. Certainly, my previous study and staff experience helped me undertake specific policy initiatives (which I will describe in Chapter 5), and I naturally gravitated toward education and research issues on the Science Committee. Stylistically, I have perhaps been overly fastidious about what goes out of the office under my name. I am certain that I spend far more time than the average member reviewing and editing mail, and I have found it difficult to delegate speechwriting to staff. I tell myself that much of this personal attention is required by the remarkable volume, diversity, and erudition of the correspondence that my district produces, but it is, I am sure, also demanded by the habits and standards (and the streak of compulsiveness) I developed over my years in academic life.

My background also has predisposed me toward an activist, but selective and specialized, legislative style. Speaker Sam Rayburn used to distinguish "showhorses" from "workhorses" in the House by way of expressing his clear preference for the latter. Today, the norms of specialization, apprenticeship, and deference that once held showhorse behavior in check have weakened considerably, and even self-effacing workhorses must pay more attention to courting the media and building public support. But the rough stylistic distinction still holds.[7] My own inclination has been in the workhorse direction. There is still something of the student in me, with an urge to master the assignment at hand, and the committee system continues to encourage and reward this sort of behavior. I have occasionally become involved in attempts to amend bills from outside my committee areas on the House floor, and I may do more of this in the future. But in my early terms, I have concentrated on a limited number of initiatives, mostly in my committee areas, on which I could work in a concentrated fashion. This is a sensible strategy for a junior member, but it also stems from my preference, rooted in prior experience, to focus on a manageable number of projects and to operate from a substantial base of knowledge.

For many members, the transition from the campaign trail to congressional life is fully as jolting as any career change.[8] I found the shift dramatic emotionally but not especially problematic. Some of the issues I highlighted in my first campaign led to specific legislative initiatives. I proposed, for example, to repeal the Nuclear Waste Policy Act's requirement for a second national repository for high-level waste (my district had been identified as a possible site for this repository). The continuity was stronger in later campaigns, after I had my committee assignments and a legislative record in housing, education, and consumer protection to talk about. My campaign experience—recall that my ads made a great deal of Bill Cobey's isolation on key votes from both Democrats and Republicans in the North Carolina delegation—also probably made me more sensitive to the few instances when I later found myself voting with a small minority. I never got myself into binds as some of my colleagues did when, in the course of their campaigns, they got pressed into taking "the pledge" to never, ever raise anyone's taxes. But, especially as Tom Fetzer's campaign was warming up, I was wary of votes that might be construed as reversals of position or might provide material for thirty-second ads. I have gradually gotten more relaxed about this, realizing that no amount of caution can prevent an opponent's media consultants from finding something on which to base an outrageous ad, that such ads can effectively be countered, and that, in any case, it is simply intolerable to have one's life and work dominated by memories of the last (or fears of the next) campaign.

I will argue in this book's final chapter that a deep and dangerous gap is opening up between campaigning and governing in our country—a gap that inspires public cynicism and threatens democratic accountability. My experience with "hot-button" attack politics in North Carolina and my decrying of its irrelevance to the "real problems of real people" over the years have made me especially concerned to maintain the continuity between what I say in campaigns and what I do as a House member. But there will always be a certain tension between campaigning and governing, and that tension can be positive and productive, as well as distracting and debilitating. For me, the move from academic life into a congressional campaign was as great an adjustment as moving from the campaign to Congress, and I have found that certain instincts and sensitivities bred in the campaign are of continuing use in the Congress, sometimes acting as a counterweight to my inclination simply to do a workmanlike job on the task before me. Traditional congressional norms, reinforced in my case by my career background, encourage members to choose a few matters for specialization and to work persistently, mainly out of the limelight, to shape policy in these areas. But constituents still expect their representatives to be their voices and votes on the full range of governmental matters, and members cannot realistically expect constituents to understand and appreciate their legislative efforts if they do not make the effort to interpret, even dramatize, them. In these respects, the sensitivities and skills acquired in the campaign are of continuing relevance.

That, at least, is the way it has worked for me. My background in teaching and research has proved serviceable in many ways. But it was fortunate that I was forced out of those routines for a demanding twenty-month campaign and that I developed the broad-gauged knowledge of national issues, the sensitivity to constituency needs and views, and the ability to communicate that was required by that effort. This does not mean that I want or need a John Carrington throwing $900,000 at me every two years! But I believe that, for much of what the contemporary member of Congress needs to do, the experience and exposure offered by the campaign, far from being diversions, are absolutely essential.

4

Finding a Niche

My first extended conversation with the new Speaker of the House, Jim Wright, was during orientation week, one month after the 1986 election. We met to discuss committee assignments. Although U.S. House committees neither enjoy the autonomy nor receive the deference they did a generation ago, they are still quite powerful relative to the status of committees in most of the world's legislative bodies. The House's legislative division of labor follows the lines of standing committee jurisdictions, and committee assignments largely determine the focus of a member's legislative and oversight efforts.

I knew how important it was to get assigned to desirable committees, and I also knew how much the new Speaker was likely to have to do with that decision. One of the critical House reforms of the 1970s was to take the committee assignment function for Democrats from the Democratic members of the Ways and Means Committee, where it had resided since 1911, and place it in the party's Steering and Policy Committee. That committee has 33 members, including the Speaker and other top party leaders, 12 representatives elected by the regional party caucuses, and 8 at-large members appointed by the Speaker. This arrangement obviously enhances the leadership's role in committee assignments—depending, in part, on how forceful the Speaker is in making his or her preferences known. Those who knew Jim Wright expected him to be forceful indeed.

Wright had visited my district once during the campaign. My memory of the visit was mainly of the relief I had felt when it was over. Wright's staff had told us on very short notice that he would be coming in on a Saturday afternoon—a time when, as luck would have it, both the University of North Carolina and North Carolina State had home football games. Our thought, in throwing together a fund-raising barbecue, was less of the money we could raise than of how we could get enough people together to convince our guest we were not dying on the vine. This we barely were able to do. Unfortunately, Wright then managed to puncture his leg on a wire protruding from my station wagon seat as I drove him to the airport. I am sure that my embarrassment exceeded his injury, but it was the kind of day that seems much funnier in retrospect than it did at the time.

Memories of this encounter notwithstanding, Wright was cordial but noncommittal about my prospects when we met in Washington in December 1986. I approached the conversation with some trepidation. I knew better than to request one of the three "exclusive" committees—Appropriations, Ways and Means, and Rules, termed exclusive because their members must drop all other standing committee assignments—for they were virtually off-limits to first-term members. There is intense competition for these powerful positions, and party and committee leaders wish to take the measure of a member before placing him or her in such a critical spot. A story had circulated among our class about a freshman who earlier had been filmed for a television feature as he made his initial rounds. He had told Speaker O'Neill of his desire to be appointed to Appropriations, Ways and Means, or Rules, and the camera had caught the Speaker as his eyes rolled heavenward. So I knew what not to request. But the assignment I most wanted—to the Energy and Commerce Committee—also seemed likely to be out of reach, and I was uncertain how hard to press my case before falling back on a second choice.

I had a particular personal interest in Energy and Commerce. My time with Senator Bartlett had involved extensive work with the Senate Commerce Committee, of which he was a senior member, and my academic work included a general study of both the House and Senate Commerce committees and an examination of the House committee's oversight role.[1] The Energy and Commerce Committee, moreover, had an exceedingly broad jurisdiction—health, communications, energy, the environment, consumer protection, transportation, and securities and exchanges—much of it vitally important to North Carolina and to my district in particular. Former North Carolina representatives James Broyhill, a Republican, and Richardson Preyer, a Democrat, had earlier risen to ranking positions on the committee, but by 1987, the state had no Energy and Commerce member and had not had a Democratic member for six years.

My problem was that Energy and Commerce had become almost as sought after as the exclusive committees by virtue of the increasing salience of its jurisdiction and the success of its chairman, John Dingell (D.-Michigan), in carving out an assertive and expansive role for it. When I began to talk with party leaders about my committee assignment possibilities, I was advised to push—at least, up to a point—for Energy and Commerce. My state's needs and my own credentials were unusually strong, and even if I did not make it, I could leave a powerful impression for possible future reference. But I was also advised that many second- and third-term members would be putting in strong bids and that I should be prepared to indicate a backup choice. If I held out too long, I was cautioned, I might end up without any desirable alternative.

I did not receive any encouragement from Wright; this suggested to me that the rumors were probably true that he and chairman Dingell, who was also on the Steering and Policy Committee, were prepared to endorse 3 members, none of whom was a freshman, for the available Energy and Commerce slots. At the same time, I was disconcerted to see that some other freshmen still seemed to regard Energy and Commerce as a good possibility—I wondered what Wright had told them that he had not told me. (None of them, however, ended up getting the assignment.) As for myself, I decided it was time to shift to Plan B, to settle on a realistic backup choice and let my alternative preferences be known.

BANKING, SCIENCE, AND SMALL BUSINESS

Although I was not initially drawn to the Banking Committee, I fairly quickly concluded, after looking at the available alternatives and how they fit my own interests and the state's needs, that it was the most attractive backup possibility. North Carolina is a major banking state, and the committee seemed poised to tackle important banking issues in the 100th Congress. The committee also is responsible for housing policy, an area in which I had some experience and considerable interest. In addition, I decided that the most desirable choice by far as my second or "nonmajor" committee would be Science, Space, and Technology, a panel of obvious importance to the educational institutions and research enterprises of central North Carolina.

I, like most of the other new representatives, called on the Steering and Policy Committee members one by one. It was not clear to what extent Wright would try to call the shots for assignments beyond the exclusive committees, Budget, and Energy and Commerce. For many of the remaining committees, the leadership might have no overriding preference and, in any case, leadership control was not absolute. So freshmen seemed well advised to seek out Steering and Policy members, to get acquainted and make as strong a case as possible for suitable assignments.

My regional representative on Steering and Policy, Butler Derrick of South Carolina, agreed to nominate me for the Banking and Science vacancies. On the day of the meeting, I anxiously awaited his call, having finished my round of visits without a sure sense of how I would fare. As it turned out, I received both assignments but by a rather circuitous route. The initial balloting for Banking slots was complicated by the late entry of members who had missed out on other assignments, and I failed to obtain a seat by one vote. I then was the first member chosen for the available seats on Science, no doubt as a consolation prize. But two additional Banking slots were later added as part of an agreement with the Republicans, and I was able to obtain one of them.

Some weeks later, after all assignments had been made, I was offered a temporary, one-term assignment on a second nonmajor committee, Small Business, presumably because the leadership saw this committee as relevant to my district and felt that such an assignment might enhance my reelection prospects. I accepted the post eagerly, for Small Business was a possibility to which I had been drawn from the beginning.

These three assignments—Banking, Science, and Small Business—were as strong a combination as I could realistically have hoped for, and I was able to make good use of each of them. The Banking Committee presented the greatest challenge in several respects: the complexity of its subject matter; the number of major policy questions on the agenda; the intricacy of committee politics, both internally and in relation to outside groups; the depth of its leadership difficulties, which continued despite a change in committee chairs in 1989; and, increasingly, the political perils associated with the policies under its care, especially savings and loan regulation. To my surprise, however, the Banking Committee proved most amenable to my own legislative projects. In my first term, I concentrated on sponsorship of a consumer protection bill, the Home Equity Loan Consumer Protection Act. In my second term, I was able to take a more active hand in the committee's two major legislative efforts, the savings and loan reform bill and the 1990 housing bill, adding several of my own amendments to each. I will describe these initiatives in more detail in the next chapter.

The Science and Small Business committees are less torn by conflicting interests than is Banking. Their histories feature promotion and advocacy for American scientific leadership and the well-being of small businesses, respectively. These missions have often attracted like-minded members to the committees and helped mute partisan conflict. Especially on the Science Committee, however, this tradition of advocacy is running up against the painful choices necessitated by an era of budget constraint. The space station, the superconducting supercollider, healthy National Science Foundation budgets—the Science Committee has historically and often effectively said, "We want it all." The trade-offs are, indeed, difficult to make, and as the committee faces the necessity of setting priorities, its bipartisan promotional consensus is coming under increasing strains.

On both Science and Small Business, I concentrated initially on securing compatible subcommittee assignments, preferably under young, aggressive subcommittee chairmen who would pursue an expansive agenda and would welcome my participation. Such criteria are often more important than the subcommittee's precise jurisdiction, for the subject matter lines are rather ill defined and an aggressive chairman generally has wide latitude in exploring policy questions of interest. Thus, I was able to secure the cooperation of Chairman Doug Walgren (D.-Pennsylvania) in bringing our Science, Research, and Technology Subcommittee to my district for a day of hearings on "workplace literacy"—examining the knowledge and skills that will be required in the workplace of tomorrow. I then used the subcommittee as a base for developing a legislative proposal to improve curricula and teaching methods in science, mathematics, and advanced technical training.

My second Science subcommittee choice, Investigations and Oversight, proved to be a mistaken one. I was impressed that the full committee chairman had elected to chair this subcommittee himself, and I knew that on other committees (such as Energy and Commerce) this arrangement facilitated aggressive oversight. Not so on Science: The Investigations subcommittee was totally inactive in the 100th Congress. In 1989, I therefore switched to the Natural Resources, Agriculture Research, and Environment Subcommittee, actively chaired by Rep. James Scheuer (D.-New York). This assignment proved particularly useful in the aftermath of a severe tornado in my district, enabling me to investigate the National Weather Service's failure to give a timely warning and to push for modernized detection systems and a relevant research effort.

I also made good use of the one-term Small Business assignment. The full committee held hearings in my district on government and military procurement, asking how small and local businesses could be included in that process more effectively, and I used my committee position to help secure a full-time Small Business Administration procurement officer for the state. Rep. Dennis Eckart's (D.-Ohio) Antitrust Subcommittee also came to the district, exploring the availability and costs of liability insurance for small businesses.

These experiences confirmed the compatibility of my committee assignments with my own policy interests and with the needs and concerns of my district. But such compatibility is not always self-evident; considerable effort and initiative are required to ensure that the fit is a good one and that it results in productive activity.

PURSUING APPROPRIATIONS

Although I was reasonably content with my committee assignments, I was predisposed to seek a move to one of the more powerful and prestigious panels, particularly if I could make this transfer early in my career. This would let me begin to accumulate seniority on the new panel and to avoid giving up a great deal of seniority on Banking and Science.

At first, I saw Energy and Commerce as my most likely move, but I gradually began to shift my sights to Appropriations.

Energy and Commerce was still appealing, and North Carolina still needed majority representation there, but the appointment in 1989 of a Republican from our state's delegation, Alex McMillan, lessened some of the urgings from constituency and other groups for me to seek appointment. And the case I could make to Steering and Policy Committee members for regional equity became weaker after two Democrats from our four-state Steering and Policy region were appointed to Energy and Commerce.

The main reason for my change, however, was that Appropriations—which had not even been in my sights as a freshman—was simply a more attractive possibility. With its control over the federal government's discretionary expenditures, Appropriations has far more power than any other committee in shaping and setting priorities for federal activity. To be sure, its power is constrained by the budget process and, more importantly, by the ongoing budget crisis (see Chapter 7), but in a time of scarcity, it is all the more important to have a seat at the table when the spending decisions are made.

North Carolina already had a senior Appropriations member—Bill Hefner, chairman of the Military Construction Subcommittee. Hefner was an effective inside player on whom many of us had come to depend for help with district-related projects. But the balance that counts in allocating committee seats is not only among states but also among Steering and Policy regions, and on that basis, my argument was very strong. Although our region—North Carolina, South Carolina, Georgia, and Tennessee—was tied for first in its number of House Democrats, it was one of the few regions with only 2 Appropriations members (most had 3 and several had 4). Fortunately, our regional representative on the Steering and Policy Committee, Butler Derrick, was a forceful advocate, and he promised to help me with whatever committee move I wanted to undertake.

Late in the 100th Congress, Derrick, Hefner, and I went to talk with Speaker Jim Wright about my committee assignment prospects. Wright was not inclined to leave Steering and Policy decisions (or much of anything else) to chance, and he had already let it be known that he wanted one of the two Appropriations slots coming open at the beginning of the 101st Congress to go to his fellow Texan Jim Chapman. (The other was bound to go to the New England region, which would be reduced to one seat with Edward Boland's retirement.) We assured the Speaker that we had no desire to challenge that decision, but we also reminded him of my personal credentials and of our region's underrepresentation and indicated that I would be seeking the next Appropriations seat that came open. Although he said that I could be assured of serious consideration for that slot, he promised nothing more specific.

As it turned out, the next Democratic vacancy occurred in March of 1990 when Rep. Daniel Akaka of Hawaii was appointed to the Senate after the death of Sen. Spark Matsunaga. By then, Wright had resigned. Tom Foley, the new Speaker, was less inclined than Wright to dictate Steering and Policy decisions, at least on early midterm appointments like this one. The result was a wide-open race for the seat. I quickly decided that it was important to run and run hard, for the race was likely not only to provide one new member for Appropriations but also to establish a presumption as to who might get future seats, based on their show of strength in this round.

A number of other members saw it the same way, including some who were senior to me (Marcy Kaptur of Ohio, Peter Visclosky of Indiana) and some from my own class (David Skaggs of Colorado, Nancy Pelosi of California). Of the additional members who considered the race, one who was from my region especially concerned me: I knew of a recent instance in which a region had forfeited an otherwise strong claim to a major committee seat because 2 members from the region ran, thus giving Steering and Policy members a perfect excuse to vote for neither of them. Consequently, it was important to establish that I was the candidate who had our region's endorsement. Derrick's vocal backing helped, as did a unanimous letter of support I secured from the Georgia delegation. Eventually, my potential rival withdrew.

Since the beginning of the 101st Congress, I had been casually visiting with Steering and Policy members, letting them know of my eventual interest in whatever opened up on Appropriations. Now, of course, I greatly accelerated that activity. My staff and I kept records of each contact, taking care to distinguish among those promising first-ballot support, those promising later-ballot support if their preferred candidate was eliminated, and those merely expressing good wishes. Individuals in this latter group ranged from one supporter of a rival who assured me he had "nothing against me" and seemed to think I should be relieved to hear it to some who were genuinely uncommitted. I asked a number of colleagues to speak on my behalf to Steering and Policy members whom they knew well, and in several instances this helped produce commitments. What I did *not* do was ask any person or group outside the House to intercede on my behalf. Steering and Policy deliberations, like leadership contests, are considered by most members to be strictly an internal affair, and outside entreaties might well hurt more than they would help.

Kaptur won the vacant seat. Although she was not a leadership favorite, she benefited from a concerted effort by midwestern members (anticipating a loss of seats in the 1991 reapportionment) to shore up their representation, from a promise to her from Jim Wright that was allegedly more specific than the ones he had given to me and others (this swayed mainly the Texas members), and from the fact that Appropriations contained few women. It was a close contest that required four ballots to resolve. My six first-ballot votes were enough to put me in second place, and I held that position throughout, surviving until the last ballot. It was a stronger finish than most had predicted, and I was quite pleased and encouraged because I felt I had strengthened my position for the next round at the beginning of the 102nd Congress. But I knew that the ground could shift over the coming months and that next time the leadership might do more to shape the decision. I therefore continued to talk to Steering and Policy members, especially the top party leaders. Most of what I heard encouraged me.

Running for Appropriations was an intense experience and, on the whole, an enjoyable one. It gave me an occasion to get to know a number of senior members better, and a good deal of camaraderie developed among most of us who were competing. We pretty well knew what commitments of support each other had, and what we did not know before the balloting we figured out by comparing notes afterward. Most Steering and Policy members had been careful in what they promised, but for those who had made inconsistent promises to several of us or who had not delivered on their pledges, the secret ballot concealed very little.

Resignations produced two Democratic vacancies for the 102nd Congress. By mutual agreement, the parties maintain a much more exact relationship between their ratio in the House and on Appropriations than they do with other committees. And the slight shift in the balance of party strength in the House produced by the 1990 elections was sufficient to add two Democratic seats if combined with one new seat for the GOP. The leadership decided to make these additions, which resulted in a total of four Democratic vacancies—good news for those of us lining up for the race. The leaders also decided to make their preferences for Appropriations and other top committee assignments known this time, and fortunately, I was on the list.

The Steering and Policy decisions were made during the presession organizational meetings in December 1990. Larry Smith (D.-Florida), a late entry who was beginning his fifth term, led the balloting. I was second, followed by Pelosi and Skaggs. Visclosky fell short with a fifth-place finish, but the leaders promised him their support for the next vacancy to occur. It was therefore a happy outcome, accommodating all of us who had made a serious run for the midterm vacancy. Having just survived a rougher-than-expected 1990 reelection contest, I was gratified to see this exercise in internal House politics turn out successfully as well. Although it seemed that I had been working at it for a long time, I realized that I was fortunate to secure an Appropriations seat as early as the beginning of my third term. I was not forfeiting a great deal of seniority on Banking or Science, and I was getting on the all-important seniority ladder on Appropriations at a relatively early point, in advance of a number of anticipated 1992 retirements.

I nonetheless had some mixed feelings as I gave up the Banking and Science assignments. Appropriations would offer more influence on a broader range of policies, but the initiatives I could take would be less visible and more incremental in nature. During my first two terms, I had been able to use committee hearings, especially the five we held in the district, to publicize issues that needed attention and to involve North Carolinians who had a stake in those issues. I had also steered initiatives in consumer protection, housing, and science education through my committees and on to final passage. Now, I would need to find new channels for working on such issues and for interpreting what I was doing for my constituents. But I knew that the Appropriations assignment was likely to open far more doors than it closed. Beyond that, there were certain characteristics of my former committees that I would not miss at all. This occurred to me forcefully in February of 1991 as the House Banking Committee wrangled over a bill to authorize additional borrowing by the Resolution Trust Corporation, the agency responsible for the S & L cleanup. The committee spent eight hours loading the bill down with amendments, only to defeat the measure at the end of the day. It was a good time, Nancy Pelosi and I agreed, to have left the Banking Committee!

Most Appropriations work is done in subcommittees, and senior members jealously guard their positions on these panels, for subcommittee chairs are based on subcommittee, rather than full committee, seniority. The subcommittees are kept small—most contained 10 members in the 102nd Congress—and members are allowed to lock in or "grandfather" two of their previous subcommittee assignments as each new congress begins. At first, it seemed that we 4 new Democratic members might have very little to choose from because subcommittee chairs were resistant to enlarging their panels and a new Democratic slot was added only to two subcommittees, Defense and Agriculture. But the availability of the Defense slot induced a middle-ranking member to give up his grandfathered rights in order to claim it. This set up a chain reaction down the seniority ladder, with the result that each new member got assigned to at least one of the more sought-after subcommittees.

I and the other new members got all the information we could in advance and carefully plotted how the bidding for slots was likely to go. My first choice was the subcommittee on VA, HUD, and Independent Agencies, which appropriated in both the housing and National Science Foundation areas where I had worked hardest for the past four years. I knew that higher-ranking committee members were unlikely to jump for that vacancy but that Marcy Kaptur, who ranked just ahead of our group in committee seniority, would likely claim it. As I considered the available vacancies and the likely preferences of those ahead of me in the order of bidding, it became clear that I could secure a seat on the Subcommittee on Transportation and that a seat on Rural Development, Agriculture, and Related Agencies would still be available to me on the second round of bidding.

These were highly desirable subcommittees, allowing me to work on a number of matters important to my district—airport development, highways, intercity mass transit planning, agricultural research, nutrition, rural housing—and putting me in a position to help broker other members' interests as well. I may someday seek a seat on subcommittees in which I have an even stronger policy interest, such as VA-HUD or Labor-HHS-Education. But full committee membership and reciprocity among subcommittees should give me increased leverage in these areas in any case. And when the opportunity comes to move, I will have to weigh the appeal of these areas against the value of the seniority I have begun to accumulate on the other panels.

INFORMAL GROUPS AND CAUCUSES

Although newly elected members of the House must give primary attention to their committee assignments, they are also confronted with a bewildering array of some one hundred caucuses and other member groupings that have grown up around the committee and party systems since the mid-1970s.[2] This proliferation has been criticized for dissipating the energies of members and heightening their special-interest orientations. "The House," Speaker O'Neill once said, "has over-caucused itself."[3] Yet most members end up affiliating with several of these organizations, and many find in them a useful supplement to their committee posts. Caucus affiliations can provide a member with outlets for policy interests that his or her committee assignments do not afford. And caucuses can bridge committee divisions, helping members from various jurisdictions to communicate and to work together.

I have been rather sparing in my caucus affiliations, constrained both by time and by the dues some of them charge. But a number of these memberships have been quite important to me, and by reviewing the most significant, I can illustrate both the variety of these groupings and what they offer to their members.

Because my committees have been focused almost exclusively on domestic affairs, I have had to look elsewhere for outlets in foreign and defense policy. I have participated profitably in the discussions with governmental, academic, and other experts organized by the Arms Control and Foreign Policy Caucus, a bicameral, bipartisan organization that also furnishes useful issue briefs for its approximately 130 members. My main organizational outlet in this area, however, has been the German Study Group, an informal organization of some 80 House members interested in German and European affairs.

My involvement began in my first term when I was invited to go to West Germany as part of a parliamentary exchange sponsored by the German Marshall Fund of the United States. Shortly thereafter, I and 7 other "founding members" set up the German Study Group with the support of the German Marshall Fund and with Lee Hamilton (D.-Indiana) as our first chairman. My turn as chairman came at a particularly opportune time—during German reunification in 1990. Along with Sen. Bill Roth (R.-Delaware), chairman of the Senate study group, I led a congressional delegation visit to Bonn, Berlin, and Budapest, meeting with Chancellor Helmut Kohl, Foreign Minister Hans-Dietrich Genscher, and our counterparts from the Bundestag and the East German Volkskammer at a critical stage in the reunification process. The German Study Group, the only organization of its kind in the House, has enabled us to sustain discussion and involvement between such visits and to include a wider circle of interested members, most of them nonspecialists in foreign affairs. We often hold luncheons for visiting parliamentarians and political leaders, and periodic sessions with the German ambassador, who has taken a lively interest in the group, have let us explore such critical issues as trade, the future of the North Atlantic Treaty Organization (NATO), and German participation in the Gulf War effort.

As a member from a district and a state with a major stake in the textile and apparel industries, I also affiliated at an early point with the Congressional Textile Caucus. This organization has helped me make a case for two major research efforts based in my district that promise industrywide benefits. However, the main preoccupation of this caucus has been trade. We have met periodically for (usually unsatisfactory) discussions with the U.S. Trade Representative, and the caucus has organized support for bills slowing the growth of textile, apparel, and shoe imports in the 99th, 100th, and 101st congresses. (Each of these bills passed by a wide margin but fell to a presidential veto.)

The Congressional Sunbelt Caucus attends to a broader array of regional interests and, through its task forces, enables me and other members to focus on infant mortality, workplace literacy, and similar issues of special relevance to the South. In the 101st Congress, for example, our Infant Mortality Task Force concluded that the South's appalling maternal and child health statistics called out for the energetic implementation of programs we already knew could make a difference—the National Health Service Corps (NHSC); community health centers; Medicaid; the Women,

Infants, and Children (WIC) nutrition program; and so forth. We then deployed our members to testify and to lobby our colleagues for NHSC revitalization and more adequate funding for many of these programs.

In the area of workplace literacy, however, my work on the Science Committee convinced me that an authoritative study would be helpful, and the Sunbelt Caucus and Sunbelt Institute, its affiliated think tank, provided a significant complement to the committee's work. The institute commissioned a study that documented the evolving workforce needs of the South, evaluated existing basic education and training programs, and made specific policy recommendations.[4] This study and a related conference organized in North Carolina under institute auspices bore fruit in workplace literacy/technical training bills I introduced in the 101st and 102nd congresses.

I have also worked with two groups composed of Democratic House members but outside the party's formal organization, the Mainstream Democratic Forum and the Democratic Budget Study Group. The Mainstream Forum began holding regular weekly meetings in 1990 under the leadership of Dave McCurdy (D.-Oklahoma). The forum is a congressional offshoot of the Democratic Leadership Council (DLC), a national organization of elected officials and other Democratic leaders who have attempted to inspire serious policy debate within the party and to maintain a broad middle-class appeal. Most Mainstream Forum participants would regard themselves as moderates, but the group is more loosely organized and more diverse ideologically than the Conservative Democratic Forum (CDF). About 40 members attend Mainstream Forum meetings at least occasionally; average attendance is about 15. Sometimes, the topic is a policy proposal spawned by the DLC or its affiliate think tank, the Progressive Policy Institute: a police corps modeled on the Reserve Officers' Training Corps (ROTC), a progressive tax policy, new approaches to family policy. Other meetings focus on pending House business and may result in requests to the leadership regarding scheduling, making certain amendments in order on the floor, and so on.

The Democratic Budget Study Group was organized in 1983 by then-freshman Democrats Buddy MacKay (D.-Florida) and Tim Penny (D.-Minnesota). I became a regular participant immediately on coming to the House in 1987 and became the group's cochairman in 1989, after MacKay left the House to run for the Senate.

All Democratic members are invited to Budget Study Group sessions, and a large percentage of them drop in at one time or another. The attendance at a typical weekly meeting is around 25, and the typical participant is a party moderate, concerned about the country's deepening fiscal difficulties. We have never attempted to organize the group formally or to mobilize on behalf of a particular position, and it is not any person's or any faction's power base, which is one reason it works so well. Many attend our sessions simply because they afford the best opportunity available to discuss budget-related issues in an open and direct fashion. Guest speakers in recent years have included Federal Reserve chairmen Paul Volcker and Alan Greenspan, the Office of Management and Budget (OMB) director, Richard Darman, and Brookings Institution economists Alice Rivlin and Barry Bosworth. We also often hear from our own committee and party leaders. They invariably accept our invitations, sometimes seeing Budget Group sessions as a way of reaching "swing" members they need to persuade. I have found this group's discussions generally to be as satisfying and enlightening as any in the House, which is why I have participated enthusiastically and have been willing to contribute to the leadership of the group.

Finally, a word about our state delegation. North Carolina's House delegation is a midsized one, currently consisting of 7 Democrats and 4 Republicans. We are not formally organized, nor do we hold regularly scheduled meetings. Our "dean" or most senior member, Walter Jones, occasionally calls a meeting of either the entire delegation or of the Democratic members, depending on the subject matter and on who requests the meeting. The delegation recently discussed the state's highway program and other matters with our Republican governor, for example, and Democrats met with our 1990 U.S. Senate nominee to discuss his campaign plans. We also frequently come together for luncheons or receptions organized by groups from the state—such as agricultural extension leaders, North Carolina homebuilders, or university researchers briefing us on cancer research needs.

This rather sporadic schedule of delegation meetings provides only a hint of the importance of state delegations as reference groups for their members and as settings for collaborative work. In fact, I would find more frequent delegation meetings useful. But with or without formal meetings, I see my North Carolina colleagues on the floor daily, exchange information and opinions with them, learn how they are inclining on matters before us, and discuss projects in which we are jointly involved. Sometimes, all the members from the state or a region within the state join together to express an opinion or make a request—for example, urging the Pentagon to leave the Army Research Office in the Research Triangle Park. More frequently, we count on well-situated members to carry the ball for the rest of us: Tim Valentine of the Public Works Committee becomes the key player in getting a more favorable formula for the return of Highway Trust Fund monies to the state; Bill Hefner and I push Appropriations projects for various delegation members; and we count on Walter Jones as Merchant Marine Committee chairman to find a way to defer oil drilling off North Carolina's Outer Banks. Often—but not always—these patterns of reciprocal assistance extend across party lines.

The state delegation's role as a reference group is especially important in roll-call voting. The party cue is often compelling, of course, and on some votes one wants to know how members from the committee of jurisdiction are voting, how certain members identified with the issue are inclined, and so forth. But on any vote involving a significant division of opinion, I generally check the voting board to see how at least some of my North Carolina Democratic colleagues are recorded. That is as effective a way as I know to double-check my own intended vote—to see if there is some impact on the state or some other consideration that I may have overlooked. I may be in a minority among my fellow North Carolinians on a given vote, but if that is the case, I want to make certain I know what I am doing.

All of this presumes widespread agreement among our North Carolina Democratic members and an inclination to trust one another's judgment. Often, in the process of checking and discussing, we persuade one another, and sometimes we agree, on a particularly difficult vote, to stick together. Average party-support scores for North Carolina's Democratic members both illustrate this cohesion and help explain why we achieve it more easily than some other delegations. The range of scores for North Carolina Democrats was 70–91 for the 101st Congress (1989–1990), compared to the much wider range of 44–98 for all House Democrats.[5]

No one understands or cares about home like one's home state colleagues, and collegial relationships within a delegation can be a tremendously important personal and political resource for a member. I am fortunate that, by and large, it has worked that way for me.

5

Policy Entrepreneurship

"The President is now the motor in the system," wrote a distinguished political scientist in the mid-1960s; "the Congress applies the brakes."[1] My staff work in the Senate during those years, when I was also casting about for a doctoral dissertation topic, led me to question this particular piece of conventional wisdom. It also put me in a good position to observe committee politics and to build on the studies of congressional committees then being pioneered by Richard Fenno, Ralph Huitt, and others.[2] I wrote a dissertation, later published as *Who Makes the Laws?* that delineated congressional and executive roles on thirteen major pieces of domestic legislation during the 89th Congress (1965–1966) and focused especially on the three committees handling the bills in the Senate.[3] I found the congressional role in legislation to be significant, even for major administration initiatives at the height of President Lyndon Johnson's Great Society program. But I also found that the congressional role varied a good deal at different stages of the legislative process and that it depended significantly on the incentives, opportunities, and resources present in various committee settings.[4]

In searching for the sources and conditions of congressional policy initiatives, I soon came to focus on the emerging phenomenon of "entrepreneurship" among senators and their aides. The 1960s were a time when public opinion seemed to underwrite an expansive governmental role, when the institutional folkways that had inhibited legislative activity down through the ranks of the Senate were beginning to erode, and when a new breed of activist senators exemplified by Hubert Humphrey, Joseph Clark, Philip Hart, Edmund Muskie, and Jacob Javits were beginning to make their mark. I particularly stressed the importance of entrepreneurship within congressional staffs—a continual search for policy gaps and opportunities, a job orientation that stressed the generation and promotion of policy initiatives designed to heighten the public visibility of the senator and his or her leadership role within the chamber. Senate committees like Commerce or Labor and Public Welfare (later renamed Labor and Human Resources) became hotbeds of legislative innovation, and the development of an entrepreneurial orientation on the part of members and aides was a critical element in the productivity of these committees in the 1960s and beyond.[5]

Policy entrepreneurship was slower to emerge in the House, where the size of the body placed greater restrictions on the independence and impact of most members and where members' electoral fortunes turned more on constituent services and district relations and less on media exposure than was true for most senators. But House members also faced a changing political environment, one that increasingly left them on their own electorally. An important element in this change, as I will show in the next chapter, was the decline of political parties—members faced voters who were less inclined to support them on partisan grounds alone, and party organizations were becoming less effective in communicating with and mobilizing the electorate. Party decline, together with the rise of television as the dominant news and campaign medium, thus gave members incentives to seek a higher public profile. For many representatives, especially those from districts where public awareness of and concern for national policy questions were high, policy entrepreneurship was a promising means to that end.

The desire for a more prominent policy role was, therefore, a powerful motivation behind the House reforms of the 1970s—reforms that, for the most part, parceled out authority and resources to subcommittees and individual members. These changes, in turn, encouraged policy initiatives down through the congressional ranks—although the fragmentation of power, ironically, also made it more difficult for the House to handle conflict and to bring many legislative initiatives to fruition.

The 1980s saw some waning of entrepreneurial activity. A few figures are suggestive: In the 97th Congress, during the first two years of the Reagan administration, the number of public laws enacted dropped to 473, the lowest since World War II. The volume of committee hearings tapered off somewhat after the peak years of the 1970s and reached a postwar low in 1986.[6] A number of factors contributed to this decline— shifts in the political climate that seemed to reduce public support for legislative activism, the advent of an administration hostile to much policy innovation, and, most important, the constraints imposed by the budget crisis on any new departures in policy, especially those that cost money. Still, authority and resources are distributed in both houses of the U.S. Congress in ways that give large numbers of members opportunities for legislative entrepreneurship. And many members continue to find it advantageous, as they consider both their electoral prospects and their standing within the legislature, to establish active policymaking roles for themselves.

I came to the House with some entrepreneurial experience (I had handled the Radiation Protection Act of 1967 for Senator Bartlett, who was its chief Senate sponsor), some awareness of the conditions of successful activism, and strong personal and political motivations to develop such a role for myself. At the same time, I realized that on most major bills I, as a new member, would need to follow the lead of like-minded senior members. As for my own legislative ventures, I felt that they should be limited in number and chosen with care. Some of the bills I introduced were a direct response to district needs or campaign pledges, such as the proposal to repeal the Nuclear Waste Policy Act's requirement for a second national repository for high-level waste and a bill to restore income tax deductibility for interest on student loans. But the project that most closely fit the traditional entrepreneurial pattern was a bill I managed to steer through the Banking Committee and on to final passage—the Home Equity Loan Consumer Protection Act of 1988.

THE HOME EQUITY LOAN
CONSUMER PROTECTION ACT

Home equity loans were a hot new financial product in 1987. The Tax Reform Act of 1986 had phased out income tax deductibility for interest on most consumer loans and credit card accounts, but it had left deductibility in place for loans secured by one's home. In response, home equity loans—second mortgages that ordinarily had a variable interest rate and an open line of credit up to a substantial portion of the value of the house—were vigorously marketed, and many consumers (including me) found them attractive and advantageous. This aggressive marketing and the possibility that, with a rise in interest rates, borrowers might find themselves in over their heads with their homes at risk made certain basic consumer protections desirable. Yet these loans were subject to little advertising regulation, and under the Truth-in-Lending Act, they were treated as an open-end product, like a credit card, rather than as a closed-end product, like an adjustable-rate or fixed-rate mortgage. Consumers could be given considerably less information than would be required in the case of other loans secured against their homes, and even this information might be provided only after they had paid nonrefundable fees or closing costs. It seemed obvious that home equity loans should be subject to disclosure requirements at least as stringent as those that applied to other mortgages. And my committee assignment gave me a good position from which to work on a measure to accomplish this.

Having discovered a promising policy gap and feeling anxious lest other members might be getting similar ideas, I hurried to draft a bill and to circulate a "Dear Colleague" letter inviting other members to join me as cosponsors. My staff and I quickly solicited suggestions from several consumer and banking groups and, most importantly, from the staff of the Federal Reserve Board, which was already working on new regulations for the timing and content of disclosures for adjustable-rate mortgages. One critical early decision was to make this primarily a disclosure bill that, while it went beyond what most industry associations preferred, still fell short of the wish lists of the consumer groups. I made this decision on the merits of the case. I did not want to place regulations on home equity loans that went far beyond what was required of comparable products; nor did I want to see these loans increased in price or made less available. At the same time, however, I wanted the bill to attract a broad base of political support. An alternative approach would have been to introduce a much more extensive bill, with the idea of compromising later if necessary. In fact, Rep. Charles Schumer (D.-New York) subsequently introduced such a home equity loan bill, to the applause of the consumer groups. But I chose to draft a bill that I thought could pass and that came close to what I thought Congress finally should produce. This approach paid off: No potential opponents got *too* upset, and the bill attracted a bipartisan group of 23 original cosponsors, including the chairman and ranking Republican member of the House Banking Committee.

Frank Annunzio (D.-Illinois), chairman of the Banking Committee's Subcommittee on Consumer Affairs and Coinage, scheduled hearings on the bill for October 6, 1987, and his top subcommittee aide, Curt Prins, worked closely with my banking aide, Paul Feldman, to undertake the consultations necessary to get a consensus bill reported. This was not a simple task. Annunzio wanted to maintain his reputation as a consumer champion, and Prins was wary of possible attacks by consumer groups, who had begun rather noisily to object to my initial draft. However, it was clear that the industry groups (which, like the consumer groups, had formed an informal coalition for purposes of negotiation and lobbying) would resist adding substantive restrictions on home equity loans to the disclosure and advertising regulations contained in my bill. It was not difficult to imagine the lenders deciding to oppose the bill; their success in defeating interest-rate caps on a related credit card bill by a large margin suggested that they might be able to do the same if the home equity bill were amended to contain such restrictions. Moreover, they could assume that if Congress was unable to act, the Federal Reserve Board would promulgate regulations they could live with. Therefore, I was eager to keep both groups at the table because I knew that the disaffection of either would break up the coalition of members who had joined in sponsoring the bill and would make its passage far less likely.

At the House subcommittee hearings, I identified several areas where I thought the bill could be strengthened and substantive restrictions ought to be considered: limiting the ability of a lender to arbitrarily manipulate the interest rate, for example, and tightly restricting the lender's right to call in a loan or to change its terms. Fortunately, the consumer groups also chose to focus on such potential areas of abuse, rather than to push hard for the kind of broad limits on the terms of home equity loans contained in the Schumer bill. Despite this, our negotiations grew quite contentious and came close to breaking down. And we were able to get a revised bill reported out of subcommittee only by promising all concerned that they would get another crack at it before the full committee undertook its final revisions.

In the meantime, the Senate Banking Committee's Subcommittee on Consumer Affairs, under the leadership of chairman Christopher Dodd (D.-Connecticut), took up the home equity issue, using my bill and Schumer's as the basis for a day of hearings on November 18, 1987. The committee leadership later decided to append a home equity loan disclosure provision to their bank powers bill—Senate Banking's most ambitious legislative project in the 100th Congress, which passed on March 30, 1988. Home equity legislation had not originated in the Senate, and the home equity title that the Senate approved was a hastily drawn proposal. Nonetheless, this temporary shift to the Senate of the negotiations among industry and consumer groups served us well on the House side: The prospect of immediate floor action forced everyone to reveal their bottom lines in short order, and we were able to use the Senate language to resolve several difficult issues that were slowing our progress toward full committee markup in the House.

The House Banking Committee approved the Home Equity Loan Consumer Protection Act by a unanimous vote on May 19, 1988, and the House passed the bill by voice vote on June 20. Although I had been happy to see the measure pass the Senate expeditiously as part of the bank powers legislation, I wanted to pass it as a separate bill in the House, where the prognosis for the bank powers bill was far less hopeful and home equity's prospects could be harmed if it became entwined in the conflicts surrounding the broader measure. This strategy, supported by the full committee's ranking minority member, Chalmers Wylie (R.-Ohio), as well as Chairman Fernand St. Germain (D.-Rhode Island), preserved both options—taking home equity to a House-Senate conference as part of the larger bill or passing it as a freestanding measure if the bank powers bill failed.

This proved to be a wise strategy, for the bank powers legislation ran into major obstacles in the House. However, both the chairman and the ranking Republican of the Senate Banking Committee—William Proxmire (D.-Wisconsin) and Jake Garn (R.-Utah), who were also the chief proponents of the bank powers bill—were reluctant to pass home equity separately because they believed it enhanced the broader bill and improved their chances for getting it approved. It was only after the prospects for bank powers were seen as completely hopeless that separate passage of home equity could even be discussed. By then, though, time was so short that the only feasible approach was for the Senate to pass the House's freestanding home equity bill and send it directly to the president, thus making further House action or a House-Senate conference on the bill unnecessary.

Feldman and I spent many hours during the closing days of the session working with allies that included several House members and aides as well as industry and consumer lobbyists, trying to secure Senate passage. The task was complicated by the fact that the Senate was conducting its business essentially by unanimous consent in the waning hours. Any one member, therefore, could block approval, and several placed "holds" on the home equity bill, hoping to use it as a vehicle or bargaining chip for proposals of their own. The Senate committee staff worked all day on October 21 to accommodate as many of these members as possible and finally, at 2:00 A.M., got home equity to the floor as part of a package of three bills. With one hour remaining before final adjournment of the 100th Congress, the Home Equity Loan Consumer Protection Act passed the Senate by voice vote and was on its way to the White House.

The home equity case suggests several conditions that facilitate and shape policy entrepreneurship in the House. In the first place, the committee environment was a relatively favorable one. The chairmen of both the subcommittee and the full committee stood to benefit if the Banking Committee was regarded as active and productive in the consumer protection area. Both were generally permissive and helpful with respect to member initiatives in this area, particularly with nonthreatening junior members like myself. These committee leaders handled certain other areas of their jurisdiction quite differently, encouraging initiatives and sharing power much less readily. But in the consumer protection area, leadership style and the effective decentralization of the committee fostered entrepreneurship and gave it a fair chance of success (Fig. 5.1).

The committee's mode of partisanship also had a positive effect. Though House Banking Committee members frequently experienced severe conflict and committee leaders often failed to manage conflict well, these divisions shifted from issue to issue and often cut across party lines. There was a tradition of cross-party collaboration on discrete measures on which I could draw in introducing and refining the home equity bill.

The political conditions surrounding the home equity issue were also favorable.[7] The bill spoke to a problem of growing public salience, one that promised some recognition and reward to legislators who addressed it. In addition, the issue was not saddled with the kind of debilitating conflict that would have discouraged legislative involvement. Members could see this as a consumer protection measure with considerable poten-

FIGURE 5.1   An exciting day on the Banking Committee.

tial public appeal, but at the same time, they could be relatively certain that support of the bill would not draw them into serious conflicts with outside groups or with their colleagues.

The relevant "interested outsiders" had good reasons for adopting a constructive, cooperative posture, although it was by no means always certain that they would do so.[8] The Federal Reserve Board, having acknowledged the need for home equity loan regulation and having begun its own rulemaking, needed to ensure congruence between congressional action and its own. And industry groups recognized that the price of noncooperation might be a more punitive and less workable bill. This led to a rather grudging decision by the American Bankers Association not to oppose the bill actively and to much more positive collaboration by other industry groups. Some of the consumer lobbyists were inclined to push for "their bill or none," to test the limits of the developing consensus. But others, most notably the American Association of Retired Persons (AARP), needed to deliver a bill to their constituents, and committee allies of the consumer groups, like Annunzio and Schumer, let them know that they would not back an absolutist stance.

Although these conditions facilitated a successful initiative, they by no means ensured it. Successful entrepreneurship requires members and their aides to *push*, to push continually, and to push hard. Furthermore, one must *shape* such an initiative to make the most of favorable conditions. In the home equity case, this approach meant taking full account of the Federal Reserve's preferences as the bill was drafted and refined. It meant consulting with and deferring to the committee leadership. It meant drafting the bill to attract bipartisan support, seeking that support, and insisting that all the major players be brought along at each successive stage. And it meant working hard to keep the intergroup negotiations on track.

Policy entrepreneurship is irreducibly personal. It does not lend itself to easy predictions or determinate explanations. One can identify the conditions that encourage or facilitate entrepreneurial ventures, but the shape and the success of such initiatives still depend on the motivation, style, and skill of members and their aides—the kind of job they wish to do and the strategic choices they make in pursuing that goal.

AMENDING THE HOUSING BILL

The House Banking Committee has eight subcommittees, but two of them—Financial Institutions, and Housing and Community Development—far surpass the others in the breadth of their jurisdictions and their attractiveness to members. Though some subcommittees have trouble attracting even 10 or 12 members, there has been constant pressure to expand both Financial Institutions and Housing to accommodate more. As a new member in 1987, I, too, wanted both major subcommittees, but I knew that, given the way the process of "bidding" for subcommittees was likely to go, there would probably be room for me only on one. Therefore, I picked Financial Institutions, considering not only its centrality to the jurisdiction of the committee but also the fact that the major agenda items that could be anticipated for the 100th Congress—bank powers, for example, and the savings and loan crisis—were likely to be in this area.

This proved to be a good choice, for congressional action on housing in 1987–1988 amounted to little more than an extension of existing programs. By 1989, however, I had more seniority, and the new full committee chairman, Henry Gonzalez (D.-Texas), who inherited the chair after St. Germain's defeat in the 1988 election, expanded the top two subcommittees even further. I eagerly claimed a seat on Housing as well as on Financial Institutions, for I saw housing as a critical area of national need where I could make a contribution. Moreover, it seemed likely that there would be a push for significant housing legislation in the 101st Congress.

Senators Alan Cranston (D.-California) and Alfonse D'Amato (R.-New York), chairman and ranking Republican on the Senate Housing Subcommittee, were nearing the culmination of an ambitious, two-year effort to draft an overhaul of federal housing policy. Gonzalez, longtime chairman of the House committee's Subcommittee on Housing, had remained aloof from this effort because of what some termed "a combination of ego, institutional rivalry, pent-up frustration from the beating liberal housing advocates in the House took when Republicans controlled the Senate in 1981–86, and a lack of desire to revamp existing programs."[9] But Gonzalez was drafting his own bill, and his elevation to the chair of the full committee, while retaining the same position on the Housing Subcommittee, put him in a strengthened position from which to push this and other housing proposals. In addition, the Bush administration, with an energetic new Housing and Urban Development (HUD) secretary in Jack Kemp and a legacy of HUD scandals to overcome, seemed more amenable than its predecessor to housing initiatives.

During 1989, however, housing, like everything else on the Banking Committee agenda, took a back seat to the legislation to recapitalize the savings and loan insurance fund and to revamp regulation of the industry—the Financial Institutions Reform, Recovery, and Enforcement Act (FIRREA). The three amendments I was able to add to this bill as it made its way through the Financial Institutions Subcommittee set the pattern for more extensive attempts to modify and augment the housing bill a year later. Two years of experience with the committee, with the issues, and with "interested outsiders" in the agencies, academia, and financial institutions made such a role much more feasible and comfortable for me and for my banking aide, Paul Feldman, than it would have been during my freshman term.

We developed two of my FIRREA amendments in cooperation with the Federal Deposit Insurance Corporation (FDIC), which was to be given major responsibility for the savings and loan cleanup. I thought the administration proposal that the FDIC chair and vice chair should serve at the president's pleasure would make the board vulnerable to White House pressure; my first amendment therefore gave them a fixed, four-year term of office. The second amendment altered the administration's proposed limits on FDIC borrowing authority, so that no notes could be issued that would put the agency in a net deficit position (and thereby implicitly obligate the taxpayer). My third amendment drew on a recommendation of the Shadow Financial Regulatory Committee, a private organization of academics and former regulators; it required regulators to reveal the economic assumptions and calculations that led them to dispose of a case in one way rather than another, so that third parties might scrutinize and evaluate their decisions. The need for such a provision had been underscored by the controversy swirling around the "December deals" entered into by the Federal Savings and Loan Insurance Corporation (FSLIC) in the last month of the Reagan administration.

These additions to FIRREA and the six comparable additions I made to the housing bill—which I will describe in somewhat more detail to illustrate their origins and the politics of their adoption—are typical of the policy entrepreneurship a variety of members undertake as a major bill is considered in committee. FIRREA and the housing bill contrasted sharply, however, in the degree of congressional responsibility for their initiation and their content. FIRREA was mainly a presidential initiative, which the Banking committees and the Congress amended at the margins. The housing bill also contained presidentially initiated elements, most notably a program pushed by Secretary Kemp to help public housing tenants and other low-income people buy housing units. But the fact that the administration put forward even this proposal when it did was partially a result of congressional pressure, and the great majority of the provisions in both the House and Senate bills were congressional in origin.

The heart of the Cranston-D'Amato bill, for example, was a new Housing Opportunity Partnerships (HOP) program, designed to use federal matching grants to encourage partnerships among local governments, nonprofit organizations, and private industry in providing affordable housing. This provision was based on a major recommendation of the well-regarded National Housing Task Force;[10] I strongly favored it as a way to introduce innovation and flexibility into the federal housing effort. The House bill concentrated more on strengthening a range of existing programs, many of which had declined disastrously through mismanagement as well as deep funding cuts during the Reagan years. But the bill also proposed several new programs, including Gonzalez's National Housing Trust Fund to subsidize mortgage costs for first-time homebuyers of moderate income and a rental housing production program initiated by Schumer (and opposed vigorously by the administration) to authorize low-interest advances to groups and agencies engaged in the construction or acquisition of affordable rental units.

My active involvement in shaping the housing bill and my public identification with the issue were facilitated when Gonzalez agreed to schedule a field hearing of the Housing Subcommittee in Raleigh in early 1990. The full day of testimony we heard reinforced several ideas for amendments that I had been working on. It also helped provide a basis for later cooperation with each of the colleagues who made the trip— Steve Bartlett (R.-Texas), Liz Patterson (D.-South Carolina), and Peter Hoagland (D.-Nebraska).

The first amendment set up a $20-million demonstration program for "soft second" mortgages. We used the Raleigh hearing (Fig. 5.2) to highlight the success of this financing technique in several local affordable-housing developments. In this financing arrangement, a bank made a loan to a borrower for approximately 70 percent of the home's value. A local government or nonprofit organization made a second loan—the soft second—to the borrower for the remaining percentage of the home's value. Principal and interest payments on the second mortgage were deferred for several years or until the house was sold again. Such schemes, several witnesses testified, were bringing monthly mortgage payments within reach for homebuyers of modest income. However, the resources for such financing were limited; "the problem," said one mayor, "is now that we know this works, we don't have the resources to replicate it."[11]

Providing such second-mortgage resources seemed to be a feasible federal role, a way of stimulating substantial public and private investments in affordable housing with a relatively modest federal contribution. I therefore proposed that we set up a demonstration program at HUD that would allow local governments and nonprofits to apply for funds for soft second mortgage financing. After a good deal of discussion, mainly at the staff level, Chairman Gonzalez agreed to include a modest authorization as part of his home ownership title in the "chairman's mark," the revised bill offered to the subcommittee for markup.

My second amendment loosened the so-called federal preference eligibility rules for public housing and rental assistance projects. By law, 90 percent of such units had to go to families in the preference categories—families who were paying more than 50 percent of their income in rent, had been involuntarily displaced, or were living in substandard housing. The administration defended such targeting as a way of giving priority to the most needy, but the people who actually had to administer these developments told a different story. "The concept of dealing only with the neediest of the poor . . . was well intended," the director of the Raleigh Housing Authority told our subcommittee, but as a result, "we have driven the low-income working families out of our public housing and we have driven the role models out, we have driven the two-parent households out and [have helped create] much of the negative environment that we are now being criticized for in public housing."[12] In other words, too rigid preference rules meant that public housing was not working as a *community*, for the neediest or for anyone else.

I was predisposed to attend to such arguments by some consulting I had done in 1978–1979, helping HUD evaluate community development programs, and by my academic work in ethics and public policy (see Chapter 10). I did enough checking to assure myself that there was hardly a public housing director in the country who did not believe the preference

FIGURE 5.2 At the Housing Subcommittee field hearing in Raleigh, North Carolina Association of Educators auditorium, January 26, 1990. *Herald-Sun* photo by Chuck Liddy, Durham, North Carolina. Reprinted by permission.

rules should be relaxed. I then proposed that up to 30 percent of the slots in public and assisted housing could go to persons who met the income eligibility requirements but fell outside the federal preference criteria. The amendment drew skeptical responses from liberal Democratic members like Gonzalez and Joe Kennedy as well as administration partisans on the Republican side. But members like Schumer and Bartlett who knew a great deal about how housing programs actually worked came to the amendment's defense, and in the end, the subcommittee adopted it by voice vote.

The third amendment raised the maximum value of a home eligible for Federal Housing Administration (FHA) mortgage insurance to $124,875 (or 95 percent of the median sale price in a given area, if that were a lower figure). Although I had proposed a similar increase the year before as part of a bill to make FHA mortgage insurance more accessible to first-time homebuyers, I was by no means the only member interested in raising the FHA ceiling, for in many cities across the country—like Raleigh, Cary, and Chapel Hill in my district—the median price of a home had risen far above the existing FHA limit. Realtors, homebuilders, and housing officials and advocates were united in seeking a more flexible limit; the private mortgage insurers were the only major group opposed.

In late 1989, the Appropriations Subcommittee on VA, HUD, and Independent Agencies included a one-year increase to $124,875 in its fiscal year 1990 appropriations bill. Gonzalez was not sympathetic to the increase, and he angrily opposed it, without success, on the House floor as an encroachment on the Banking Committee's prerogatives. Nonetheless, he recognized the growing impatience of members with such arguments and knew that I and several others were ready to propose farther-reaching changes in FHA mortgage insurance criteria as amendments to the housing bill. Gonzalez therefore elected to include a permanent increase to $124,875 in the chairman's mark, assuming correctly that we would be willing to accept that and declare victory.

My fourth amendment expanded an FHA demonstration program to insure "reverse mortgages" for elderly homeowners. The AARP and other housing advocacy groups put great stock in the concept, which allowed cash-poor homeowners to draw down a portion of their equity to meet monthly expenses and still remain in their homes. But these groups were dissatisfied with the scale and the scope of the existing demonstration, which involved only 2,500 participants, and they began talking with several members' staffs about expanding the program. Schumer and I decided to offer an amendment to the housing bill to increase the demonstration to 25,000 participants and to clarify and expand the options available to borrowers. We consulted with administration representatives and Republican members to head off any possible opposition and got the amendment adopted in subcommittee by voice vote.

My fifth amendment required that consumers be clearly informed what they must do, in paying off FHA-insured mortgages, to avoid additional interest charges beyond the date of payoff. This problem was brought to my attention by a couple of letters from constituents who had been charged interest for an entire month even when they had paid off their mortgage early in the month. My first inclination was simply to forbid such charges, but Feldman's conversations with regulators and industry representatives convinced us that a flat prohibition would have costs and complexities beyond what we had anticipated. As a result, we settled for a disclosure and notification requirement, and this we were able to get added to the bill without dissent.

The sixth amendment, which I offered in collaboration with Tom Carper (D.-Delaware), Patterson, and Hoagland, was by far the most complex and controversial of the lot. We developed our own compromise solution to the vexed question of whether and under what conditions landlords who were eligible to prepay federally subsidized mortgages and to convert their properties to uses other than low-income housing should be allowed to do so. I felt that the owners clearly had a right to prepay because their contracts so stipulated and that for the government to renege on this promise would discourage future private participation in low-income housing ventures. At the same time, it was clearly desirable that prepayment and conversion not occur on a large scale, for hundreds of thousands of lower-income tenants would then risk eviction.

The chairman's mark, reflecting the views of low-income housing advocacy groups and of members like Gonzalez, Kennedy, and Barney Frank (D.-Massachusetts), essentially forbade prepayment. An amendment, sponsored by Bartlett and Doug Barnard (D.-Georgia) and backed by the realtors and other supporters of the owners, upheld the right to prepay, while providing certain incentives for owners to remain in the program and protections for tenants who might be displaced. My collaborators and I were not entirely happy with either proposal, and we realized that we might well be the swing votes that determined which approach the committee approved. We therefore decided to work with Bartlett, to see if we could devise some modifications that would let us support his proposal with more enthusiasm. We chose this course because we were in fundamental agreement with him on the right to prepay and because he and Barnard had already gone some distance to develop a balanced solution and seemed willing to go further. Our proposal strengthened the incentives for owners and the protections for tenants—requiring direct relocation assistance from owners, for example, and facilitating the transfer of properties to nonprofit organizations—and was accepted by Bartlett as a friendly amendment. Thus augmented, the Bartlett-Barnard amendment passed the full committee by a 29–19 vote. In the meantime, our group announced that we would continue to work on the prepayment issue and would bring further refinements to the House floor. We used the seven weeks between the committee vote and floor consideration on August 1 to devise a more comprehensive amendment that gave nonprofits and others who intended to use the property for low-income housing a clear right of first refusal when an owner elected to prepay his or her mortgage and sell the property. It also extended the low-income use restrictions for those who elected to stay within the program and provided some incentives for owners to improve services for the elderly living in their units. The latter provision as well as the first refusal requirement helped attract the support of the AARP. Some low-income housing advocates worked with us in devising the floor amendment, although others kept their distance. We continued to consult with Bartlett and the groups working with him as well. In the end, our amendment passed by a vote of 400–12. Among the opponents, however, were Gonzalez and Kennedy, who were still unreconciled to their defeat in committee. Some Republicans had felt Bartlett went too far in accepting our amendment, but they decided to vote yea after Kennedy opposed it in intemperate terms.

Frank and most other committee liberals also voted for our amendment, recognizing that it moved the bill toward the committee's original position. Frank withdrew his own proposal, which would have moved even further, when he saw the size of our vote. He pledged, however, to work in conference to move toward the Senate position, which severely restricted prepayment. This he was able to do, although the conference agreement remained close to the balance we had struck.

All six of my amendments, in fact, survived in conference, although I was not there to defend them in person. Because of my relatively junior status, I had not expected to be appointed to the conference committee. But when a senior member like Carper was also omitted and when I saw members at my seniority level and below being named, it became clear that Gonzalez was not taking our disagreement lightly. (The Speaker, who is formally responsible for naming conferees, only rarely deviates from the chair's recommendations.) Consequently, I had to request help in protecting my interests from several conferees, and most were happy to oblige. Schumer, of course, looked out for the reverse-mortgage provisions he and I had authored, and he and Frank and Chalmers Wylie, the ranking Republican member, also helped ensure that the second-mortgage demonstration project was retained. Bartlett helped persuade HUD officials not to press for the deletion of the federal preferences amendment. As the budget conflict between Congress and the White House dragged on through September and October, so did the conference on the housing bill. Finally, on October 25, 1990, the conference report cleared the House and was on its way to the president, a much more significant bill than many had believed possible when Congress had begun working on it in earnest less than five months before.

These FIRREA and housing amendments demonstrate the range of sources from which legislative initiatives may flow—agencies, advocacy groups, constituency complaints, one's own ideas and experiences, discomfort with the existing alternatives—and the sorts of alliances and compromises that are essential to their success. Like the home equity bill, they demonstrate the centrality of creative and persistent staff work to successful entrepreneurship and the importance of agency and group support. They also show the Banking Committee to be more amenable to policy entrepreneurship than is at first apparent: Though the committee has a reputation for arbitrary leadership and persistent conflict, it remains quite permeable in terms of members' ability to shape its legislative product. Its patterns of conflict, moreover, are sufficiently fluid to permit the assemblage, from issue to issue, of all sorts of coalitions, often across party lines. One has to work at it; nothing seems to come easily on the Banking Committee. But despite the obstacles and frustrations and despite the more general decline of policy entrepreneurship in Congress over the past dozen years, the committee's work demonstrates how strong the incentives for this kind of legislative role remain and how often such efforts are rewarded with success.

6

The Party Connection

Newly elected members of Congress quickly confront the realities of party leadership and control. This comes as a surprise to some, for the conventional wisdom has it that American parties are in decline, and many members' campaigns, run independently of their party to a large extent, seem to confirm this view. But despite a continued weakening in the hold of the major parties on the electorate, the congressional parties over the past twenty years have become more active and their operations more extensive than at any other time in American history. Party solidarity in roll-call voting has displayed a remarkable comeback from its low point in the 90th–92nd congresses (1967–1972). Party cohesion and control in the House of Representatives fall short of what is to be found in parliamentary systems or even in many American state legislatures, and in the U.S. Senate, the party reins are looser still. But the parties retain a central role in both the present functioning of the Congress and in periodic efforts to improve its performance.

In this chapter, I will illustrate the party role in Congress by describing my own interactions with the Democratic Party during my first five years in the House. But I should stress at the outset that not every member's story would be the same. This underscores an important fact about congressional party organizations: Though they perform crucial institutional functions and though every representative must come to terms with them in some fashion, members retain a great deal of independence and discretion in their voting behavior on the floor and in how they relate to the broad range of party functions and activities. This is mainly because of the way in which members get elected. Parties *outside* the Congress have, indeed, declined in their hold on voter loyalties and in their control of critical campaign resources.

Congressional representatives are increasingly on their own electorally and less dependent on the parties in their constituencies. They face electorates that are less inclined to vote for them on party grounds alone and a public that is largely unaware of and unconcerned about their party regularity once they are in office. They are generally nominated not by party caucuses or conventions but by direct primaries, and the number of

73

districts with party organizations strong enough to control the nomination process has declined substantially. Candidates must raise their own funds and build their own organizations at the primary stage and often for the general election as well. National partisan swings have become less and less determinative of election outcomes in most congressional districts, and ticket-splitting has become endemic. Understandably, members are less likely under these circumstances to see their ties to the organized party, either at home or in Congress, as crucial to their electoral fortunes.

Representatives increasingly relate to their districts directly, in ways unmediated by party. District service operations have grown, responding to and sometimes stimulating expanded expectations on the part of constituents as to the role and obligations of government. The growth of television as the dominant medium of political communication, both in campaign advertising and in the daily news, also offers manifold opportunities for more frequent and more direct communications with voters than was ever afforded by traditional friends-and-neighbors or clubhouse channels. The same is true of the computerized mail technologies utilized in campaigns and in most congressional offices. There is very little in all of this, then, that encourages party loyalty in Washington. It is true, as Richard Fenno stressed, that effective servicing of their districts can build up members' political capital and give them increased leeway for what they do in Washington.[1] But it is also true that much of this activity, especially roll-call voting, seems more visible now than formerly, particularly when one contemplates the use an opponent might make of it in thirty-second television commercials in the next campaign or in fire-breathing direct mail solicitations. Such prospects can make the blandishments of party leaders pale by comparison.

The decline of the party in the electorate and of traditional party organizations, along with the rise of new modes of political communication, have therefore weakened key incentives to party regularity in the Congress. As I will stress further in Chapter 10, this makes the question of what contribution one will make to the effective functioning of one's party more a matter of individual discretion and responsibility than it was for many members in the past. But it also leaves an important question unanswered: How is it that, in the midst of these unmistakable party weakening forces, the *congressional* parties—and particularly the Democratic Party in the House, which has controlled the chamber since 1955— have been able to substantially strengthen their leadership role?

The answer, basically, is that more and more members have come to believe that enhanced party operations serve their political and policy goals.[2] In the 1970s, increasingly restless members used strengthened party organs to rein in the senior committee chairmen who had dominated both chambers since the late New Deal. But as old power centers were weakened and authority and resources were dispersed more widely, the impossibility of running a legislature on the premise of "every person for him- or herself" became more apparent. Thus, the 1980s have seen the congressional parties, especially the House Democrats, expanding their operations and commanding greater loyalty from their members, even as the district-based incentives to party regularity have continued to weaken.

THE "NEW CENTRALIZATION" IN THE HOUSE

The trends I have delineated—weakened party ties, candidates and incumbents more and more on their own as they seek media exposure and name familiarity—produced a rising tide of discontent with House operations and eventually, in the 1970s, major organizational changes. Members became uncomfortable with norms and structures that denied them both visibility and leverage until they had accrued years of seniority. Many also became critical of the conservative bias of institutional arrangements that gave disproportionate power to long-entrenched southern Democratic chairmen. The elections of 1958, 1964, and 1974 in particular brought large numbers of liberal activist Democrats into the House. In the meantime, black enfranchisement and party realignment in the South gradually produced a new breed of Democratic House members from that region, much closer to the party's mainstream.

These crosscurrents produced significant shifts in ideology and policy preference within the House's majority party. Members came to see significant advantages in strengthening party organs, not by virtue of any party ties outside the chamber but as a means to their personal and policy goals within. This is not to say strengthening the party was a dominant goal of congressional reform. Its initial and main thrust was, in fact, *decentralization*—the dispersal of authority, resources, and visibility throughout the chamber—producing from 1965 to 1978 the organizational phase that Roger Davidson termed the "rise of subcommittee government."[3]

Congressional reform, however, had a centralizing component from the first. The reformers' main target was committee oligarchs, rather than party leaders, and revitalizing the House Democratic Caucus proved necessary in order to rewrite the rules, depose recalcitrant chairmen, and otherwise effect the desired transfer of power. The leadership, moreover, was the only available counterweight to bastions like the House Rules or Ways and Means committee. Therefore, two key early reforms removed the committee-assignment function from Ways and Means Democrats and placed it in a leadership-dominated Steering and Policy Committee and gave the Speaker the power to nominate the chairman and the Democratic members of the Rules Committee. For some reformers, such as Rep. Richard Bolling (D.-Missouri), the strengthening of party organs was quite deliberate, aimed at giving a true "majority of House Democrats . . . effective control of the House" and enabling them to enact their legislative program.[4] For others, it was mainly a means to the end of breaking up oligarchical power. The effect, in any event, was to strengthen the party involvement of younger members and to enhance the role of the leadership, even as the actual decisions of the caucus were helping atomize congressional power.

This atomization, as it proceeded through the 1970s, gave more and more members a stake in the new order, but it also created new problems for the institution that only strengthened parties could solve. The proliferating bases from which issues could be publicized and initiatives generated could also encourage conflict and obstruction when the time came to mobilize the chamber. Consequently, there was widespread support for leadership efforts to overcome organizational fragmentation, sometimes through extraordinary devices such as the Ad Hoc Energy Committee (1977) and more generally through increases in the Speaker's referral powers, the development of leadership agendas, and the strengthening of whip operations.[5]

The decline in the deference paid to committees, individual members' desires for visibility, and rules changes such as the institution of the recorded teller vote resulted in increased amending activity on the House floor. In time, though, many members came to see this as more of a threat than an opportunity, as measures they favored were damaged or delayed and as members of the opposition party used the amendment process to force politically charged record votes. Thus, the leadership began, with widespread member support, to pass more bills under "suspension of the rules" procedures that forbade amendments, to employ more special rules that restricted amending activity, and to otherwise rein in floor activity.[6]

As the next chapter will demonstrate, modern budget politics has also strengthened the role of the congressional leadership. The budget process reforms instituted in the mid-1970s had this effect by virtue of the control party leaders assumed over appointments to the new budget committees and the necessity, created by the process, for negotiations among committees and between Congress and the White House. Even more determinative was the budget crisis that lasted through the 1980s. "Looming deficits and the need to reach painful decisions about priorities . . . pushed legislative structures and practices toward greater centralization."[7] Budget measures became more complicated, comprehensive, and conflictful, spilling over established timetables and processes and committee jurisdictions. Working out budget deals year to year with the Republican administration increasingly became a critical leadership function.

Many majority members of the House therefore became willing to support an enhanced party role, and as the party organization developed, it was able to reinforce these tendencies with a reward structure of its own. Meanwhile, the *costs* of cooperation were decreasing for many members as well. I have indicated how the political and budgetary climate of the 1980s made for less freewheeling policy entrepreneurship. Members had less to lose by being reined in and more to gain as the leadership sought to overcome some of the adverse conditions making legislative action difficult. Nor did the House Democrats have as much trouble uniting under the party banner as they had in the recent past. Plenty of diversity remained, but the north-south gap that had bedeviled the party and had fueled much of the early reform effort continued to narrow. Thus, the potential costs of assertive Democratic leadership in terms of disaffection and division were greatly reduced.[8]

It now appears that these trends toward strengthened leadership may well have reached a high point during my first term in the House, the 100th Congress of 1987–1988. As Roger Davidson observed:

Part of the equation was the advent of a new Speaker: Jim Wright (D-TX), who had few inhibitions about exploiting the powers of the office. Even more important, however, were contextual factors that at last made vigorous party leadership feasible. First, after dominating the Washington scene for six years, President Reagan was irrevocably damaged by the 1986 elections and the Iran-contra scandal that broke shortly afterwards. With both houses of Congress in Democratic hands, the legislative initiative traveled down Pennsylvania Avenue to Capitol Hill. Democrats and their allies at last saw a chance to push their long-deferred legislative agendas. Moreover, Democratic office-holders again found reason to identify themselves with a partisan agenda: Not only was the party label worth more than in Reagan's heyday, but Democrats were anxious to compile a record of achievement to carry them into the 1988 elections. Finally, in order to pass a partisan agenda, both committee leaders and the rank and file understood that leadership coordination would be essential.[9]

Speaker Wright saw to it that the first five bills introduced, numbered H.R. 1 through H.R. 5, were those he regarded as lead items on the Democratic agenda. Two of these, the Clean Water Act and an ambitious highway bill, were passed shortly after Congress convened in January 1987; by April 2, both had again been whipped through over President Reagan's vetoes. The remaining three bills, an omnibus trade measure and reauthorizations of elementary and secondary education and housing programs, were all passed over the course of the next two years, as were significant welfare reform, Medicare expansion, fair housing, farm credit reform, plant closing notification, and homeless assistance measures. The

100th Congress could fairly be regarded as the most productive since the Great Society congresses of the mid-1960s, and strong leadership in the House was a critical part of the equation.

The 101st and 102nd congresses found it difficult to maintain this level of productivity, although the falloff was not as great as many commentators suggest. The leading agenda items were neither as obvious nor as easy to pass as the clean water and highway bills had been in 1987. The ethics troubles of Speaker Wright and of Majority Whip Tony Coelho deepened quickly as the 101st Congress began, leading to the departure of both men by mid-1989. The 1988 presidential elections left Democrats without a clear programmatic thrust and with more than a touch of defensiveness; moreover, the White House vacuum they had moved to fill in 1987 and 1988 was no more. And the long-term constraints imposed by enormous budget deficits and divided party control of government remained.

Still, there was no major reversal of the trend toward extensive and active leadership operations that had been so evident in the mid-1980s. The new Speaker, Tom Foley, though not as aggressively partisan as Wright, nonetheless became increasingly assertive in defining party goals and in using the leadership tools at his disposal. Nor was there any doubt that in so doing he was following the wishes and expectations of most caucus members. Majority Leader Dick Gephardt, who had a relatively high public profile by virtue of his 1988 run for the presidency, emerged as a forceful party spokesman. Whip and caucus operations, under the leadership of Bill Gray (Pennsylvania) and Steny Hoyer (Maryland), respectively, continued largely unchanged.

President George Bush, to be sure, proved a formidable adversary, stymieing congressional action in areas ranging from civil rights to the minimum wage to the protection of Chinese nationals seeking to delay a return home after the Tiananmen Square massacre. But in other areas, he proved far more flexible than President Reagan, cooperating with the Congress to produce major clean air, handicapped rights, and housing legislation. In either event, under conditions of both confrontation and cooperation, the need for strong party leadership was apparent to and therefore generally supported by most Democratic members.

Leadership strength is, of course, a relative concept. The House leadership system that in 1988 could plausibly be described as "more centralized and concentrated . . . than at any time since the days of Joseph Cannon" looks considerably less so when compared to its parliamentary counterparts or when whips are scrambling to patch together winning coalitions on difficult issues.[10] The dispersal of authority and resources to 148 subcommittees remains as an enduring legacy of "reform" (and of the underlying electoral realities). There is also an unmistakable fragility to leadership strength, which is now based less on "strong parties external to the Congress" and more on the acquiescence of freewheeling individual members.[11] Power relationships could no doubt shift with changes in majority party size, White House control, or the nation's policy agenda. Still, the party role looms large in the contemporary House—a role I will now attempt to elucidate further through a description of my own "party connection."

ELECTORAL SUPPORT

As a candidate for Congress, I had unusually strong party credentials. I had paid my dues through local party service and as a foot soldier in other Democrats' campaigns, and my background as executive director and chairman of the North Carolina Democratic Party was the main factor giving me credibility as a congressional candidate. I chose the county Democratic conventions in my district—simultaneously held on April 13, 1985—to announce my candidacy, believing (as I still do) that party activists were an essential core of my political base. After surviving the primary, I received substantial support from the Democratic Congressional Campaign Committee and integrated my grass-roots campaign with that of county party organizations. My campaigns thus illustrate the role the party still can play. But they also demonstrate the limits of that role, even when a candidate has an inclination (which many candidates do not) to run as part of the party team.

The state party chairmanship may actually be emerging as a more promising launching pad for a congressional candidacy. Among the Democratic state chairmen with whom I served, four—Nancy Pelosi of California, Bart Gordon of Tennessee, Dave Nagle of Iowa, and Chester Atkins of Massachusetts—are now House colleagues. This probably says less about the potency of state parties than about the changing nature of the chairmanship. It has become a far more public role, giving the individual in that post media exposure, identifying him or her as a spokesperson on key issues, and so forth. Certainly, it was the public role I assumed during the Senate and other campaigns of 1984, much more than my behind-the-scenes organizational activity, that gave me credibility as a potential candidate.

As recounted in Chapter 2, however, neither my recognition among party activists nor my wider exposure as a party spokesman gave me anything approaching a decisive edge in a Democratic primary. That came only as we formulated a television message and scraped together enough money to put it on the air. Relatively little of that money came from party sources; Democratic Party activists are generally able to contribute only modestly. North Carolina party organizations, like others in states with a one-party past where nomination was once tantamount to election, have a tradition of remaining neutral, financially and otherwise, in primary contests. The same is true, in most cases, for the DCCC. Nonetheless, I called on its leaders during the primary season, knowing that a direct contribution was out of the question but hoping to convince them that I would be a strong, perhaps the best, general election candidate, so that they might informally pass the word to potential contributors that I was a good prospect. This happened only to a very limited degree, however. The fact is that it was not within the power of local, state, or national party organizations to deliver the Democratic nomination. I and my fledgling campaign team, including, to be sure, many active local Democrats, were largely on our own in pursuing this goal.

That changed some but not entirely after the primary. The DCCC was targeting four Democratic challengers in North Carolina in 1986—three of us who were attempting to regain seats that had been lost in 1984 and a fourth, D. G. Martin, trying again for the Charlotte seat he had failed to win by only 321 votes in 1984. Tony Coelho was an unusually active and aggressive DCCC chairman, greatly stepping up fund-raising activity and moving from the group's natural tendency to simply shore up incumbents to a strategy of targeting those races where an infusion of funds could have the greatest impact. Martin's Charlotte race, where Coelho strongly disagreed with some of the candidate's tactics, showed how intrusive the chairman and his aides could be, using their financial support as leverage to try to move the campaign in certain directions. The DCCC leadership apparently had no such problems with my campaign, although we had many quibbles along the way. The committee contributed $39,848 to my effort, which, when added to the state tax checkoff monies funneled through the state Democratic Party, came close to the legal maximum.

The state party, having lost the organizational resources of the governorship in 1984 and having nothing like the Hunt-Helms Senate race to attract contributions and participation in 1986, was not in a position to replicate the state-level voter-contact operations undertaken two years before. Several congressional campaigns were weakened as a result. I was fortunate, however, in having relatively active Democratic organizations in most of my counties and a tradition of extensive phone bank and get-out-the-vote activity in Raleigh and Chapel Hill. We therefore decided after the primary to run our voter-contact operations as part of a Democratic "unity campaign," and our Senate candidate, Terry Sanford, did the same.

Although my campaign thus evinced relatively strong participation both by the national campaign committee and by local party organizations, it could not, when compared either to parliamentary elections in other Western democracies or to earlier American practice, be judged a party-centered effort. We gained numerous foot soldiers and saved scarce campaign dollars by combining forces with other Democratic candidates in our canvassing and turnout operations, but even here, we gave as much as we got. Party precinct structures were spotty at best, and the cadres of volunteers often needed shoring up. So, activists from the Price campaign helped make the party efforts work, as well as the reverse.

In other facets of the campaign, the party role was far less prominent. The state party organized a rally in each congressional district for all the Democratic candidates, and most county parties did the same thing locally. But most of my campaign appearances and fund-raising events were organized by our campaign alone. The state party had an able research director on whom we drew, and the state party chairman sometimes held press conferences or issued broadsides in collaboration with various congressional campaigns. But by and large, in devising a press strategy, in formulating a message, in putting together an advertising campaign, and in raising the money to pay for it, we were still on our own.

In the two reelection campaigns I have waged since 1986, both against aggressive and well-financed opponents, the party role has slipped somewhat. This is not because of any changed strategy on my part; rather, it reflects changed priorities and capacities on the party side. The DCCC contributed far less in 1988 and 1990 than it had in 1986. Mine was still a targeted race, but the DCCC was strapped for money and perhaps regarded me as better equipped than others to raise my own funds. The state party declined further in the financial resources and campaign services it was able to offer candidates. But we continued to cooperate actively in voter-contact operations with county party organizations, and, especially in 1990, we developed synergetic relationships with other Democratic campaigns—such as Harvey Gantt's Senate race, which attracted much participation and enthusiasm, and several targeted state legislative races in my district.

Besides trying to make the most of the party potential in my own campaigns, I have attempted to keep my local party ties in good repair between elections—attending and speaking at meetings, helping organize and promote events, consulting with party leaders. I value these organizations and believe elected officials can do much to enhance their role. Politicians who complain of the party's weakness and irrelevance and treat the organization accordingly often are engaged in a self-fulfilling prophecy; we do have significant choices as to how we relate to party organizations, and the choices we make have a considerable potential to harm or help. I am not suggesting, of course, that candidates or office-holders should be expected to sacrifice their basic interests to those of the party. I am, rather, suggesting that normally a *range* of viable strategies of campaigning and governance are available, some of which tend to reinforce and others to undermine party strength.

The parties, however, must also help themselves. The national committees, the House and Senate campaign committees, and many state parties have done more than is commonly recognized to remodel them-selves—increasing their financial base and their capacity to recruit can-didates and to offer a range of supportive services—although these advances seem to be leveling off at present. Much depends on the quality of party leadership at all levels. Local parties are not tidy organizations, and they would lose much of their vitality if they were. Gone forever is the patronage system that bound loyalists to "the organization" and assured tight leadership control. Today's party activists are motivated mainly by issue and candidate enthusiasms, and they often give organi-zational maintenance a decidedly lower priority. Candidates and office-holders who would work with the party must recognize this and adapt to it. At the same time, partisans and their leaders need to understand that if they allow the party to degenerate into contending factions—each pushing for its own "pure" policy position or preferred candidate, unable or unwilling to work together after the nomination and platform battles are over—candidates and officeholders will be tempted to distance them-selves, seeing in the party tie more hassle than help.

Public policy at all levels also can strengthen or weaken the parties' electoral role.[12] Here, I will mention only an area that has concerned me directly both as state chairman and as a member of Congress, the regu-lation of campaign finance. Campaign finance reform, however necessary or laudable in many respects, has too often handicapped the parties and contributed to their irrelevance—a problem to which Common Cause and other reform advocates are still largely insensitive. What we should be doing is *strengthening* parties as a counterweight to more narrowly based groups and as a vehicle for healthy and broadly based political participa-tion. At a minimum, this means preserving and expanding the provisions in law for parties to make "coordinated expenditures" on behalf of congressional candidates above and beyond their direct contributions.[13] It also means being very careful, in cleaning up the so-called soft money abuses, not to penalize or discourage voter registration or get-out-the-vote and other party voter-contact activities on behalf of the entire ticket, federal candidates included.[14] In fact, such activities should be given a protected position in the law. And as we consider reinstating tax incentives for small individual contributions, we should try to encourage support of parties by making available a tax credit or deduction for party contribu-tions, separate from what is provided for contributions to candidates.[15]

THE PARTY NETWORK

Newly elected members of Congress, when they come to Washington for the week of organizational meetings before the session begins, imme-diately confront the fact that the the House is a party-led chamber.

Representatives attend orientation sessions organized by the majority and minority leadership, vote to choose party leaders and adopt caucus rules, and begin to jockey for committee assignments in a process that is controlled by the parties. As I and other new Democratic members lobbied the Steering and Policy Committee for our preferred committee positions, we came to regard party leaders as the gatekeepers of the institution. This continued for me throughout most of my first two terms as I laid the groundwork for my 1991 move to the Appropriations Committee.

New members soon have the opportunity, however, to become part of the party network themselves, at least at its outer reaches. Not everyone chooses to do so, but many do—for party participation is a way of placing oneself in the crosscurrents of information and influence, and for some, it is a pathway to power within the institution. The leadership ladder is quite crowded these days, with numerous members competing for every appointive and elective leadership post. But any member who wishes to can become involved in the work of the caucus and the whip organization. This is a legacy of the 1970s, when these organizations were revitalized and expanded, but it also represents a deliberate strategy of inclusion by party leaders, who recognize that members are more likely to be cooperative and helpful when they feel they are being informed and consulted and have a role to play in party affairs.

The House Democratic Caucus meets, on the average, about every two weeks. Sometimes, the purpose is to ratify committee assignments coming from the Steering and Policy Committee or rules changes coming from the Committee on Organization, Study, and Review (OSR). More often, the caucus is called to discuss a pending legislative battle of major importance, as occurred during the protracted budget battles of 1990 when frequent caucuses let the leadership report on the twists and turns of negotiations but also enabled the membership to communicate a sense of what was politically feasible. More rarely, the caucus may debate the party's long-range agenda and political strategy, as happened when the leadership scheduled a series of meetings in 1991 on future strategies for health care, middle-class tax fairness, and other issues.

I came to the House predisposed to be active in the Democratic Caucus. I have served since 1989 on the caucus's OSR Committee and was appointed in 1990 to coordinate the caucus's nine issues task forces. I have also participated fairly consistently in the work of the Message Board, an arm of the caucus that attempts to publicize the party's legislative efforts and to put a Democratic spin on the day's events. The main aspect of this that involves members like me is the attempt to coordinate and give a consistent theme to statements on the House floor, particularly during the period reserved for "one-minute" speeches at the beginning of the day. I have thus joined with colleagues in challenging the president to offer a serious national energy policy, in insisting that we must move beyond presidential rhetoric in improving education, and in other coordinated messages. The purpose, in part, is to counter House Republicans, who have often been more aggressive than we in taking advantage of the national platform that the House floor, as telecast by C-SPAN, offers. However, the real competition is in the White House, and we are reminded almost daily of the advantages the president has over the majority party in Congress—no matter how energetically led or how well-coordinated its message is—in capturing public attention and framing the day's issues.

The OSR Committee is a housekeeping committee, highly responsive to the Speaker, that screens proposed rules changes for the caucus and renders judgment on requests from members or committees for waivers of the rules or for the adjudication of rules disputes. The committee emerged briefly from obscurity in 1974 when the highly controversial recommendations on committee reorganization of the Select Committee on Committees were sent to OSR for a thorough reworking. But in normal times, OSR operates behind the scenes—a good place for a member to learn the organizational ropes and to work with party leaders on internal House matters.

The task force project I coordinated in 1990 was the fifth in a series of election year efforts begun when Democratic Caucus Chairman Gillis Long formed the Committee on Party Effectiveness (CPE) in 1981–1982. The CPE was an ambitious effort to involve caucus members, many of them quite junior and from outside the relevant committees, in broad policy discussions, to formulate positions that could inspire agreement among Democrats, and, in some cases, to nudge reluctant committee leaders along.[16] By the time I came to the House, the CPE was not a committee at all but a series of caucus-sponsored "party effectiveness" luncheons on important national issues, often featuring outside experts. I found these sessions quite valuable but also saw the need for more focused discussions, aimed at the production of a preelection document trumpeting Democratic achievements and aspirations. I was therefore pleased when Caucus Chairman Steny Hoyer asked me to coordinate the task force effort. The fact that I had an able political scientist, Paul Herrnson, on my staff for the year as a Congressional Fellow made me more confident in taking on the assignment.

Our effort was not as far-reaching as Long's party effectiveness projects. Our nine task forces contained a mix of members, both on and off the relevant committees, and though a number of committee chairmen cooperated fully in the effort, others displayed disinterest and even some hostility. We kicked off the process at the caucus's annual retreat in February. In the ensuing months, several of the task forces met repeatedly and hammered out consensus positions; in other cases, the leaders did little more than order up staff-produced drafts. In any event, after much cajoling and editing, we produced an issues handbook, *Investing in America's Future*, that served as a useful resource in 1990 and laid some groundwork for the 1992 national platform. How useful the task forces were as outlets for their members, however, varied greatly from case to case.

My second party connection has been through the whip organization. I learned very quickly that the most valuable meeting of the week in the House is the Thursday morning whips meeting, where plans for the coming week are discussed and strategy debated in a wide-open fashion. I began to attend these meetings regularly, although I was not formally part of the organization, and to volunteer from time to time for the ad hoc task forces put together by the whip's office to count votes and mobilize support on specific bills. By 1991, I had been designated an at-large whip and was helping with whip operations on most major bills.

The whip organization and its vote-gathering efforts enlist a good portion of the Democratic membership. Besides the majority whip— currently David Bonior (Michigan), who was elected by the caucus after Bill Gray's resignation in mid-1991—and 3 chief deputy whips appointed by the Speaker, the organization includes 15 deputy whips and 60 at-large whips appointed by the majority whip, as well as 14 assistant whips (or zone whips) elected by the regional party caucuses. On a bill the organization is whipping, the zone whips normally do the first count, after which the other components of the organization, more directly linked to the leadership, go to work on members whose votes appear problematic or who need shoring up. This further checking and communicating is done by deputy and at-large whips. On particularly important or difficult matters, an ad hoc task force is often appointed, which brings into the mix committee leaders and other members particularly influential or interested in the issue at hand. These task forces are essentially open to all comers, and they can be an important avenue of participation for junior members.

My own involvement in whip operations has been useful in at least three ways. First, it has let me help mobilize support for measures that I thought were important, such as the 1990 housing bill, on which I had worked extensively in committee. Second, it has made me a partner, albeit a junior one, in leadership undertakings. This can be intrinsically satisfying, and it can also bring other rewards. Indeed, those of us who were trying throughout 1990 to position ourselves to gain the next Appropriations Committee seats joked about what a coincidence it was that we so often found ourselves on the whip's task forces. Finally, it has brought me into discussions of floor strategy and the last-minute alterations needed to maximize votes on various bills. Certain committees, most notably

Judiciary and Education and Labor, tend to bring bills to the floor that are acceptable to the liberal majorities on those committees but need further work if they are to gain the full assent of a healthy majority of Democratic members. This happens more than it should, and whip task forces are hardly the ideal place to work out accommodations. But on bills like child care in 1990 and civil rights and striker replacement in 1991, the vote counts and feedback garnered by the whip organization have served as a reality check for committee leaders and have given members like me a means of pushing for needed refinements in advance of floor consideration.

Thus, for me and for many other members, finding a place in the House has proceeded along parallel tracks, not just in the committee system but in the sprawling party infrastructure as well. These party structures are highly permeable, and their boundaries are frequently unclear. They serve critical functions in the House—disseminating information, gathering intelligence, forging a policy consensus beyond committee enclaves, gathering votes. And they also provide a substantial number of members opportunities for participation and influence.

PARTY VOTING

Party voting in the House has increased steadily and substantially since the early 1970s. About half of the House's roll-call votes now find a majority of one party arrayed against a majority of the other, compared to one-third twenty years ago.[17] More significantly, as Figure 6.1 shows, individual members have become more and more inclined to stick with their party on such divided votes. Party voting has reached levels since the early 1980s not seen since the party polarization of Harry Truman's presidency. In part, this is a reflection of another period of national polarization. Ronald Reagan's presidency was a highly ideological one, and both the content of his proposals and his uncompromising style prompted sharp partisan divisions on Capitol Hill. Democrats, by virtue of the political threat Reagan posed and the impact of his policies on their constituencies, were constrained to develop and promote distinct alternatives and to unify against a common adversary. They were aided in this by the continued, albeit incomplete, closing of the gap between the northern and southern wings of the congressional party.

This growing divergence between and convergence within the congressional parties helped underwrite—indeed, created pressures to develop— the elaborate party machinery I have described. That machinery, in turn, has helped strengthen and solidify the partisan voting trends, although the precise impact is impossible to quantify. Heightened activity by the congressional campaign committees in recruiting and financing candidates, especially on the Republican side, has probably strengthened party

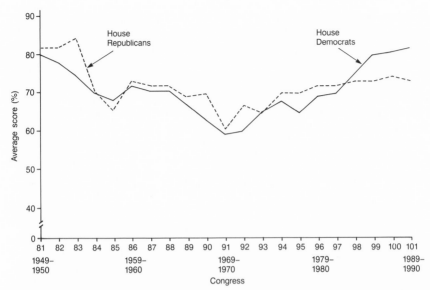

FIGURE 6.1 "Party unity" voting for House Democrats and Republicans (average individual support for party on votes dividing party majorities), 81st–101st Congresses (1949–1990). Based on data in *Congressional Quarterly Almanacs.*

identification among incoming members. The increased resources of party leaders—staff positions assigned to leadership offices, not including the campaign committees, now number 58 on the Democratic side and 44 for the Republicans—facilitate a dominant role for the parties in intra-House communications, help the leaders perform services and do favors for large numbers of members, and give these leaders a strengthened hand in shaping the House's policy agenda and assembling complex budget packages.

The party voting statistics also reflect the enhanced powers of the Democratic leadership in scheduling and structuring floor debate. Firmly in control of the Rules Committee, party leaders may, for example, make in order a Republican substitute to a pending bill that they know they can defeat on a party-line vote but refuse to permit the consideration of amendments that would be more threatening and/or might divide the Democratic vote. Such tactics, to be sure, can alienate Democrats as well as Republicans. I can certainly recall instances when I thought a rule should have been granted for an amendment, often proposed by a moderate Democrat, that had merit and deserved an up-or-down-vote, regardless of the fact that it had the potential to divide our party or was opposed by the floor manager or by the interest groups backing the bill.[18] Sometimes, moreover, when committees report bills that are unrepresentative of the caucus or are fraught with symbolic politics—the perennial "omnibus crime bills" often qualify on both counts—members need for both substantive and political reasons to vote for moderating amendments, preferably offered by Democrats. A strategy that denies them that opportunity may backfire, leading Democrats to vote for more extreme Republican countermeasures as the only available alternatives.

Thus do members frequently and legitimately debate *how* the leadership's scheduling and structuring powers ought to be used. Few doubt, however, that they are a useful and necessary instrument of majority control. The trend in Figure 6.1 reflects the increasing exercise and acceptance of these powers.

Expanded whip operations have also helped solidify the trend. Whip counts enable the leadership to schedule votes only when a Democratic (and House) majority is in hand. Furthermore, whip contacts help create such results, informing members of the leadership's wishes and intent, providing channels for interpretation and persuasion on pending measures, and generating feedback that helps the leadership avoid trouble, sometimes by making last-minute alterations in content or strategy. This is not to say the whipping process works ideally as an early warning system: *late* warning system is more like it—often picking up problems or grievances that committee or party leaders should have identified and could have dealt with more adequately at an earlier point. Still, the whip system permits the leaders to bring measures to the floor with confidence and to maximize the party vote in their favor once they get there.

House leaders are also able to use their control over the Steering and Policy Committee to encourage party regularity (the same is true of the Committee on Committees on the Republican side). But the limitations, intended and otherwise, on the use of this power are at least as impressive as the instances of its exercise. For one thing, most members are not usually seeking new committee assignments or other appointments that are within the authority of the leadership to grant. And the leadership does not always use the leverage it does have to reward party regularity. During the early 1980s, for example, the Democratic leadership fluctuated in its treatment of the so-called boll weevils—conservative Democrats who were prone to vote with the Reagan administration: Sometimes, the leaders attempted to win their loyalty and cooperation through generous treatment and choice committee assignments, but at other times, they passed over them in favor of their loyalist rivals.[19] The approach taken was, to some extent, dictated by the political situation the Democrats faced—they were more accommodating to the conservatives when their House majority was shaky and Reagan was riding high, less accommodating when they had regained the initiative. But the fluctuations also reflected the continuing dilemmas of House leadership. The fluidity of member coalitions from issue to issue and the need to assemble extraordinary majorities in the face of likely vetoes from a Republican president make it risky to write off swing votes or to invoke sanctions against them. Sanctions, moreover, are likely to have only a limited impact if members see them as running counter to the imperatives of "voting their district."

These fluctuations between using the carrot or the stick have become less extreme in recent years, partly because nothing like the boll weevil insurrection has confronted House Democrats. But Steering and Policy leverage still is not utilized in a wholly consistent fashion. When Jim Wright became Speaker, he left little doubt that he intended to reserve choice committee assignments for party loyalists; he once even floated the unheard-of idea of putting members on probation for their first term in a new assignment.[20] But two midsession committee appointments in the 101st Congress after Wright's resignation raised questions about the new leadership's intent. A choice Energy and Commerce slot was awarded in early 1990 to a member who had voted against the leadership on the highest-profile party test of the previous fall, a capital gains tax reduction. And the Appropriations slot that opened up in the spring of 1990 was awarded to the only one of the five major contenders who had defected on the most visible leadership vote of that session (in this case, the leadership of both parties), the pay-raise/ethics package. As one of those five contenders, I took special note of the discussions that followed these episodes and concluded that the pattern was unlikely to continue. Indeed, the leadership's hand was far more evident in the committee assignments made by Steering and Policy at the beginning of the 102nd Congress, and I was elected at that point to Appropriations as part of a slate endorsed by the Speaker.

My party voting score was 84 percent for my first term in the House, 91 percent for my second—somewhat above the average scores indicated in Figure 6.1 and relatively high for a southern member. These scores, for the most part, have come naturally; that is, they reflect a congruence among Democratic Party positions, my own values and beliefs, and what I take to be the interests of my district. They also, of course, reflect the leadership practices and powers I have described: setting agendas, scheduling and structuring decisions, informing and persuading, modifying and accommodating—all designed to facilitate party support among members like me. My record does contain some defections, mostly on minor matters but occasionally on important ones, as occurred when I found myself at odds both strategically and substantively with Speaker Wright on some key budget votes in late 1987 (see Chapter 7). I had a few uncomfortable moments with Wright and Coelho, particularly during my first term when I had little opportunity to play a part in shaping decisions and they, no doubt, were sending some signals to me. But I have much more often been treated as a member of the team and reinforced in my basic inclination toward party loyalty.

As I stressed at the beginning of this chapter, not every member's story would be the same. No two representatives have exactly the same mix of personal predilections, electoral constraints, and district interests, and we work in a system that gives those individual differences unusually free rein. By world parliamentary standards, the U.S. House, despite its strengthened party operations, would never qualify as a tight ship. Every member has reason to take advantage of that freedom from time to time, but we also have reason to reflect on the frustrations and failures its excesses bring to the institution. The party structure is the most important mechanism we have to contain those excesses and to impose a measure of collective responsibility on ourselves. The precise rewards and costs of party loyalty will differ for members who are differently situated, but for all, I believe, there ought to be a presumption in its favor, for it is the party connection that enables a House of disparate parts to function. Ultimately, that lets the individual member move beyond good intentions to what Edmund Burke called "doing his duty with effect."[21]

7

Budget Politics

The easiest vote on a budget is almost always no. I learned that early in 1987, my first year in Congress. Four competing versions of the budget resolution—the blueprint within which all subsequent spending and revenue measures must fit, adopted early in each congressional session— were before the House. President Reagan's proposed budget received a grand total of 27 votes, rejected by Republicans and Democrats alike. A proposal put forward by Rep. William Dannemeyer (R.-California) that anticipated a return to the gold standard attracted 47 hardy souls. And the Black Caucus's alternative budget received 56 votes. What the House finally passed by a 230–192 vote and what I voted for as the best of the available alternatives was a budget resolution reported by the Democratic majority on the Budget Committee in collaboration with the House Democratic leadership.

In the course of these sequential votes, it occurred to me that some 140 of my colleagues were voting for no budget whatsoever.[1] And I would wager that not one of these members paid any serious political price for ducking the issue in this fashion. For those of us who felt it was our responsibility to put a budgetary framework in place, however, the political costs were all too evident. In my case, the reward was the thirty-second ads described in Chapter 2, alleging my eagerness to raise everyone's taxes.

The budget battles of 1987 were child's play compared to those that followed. The 101st Congress stayed in session until nine days before the 1990 election, locked in a struggle to finalize spending and revenue measures for fiscal 1991 and to conclude a five-year budget agreement between Congress and the White House. A relatively ambitious deficit-reduction plan was finally approved—for which, ironically, Congress and the president got almost no political credit but a great deal of public criticism because of the messiness of the process by which we got there. I often recalled those four 1987 votes in explaining to constituents why, in 1990, it was so difficult to get a majority for any plan, particularly for one that made an appreciable dent in the deficit. Yet, in the end, a plan was adopted—in an election year and with different parties in charge of the executive and legislative branches.

In this chapter, I will recount the budget battles of these four years and offer some reflections on the politics of the budget process and the outcomes it produces. I am sometimes asked what has alarmed me most since coming to the House and what has most changed since I first worked in Congress and began studying it twenty-five years ago. The answer to both questions is the same: the continuing and deepening fiscal crisis in our national government—a crisis rooted not simply, as some believe, in economic profligacy and mismanagement but more fundamentally in political irresponsibility and intragovernmental gridlock. It is this crisis that the budget process attempts, often ineffectually, to address.

It is not surprising that many who have witnessed this deepening dilemma have suggested tinkering with the budget machinery further or even adopting a balanced-budget amendment to the Constitution—indeed, I have done some of that myself. But my argument will be that our problem is not mainly inadequate laws or flawed machinery but rather the massive budget shortfalls created by the Reagan administration's experiment with supply-side economics and the subsequent absence of sufficient political will or public consensus to rectify the situation. If the 1990 budget agreement, preceded by a bipartisan executive-congressional summit, suggested that the seriousness of the problem was finally being recognized, the fitfulness of the process and the limitations of the final product also confirmed that the difficulties were far from overcome.

REAGANOMICS AND THE BUDGET

The budget process instituted by the Budget and Impoundment Control Act of 1974 has significantly altered congressional operations. The act was a response to President Richard Nixon's extensive impoundments of appropriated funds and his accusations that Congress was fiscally irresponsible, but it also reflected long-term congressional concern about failures of budgetary coordination and control. New House and Senate Budget committees were authorized to bring to the floor, early in each congressional session, a budget resolution that would set overall spending limits and bind other committees as they passed individual authorization, appropriations, and tax bills. The Budget committees have continued to operate in a context of fragmented power; they lack specific spending and taxing authority, and the House especially has limited its Budget Committee's independence and continuity of membership. Moreover, the targets and limits set by the budget resolutions have sometimes provoked defiance by one committee or another. Still, "for every confrontation there have been dozens of legislative decisions routinely made with fidelity to the budget process."[2]

During the first year of Ronald Reagan's presidency, the concentration of budgetary power reached new heights, albeit under conditions that enhanced presidential, rather than congressional, control and with results that mocked the ideal of fiscal responsibility. In late 1980, Congress had experimented for the first time with implementation of the budget act's "reconciliation" provisions, originally designed to bring final congressional spending decisions on individual bills into line with the comprehensive fiscal blueprint adopted in the budget resolution. This procedure was moved to the beginning of the congressional budget cycle in 1981 under a plan promoted by David Stockman, Reagan's budget director, and Sen. Pete Domenici (R.-New Mexico), new chairman of the Senate Budget Committee. The first budget resolution that year included a set of authoritative instructions to Congress as it went about its work, greatly increasing the constraints the budget process placed on appropriations, on the authorizing committees, and on entitlement programs.

The Reagan administration exploited the reconciliation process—and political momentum from the 1980 elections—to push through a series of omnibus bills that reduced revenues over the next five years by nearly $700 billion, reduced domestic spending by more than $100 billion over three years, and paved the way for substantial increases in defense spending, doubling such outlays from $133 billion in 1980 to $266 billion in 1986. The numbers, obviously, added up to massive annual deficits and eventually to a tripling of the national debt. As a repentant Stockman observed after the president's successful 1984 reelection campaign, "The White House proclaimed a roaring economic success . . . when, in fact, [its policies] had produced fiscal excesses that had never before been imagined."[3]

That feat was not matched by the administration in subsequent years. Shifts in the political climate induced by the recession of 1982–1983 soon weakened the president's hand, and Congress found his budget proposals less and less palatable. But consensus within the Congress was difficult to achieve as well; the Budget committees in the Senate, under Republican control from 1981 to 1986, and in the Democratic House often produced widely disparate resolutions, and both were challenged by restive appropriations and legislative committees. Just how badly the process had deteriorated—and how difficult it was going to be to secure the cooperation between the parties and between the branches of government needed to make the machinery work—became evident as my first term in Congress began.

President Reagan proposed his fiscal 1988 budget in early 1987. He acknowledged that it would be $108 billion in deficit, while other analysts predicted as much as a $135-billion shortfall. But the Reagan budget was not accepted even by members of his own party: It received 11 votes in the Senate and, as already noted, only 27 votes in the House. Republican opposition was partly attributable to the reluctance of members to vote for *any* budget, but it was also stemmed from many of the particulars of Reagan's proposal: the total elimination of vocational education funding, almost $2 billion in student aid cuts, and devastating cuts in Medicare and veterans' health care.

"This is the only democracy in the world," quipped Majority Leader Tom Foley, "where the members of the executive's own party will consider it a dirty trick if you ask them to vote on his budget." Republican Budget Committee members also refused to cooperate as the committee formulated its own budget resolution, and when that resolution passed the House on April 9, 1987, it was with Democratic votes alone. Many seemed to take to heart the counsel of GOP Whip Trent Lott (R.-Mississippi): "You do not ever get into trouble for those budgets which you vote against." To which Foley retorted, "'Don't vote and you won't get into trouble.' What a motto for statesmanship!"[4]

During most of this century, the budget process has been presidentially driven and has relied heavily on executive-congressional cooperation. For all of its jealous guardianship of the power of the purse, the House has depended on the executive to propose a viable budget and has generally altered that document only marginally.[5] The process, instituted in the 1920s, assumed that Congress was ill suited to undertake budgeting on its own and that executive leadership was required. The budget reforms of the 1970s did not alter that fundamental reality, although they did leave Congress somewhat better equipped to develop its own budget in the event of severe intragovernmental conflict or executive default. That is basically the test that the 100th Congress faced, and it is hardly surprising that the results fell considerably short of the ideal.

The Democratic budget resolution called for a deficit of some $1 billion less than the president's budget had; it directed House committees to match $18 billion in new revenues with equivalent reductions in projected spending, equally divided between military and nonmilitary accounts. Although subsequent House action largely remained within these guidelines, there were some departures from the Budget Committee's formula. This was partly because of the need to compromise with the Senate, whose budget resolution was not as stringent because it cut defense spending less and anticipated revenue from the sale of government assets. It was also partly attributable to the ambiguity of the "section 302" process (named after the relevant portion of the Budget Act, now numbered 602) that assigned spending ceilings to individual Appropriations subcommittees and to the desire of the subcommittees to stretch these limits.

Further deviations occurred when the Ways and Means Committee came up not only with the requisite revenue measures but also with an ambitious scheme for welfare reform.

I therefore had a difficult decision to make when confronted with the postappropriations reconciliation bill on October 29. Democratic leaders, in touting the earlier budget resolution, had pledged that any revenue increases would be at least matched by spending cuts and that all revenue increases would be earmarked for deficit reduction. But neither of these criteria was met by the reconciliation bill and the accompanying spending measures. As a result, I did something I was reluctant to do: I voted against the leadership on a key budget measure. I never doubted that this was the correct vote—both in maintaining my own credibility and consistency and in holding the party to its own professions—but it was nonetheless a tough one, made more so by the narrow margin of the bill's passage (206–205) and the obvious embarrassment this caused the leadership.

In the meantime, the budget landscape had shifted in ways that created intensified pressures on both Congress and the president to reach a settlement. Although the House had passed most of its appropriations bills on time, it had become increasingly clear over the spring and summer that the closely divided Senate was going to have difficulty acting on them and that, in any event, the president was likely to veto anything that was sent him. As the prospect of deadlock loomed, a number of members, some of whom had opposed the original Gramm-Rudman-Hollings (G-R-H) law of 1985, came to see in the reinstatement of this measure, minus the constitutionally questionable provisions that had led to its rejection by the courts, a way to force all parties to the table and to guarantee that significant deficit reduction would take place.

The basic concept of G-R-H was to impose increasingly stringent deficit-reduction targets on the budget process over five years, so that at the end of this period, the budget would be in balance. If the target were not met in a given year, uniform percentage cuts would be imposed across all accounts—except Social Security and some other mandatory program— to bring the budget into line. Presumably, the threat of such an indiscriminate "sequestration" would give all parties the incentive to reach a settlement. The administration, which had paid lip service to Gramm-Rudman-Hollings originally, was notably unenthusiastic about its revival, rightly perceiving that it might force President Reagan to modify his rigid stances on new revenues and/or defense spending, which were making substantial deficit reduction impossible. Proponents therefore chose the one legislative vehicle for the G-R-H proposal that they knew the administration had to request: an increase in the debt ceiling. After protracted negotiations, during which the administration was able to get the deficit reduction target for 1988 reduced to $23 billion from the $37 billion contained in the congressional budget resolution, the debt ceiling increase with G-R-H attached was cleared in September.

It was not apparent, however, that even the threat of sequestration would bring the administration to the table. Congressional leaders speculated that the president might be willing to see the indiscriminate cuts occur, assuming that Congress would receive the blame for the ensuing damage. What changed all that was the stock market crash of October 19, which made the adverse impact of the budget crisis on the national interest plain for all to see and created political perils for anyone who appeared to be stalling the process.

By this time, the fiscal year had ended, and Congress was forced to resort to a series of "continuing resolutions"—omnibus short-term appropriations measures—to keep the government running. Negotiations between congressional and administration leaders dragged on. It was in this context that the 206–205 reconciliation vote of October 29 occurred, but because of the closeness of that vote, it largely failed in its intended purpose of strengthening the House leadership's hand in negotiations. Finally, the negotiators reached agreement on a package that included domestic spending cuts of about $8 billion for 1988, defense cuts of some $5 billion, and another $5 billion in federal asset sales. Additional revenues would total $9 billion in 1988, produced through tightening some loopholes and continuing some taxes that were to expire, but neither excise tax increases nor any change in personal or corporate income tax rates were included. This package produced $30 billion in deficit reduction for 1988, and its second-year provisions were to net a reduction of $46 billion for 1989. These figures were well within the Gramm-Rudman targets, although they fell considerably short of what many had hoped for as the negotiations began. The fiscal 1988 agreement was packaged in two omnibus bills—a full-year continuing resolution and a reconciliation bill—that finally cleared the House and Senate in the early morning hours of December 22, 1987.

This agreement resulted in reduced budget conflict during the second session of the 100th Congress, with both the House and Senate producing most of their fiscal 1989 appropriations bills on schedule. The lull, however, was deceptive. The budget crisis had not gone away, and the Gramm-Rudman targets for 1990 and succeeding years were going to be far more difficult to meet than those for 1988 and 1989. The demands for spending were intensifying—to sustain the Reagan defense buildup; to cover rising Social Security, Medicare, agriculture, and other entitlement costs; to fund major projects in science and space; and to deal with the backlog of need from the Reagan years in areas such as housing, education, and infrastructure. The collapse of the federal savings and loan insurance fund required a massive infusion of public funds, and an ominous slowdown in the economy threatened to exacerbate all of these problems. The confluence of these factors was to make the budget the most serious and difficult problem faced by the 101st Congress, but it also was to compel a budget agreement going beyond anything attempted or achieved in the Reagan years.

THE CAPITAL GAINS DISTRACTION

George Bush, who had derided Ronald Reagan's supply-side dogmas as "voodoo economics" when he was a presidential candidate in 1980, was widely expected to take a more flexible and cooperative approach to budget matters than had his predecessor. But such hopes were dashed as he assumed a rigid campaign stance on taxes—"Read my lips: no new taxes," he declared in his acceptance speech at the 1988 Republican National Convention—and as he essentially threw the budget problem in Congress's lap at the beginning of the 101st Congress.

The Bush budget submitted in February 1989 was not a conventional budget at all but a set of recommendations for marginal adjustments in the fiscal 1990 budget prepared by the outgoing Reagan administration. Bush sought to establish an activist image for the incoming administration by asking for increases in antidrug, science and technology, and environmental cleanup funding, but he declined to specify where the funds would come from. He managed to reach the G-R-H deficit-reduction target only by relying on extremely optimistic economic assumptions and by proposing reduced overall outlays in Medicare, agriculture, defense, and a large cluster of nonpriority domestic programs. It would be left to Congress, however, to identify the specific reductions. This suggested to most Democrats that Bush was no more willing than his predecessor to face budget reality and that he expected us to take the fall for the painful cuts that would have to be made. "He's saying, 'I'll take care of the increases, and you can be in charge of the cuts,'" one member quipped.

Still, the administration's approach gave the Democratic leadership a strong incentive to seek a bipartisan budget agreement—one that would spread the blame—and the budget resolution passed by both houses in early May was the result of nine weeks of negotiations between congressional leaders and the White House. The budget resolution hit the G-R-H target, but only because it retained many of the White House's optimistic economic assumptions. A good number of Bush's proposed cuts in Medicare and other domestic programs were rejected, and some limited initiatives in maternal and child health, child care, education, and drug control were incorporated. The resolution anticipated $5.3 billion in revenues from tax law changes, the same amount proposed by the administration (which claimed that such changes need not violate Bush's "no new taxes" pledge) but left the specifics to the Ways and Means Committee. "This is not an heroic agreement," said Speaker Jim Wright, although he also praised the deal as a "very good start in the direction of better cooperation and better performance."[6]

Disappointment ran rather deep among members who had hoped for a fresh start on budget policy. Office of Management and Budget Director Richard Darman ostensibly shared that disappointment, although he had been the main architect of the Bush strategy. "Collectively we are engaged in a massive *Backward Robin Hood* transaction," he said in a widely publicized speech in mid-1989, "robbing the future to give to the present." He went on to hold out the hope that the admittedly "modest" fiscal 1990 agreement could, with "good will and responsible leadership," be followed by a more substantial multiyear package.[7]

What the ensuing weeks brought, instead, was a bruising battle over the capital gains tax. President Bush had included a reduction in the capital gains tax rate as part of his original budget proposal, counting on the reduction to prompt a short-term turnover of assets and thus increase revenues by some $4.8 billion in fiscal 1990. Congressional Budget Office (CBO) estimates were considerably less optimistic for the first year, however, and they projected revenue *losses* over a five-year period of some $25 billion. In any event, the Democratic leadership—Wright had by now resigned, and Tom Foley had been elected Speaker—regarded the proposal as fiscally irresponsible and antithetical to tax reform. (The tax reform legislation of 1986 had predicated its reduction in the top marginal rate to 28 percent on the repeal of tax breaks such as that accorded capital gains.) But the proposal had majority support on the Ways and Means Committee—all the Republicans, plus 6 Democrats—and when capital gains was brought to the House floor, the new leadership team, in its first major test, suffered a 190–239 defeat.

In pressing its advantage on capital gains, the administration jeopardized the long-term prospects for deficit reduction. Foley left no doubt about this in a somber appearance before our Democratic Budget Study Group on September 13. The prospects for a multiyear, bipartisan budget agreement were "rapidly collapsing," he said. What bothered him as much as the upper-income bias of the capital gains break was the *political* "giveaway" it represented. If the administration got this now, what incentive would the White House have to return to the table and negotiate a more balanced tax package later? Moreover, in further increasing the deficit for the benefit of (mainly) upper-income taxpayers, would not a capital gains reduction make it both more necessary and more politically difficult to hit middle-income taxpayers later?

Foley subsequently secured the agreement of Minority Leader Robert Michel to delete a number of contentious provisions, including capital gains, from the pending budget reconciliation bill. That would have allowed the terms of the spring budget resolution to be met with little controversy and would have improved the climate for future negotiations. But Darman rejected the deal, choosing to push capital gains to a vote. "They have put all their chips on winning capital gains, and it has little to do with deficit reduction," observed House Budget Committee Chairman Leon Panetta (D.-California). "That poisons the well for the relations you need if you're going to tackle this seriously."[8]

Senate Finance Committee Chairman Lloyd Bentsen (D.-Texas) and Majority Leader George Mitchell (D.-Maine) managed to keep the capital gains provision out of the Senate reconciliation bill. Meanwhile, the new fiscal year began. Because the budget reconciliation and most appropriations bills had not yet passed, a continuing resolution was approved to keep the government running, and on October 15, the first stages of G-R-H sequestration were imposed. Feeling the heat, the Senate passed a stripped-down reconciliation bill. But the heat was not sufficient to force a quick House-Senate conference agreement. Republican members and the administration insisted on retaining the capital gains provisions in the House bill, while House Democrats demanded accommodation on other extraneous items, such as child care assistance and revisions of Medicare's physician payment system.

The logjam began to break on November 2 when Bush announced that he was willing to drop his demand that a capital gains tax reduction be included in the bill. But he simultaneously demanded $14 billion in "real" deficit reduction, as OMB defined it, prompting angry Democratic charges that Darman was "moving the goal posts" as the game neared its end. Finally, with most of the extraneous reconciliation provisions either dropped or passed separately, the House approved the reconciliation conference report late on November 21. The bill picked up $4.6 billion, some one-third of its savings, by reducing all accounts to what they would have been had sequestration remained in effect through January. The final result fell considerably short of the already modest spring budget agreement. And it left exhausted members wondering how they would ever find and agree on the $40 billion in additional savings that G-R-H would require in the next budget cycle.

BUDGET SUMMITRY

Despite the lingering animosities from the 1989 budget battle, both congressional and administration leaders had strong incentives to seek some sort of major bipartisan deal as the fiscal 1991 cycle loomed ahead.

It could not be a Band-Aid agreement of the 1987 or 1989 variety. The new G-R-H target required more than that and made across-the-board sequestration to meet the target an unthinkable alternative for both Congress and the White House. The constant budget wrangling was bringing both branches into disrepute, yet we had remarkably little to show for our efforts. The White House was locked into a rigid position on taxes and displayed only minimal flexibility on defense; neither party felt it could afford to tamper with Social Security; and congressional Democrats were unwilling to sacrifice domestic programs, which already had borne the brunt of Reagan-era cutbacks. No one, therefore, could imagine where savings of the magnitude required were going to come from— unless a new kind of agreement (Darman liked to speak of the "deal of the century") could be reached. Those of us who had long advocated a major effort to break the budget impasse imagined that our day finally had come. As it turned out, however, things would get far worse before they got even marginally better.

The budget submitted by the president on January 29, 1990, anticipated a fiscal 1991 deficit of $64.7 billion, falling beneath the $74 billion G-R-H ceiling. But it reached the target only by leaving the costs of recapitalizing the savings and loan insurance fund off-budget, making impossibly optimistic economic assumptions, and engaging in a good deal of smoke-and-mirrors accounting. The CBO estimated that Bush's budget would, in fact, produce a deficit of $131 billion. Democratic congressional leaders were ambivalent about highlighting this discrepancy, however, because it made their task of putting together and passing a budget resolution that hit the G-R-H target all the more daunting. "For us to play a 'real' game while they're playing an 'unreal' game," Majority Leader Gephardt told the Budget Study Group in February, "simply creates political pain for us." The Democratic budget resolution therefore retained many of the president's economic assumptions and dubious revenue projections, while requiring greater savings in defense, reducing Bush's proposed Medicare cuts, and adding $6.2 billion for new activity in education, health, and other domestic areas.

The House passed the budget resolution on May 1 with Democratic votes alone. The Republicans had no desire to vote for the president's budget, however, and their ranking Budget Committee member, Bill Frenzel (R.-Minnesota), who had been authorized by the Rules Committee to offer the Bush budget on the floor, declined to do so. This prompted as angry a whips' meeting as I have ever witnessed: Democratic members were sick of casting tough budget votes while Republicans ducked the issue. Foley, who had thought he had a commitment from Frenzel to call for a vote on the Bush budget, vowed that it would never happen again.[9]

In the meantime, it had become clearer than ever that the normal budget process was not up to the task before us. The economic indicators and deficit projections had worsened to the point that even OMB could no longer paper over them. The House had produced its budget resolution tardily and with great difficulty, and in the Senate—where the Democratic margin was slimmer and disagreements about spending priorities deeper— the prospects were far worse. Both Congress and the White House needed a budget deal that went considerably beyond what the regular process was likely to produce, if, indeed, it could produce agreement at all. Thus, the budget summit of 1990 got under way. Bush invited congressional leaders to the White House for a preliminary discussion on May 6, after which full-scale talks involving 17 congressional and 3 White House negotiators began.

Our Democratic Budget Study Group brought Panetta and Frenzel in for a progress report on May 23. It was clear that not much was happening; "so far it's been like a bunch of strange dogs sniffing at each other," Frenzel said. Noting that the negotiators would need to find some $50 to $60 billion in first-year savings, he warned that "if you are a defense hawk, or welfare-bleeding heart, or anti-tax zealot, there's no comfort in this for you." Yet Panetta reported a lack of a real sense of urgency despite the magnitude of the problem, and he reminded us that it had taken a stock market crash to produce even the modest 1987 agreement. Most of us agreed that the threat of sequestration was, as yet, unreal for our constituents, while antitax sentiment was high. This meant that the pressures the negotiators felt to push toward agreement were matched by a desire to avoid blame for unpopular moves on taxes or entitlements.

It was the White House's John Sununu who made this clearest. Addressing Republican fears that Bush's agreement to talks with "no precondi-tions" indicated a weakened antitax position, Sununu put his own gloss on the agreement: "It is [the Democrats'] prerogative to put [taxes] on the table, and it's our prerogative to say no. And I emphasize the 'no'."[10]

This led Foley and other Democrats to wonder out loud whether the Republicans were negotiating in good faith and whether the talks should continue. But House Democrats were hardly in a position to go it alone. We could and did pass appropriations bills within the terms of our own budget resolution, but we knew they were unlikely to clear the Senate, to say nothing of the White House. Nor were we in a position to unilaterally unveil our own long-term budget plan; the political liabilities would have far exceeded the benefits, with the president retaining the antitax high ground. Consequently, it was in our interest to keep everyone at the table but also to insist on a serious offer from the president before revealing our own hand.

This finally came on June 26 when Bush, after a protracted meeting with the bipartisan congressional leadership and his own negotiators, issued a statement acknowledging that "tax revenue increases" would have to be part of any realistic deficit-reduction plan.[11] But if the president expected this declaration to jump-start the negotiations or win him praise for his political courage, he was to be sorely disappointed. A howl of protest went up from the Right, and the House Republican Conference soon passed a resolution opposing any new taxes as a means of reducing the deficit. Among Democrats, there was some satisfaction that Bush at last had uttered what anyone who had looked at the budget dilemma for five minutes knew to be true and some relief that the president finally seemed willing to invest political capital in order to reach an agreement. But few of us saw much reason to praise him for rescinding a demagogic promise he should never have made in the first place. Rather, we sought to use Bush's reversal to shift the focus of the budget debate.

For ten years, presidents Reagan and Bush had managed to frame the debate as taxes versus no taxes; naturally, there was little doubt of the popular response to such a proposition. In truth, though, that was always a contrived issue. People continued to pay taxes, and middle-class people, despite the antitax rhetoric, bore an increasing share of the overall tax burden through the 1980s. The question Reagan and Bush never asked was how the tax burden was *distributed*, what share of the load different income groups were bearing. They and we both knew that the tax fairness issue was Democratic turf. President Bush's reversal offered us the opportunity to shift to this more advantageous political ground and also, we hoped, to influence the shape of the final agreement.

I therefore joined with 133 other House Democrats in sending a letter to Speaker Foley suggesting that any new taxes should target those upper-income persons who had benefited most from the Reagan policies. I also joined with several other members affiliated with the Democratic Leadership Council (DLC) in publicly insisting that any acceptable agreement would have to make the tax system more progressive. At the same time, one of the key negotiators, Senate Majority Leader Mitchell, made it clear that any consideration of a capital gains tax cut, still a key administration goal, would require an adjustment in the top marginal rate for the wealthiest taxpayers as a likely quid pro quo.

The deep partisan divisions prompted by the tax issue, as well as the disarray in GOP ranks, made it very difficult to move toward a broad agreement. It also became clearer than ever that an agreement had to be reached, as deficit projections soared and the amount of the projected sequester reached $100 billion. The negotiators, after a flurry of activity in late July came to naught, resolved to return to the table immediately after the August recess and to try to finalize an agreement in a matter of days, still in time for the new fiscal year.

The September talks, held in semiseclusion at the Andrews Air Force Base, produced long-awaited specificity as to what the White House and the Democratic congressional leadership were willing to support, as well as a developing consensus on the magnitude of the spending cuts to be sought in various areas. But on the tax issue, each side remained immovable: The White House insisted on a capital gains tax reduction but refused to combine it with any adjustment in the top rates, while the Democrats insisted that capital gains cuts were acceptable only if combined with other changes that made the tax code more progressive.

Finally, on September 30, the last day of the fiscal year, President Bush appeared with the summit participants to announce that an agreement had been reached. The negotiators had dropped both capital gains reductions and top-rate increases from the package and thus had fallen $10 billion short of their goal of $50 billion in first-year savings. They also had backed away from any alterations in Social Security. But the plan still projected $500 billion in savings from the current-services baseline over the next five years, with some $134 billion of this coming from tax increases, $65 billion from debt-service savings, and $301 billion from spending cuts. Almost two-thirds of these cuts were to come from defense and the rest mainly from entitlement programs like Medicare, agricultural price supports, and civil service retirement. Domestic and international discretionary spending were to be frozen at the baseline level, that is, increased only for inflation. Substantial budget process and enforcement reforms were also proposed. G-R-H would be extended through 1995 in revised form, with spending caps set for domestic discretionary, international discretionary, and defense spending that, if violated, would trigger across-the-board cuts within the appropriate category. Enforcement by sequestration would remain, but excesses in one area would not trigger sequesters in another. New pay-as-you-go rules would require tax reductions or entitlement increases to be accompanied by whatever additional revenue or entitlement measures were required to offset their budgetary impact.

We passed a continuing resolution to head off sequestration and keep the government running through October 5 and prepared anxiously for what was sure to be a close vote on the summit agreement. House Minority Whip Newt Gingrich (R.-Georgia), who had pointedly skipped the White House announcement, began to organize Republican opposition to the plan in defiance of the president and his own minority leader. Gingrich's point of departure was not any alternative plan for reducing the deficit— he had none—but rather a dogmatic insistence that taxes not be raised and a conviction that the GOP, politically, could not afford to abandon that position. As the *Washington Post* editorialized:

> The balking Republicans say they are against all tax increases. But they are of course against the deficit as well—and no more willing or able than Ronald Reagan or George Bush has been to name the spending cuts that by themselves might bring the deficit out of the red zone. Instead they continue to parrot that what the country needs is more tax *cuts* to grow its way out of the deficit. You last heard that sort of happy talk about $2 trillion in debt ago.[12]

Speaker Foley and other House Democratic leaders, while acknowledging the agreement's deficiencies, nonetheless strongly urged a yea vote. They presented the package as the best that could be attained after five months of negotiations and warned that we would reject it at our political peril. The shakiness of our Senate majority put us in a poor position to push a budget measure through on our own; "We're only as strong as our weakest Senator," Gephardt lamented at one point. Moreover, time had run out. We faced an imminent government shutdown, for which the Democratic Congress was likely to take the fall. "We're about to hand the President a pardon and a machine gun," Foley told a Democratic Caucus meeting as the negative whip counts came in. Democratic rejection would take the spotlight off GOP disarray and Gingrich's rebellion and would give the president an excuse to "do anything he wants," perhaps to assume extraordinary powers to avert governmental breakdown.

Such pleas were to no avail. The Democrats' main objection to the agreement was its regressive character. The tax package had some progressive elements—luxury taxes, for example, and cuts in allowable deductions for those earning over $100,000—and nonentitlement domestic programs had been spared further cuts, but by any measure, the wealthy got off lightly. The problem with the package, commented Charles Schumer, was that "Democrats think it's a Republican budget and Republicans think it's a Democratic budget."[13] As it became clear that the package was in trouble and after meeting with the president, Foley issued a statement stressing that Ways and Means and other committees, in writing the legislation to implement the agreement, would be free to alter its distributive impact: "The President and the Bipartisan Leadership always understood that many of the policies set forth in the budget agreement are for illustrative purposes only and that the committees of jurisdiction retain the right to achieve the savings required through alternative policies."

But despite such scrambling and all the importuning, including a national television address by the president, the budget agreement was rejected on October 5 by a vote of 179–254, with a majority voting nay among both Democrats (108–149) and Republicans (71–105).

One reason for the skittishness in both parties was the chorus of protest that came from affected constituencies, prompted in large part by the tendency of the media, especially television, to cover the budget agreement by focusing on its supposed "victims." I knew we were in trouble when I saw the network news coverage immediately after the agreement was announced: motorists at the gas pump, frail nursing home residents (who, in fact, probably would not have been affected by the proposed Medicare premium increases), and others bewailing their victimization. Not much was made, however, of the potential victims of sequestration (including 113,000 children dropped from Head Start, 1.4 million students losing their Pell Grants, and 83,000 inpatients and 1.7 million outpatients losing their Veterans Administration [VA] medical care) who would suffer if we did *not* act, not to mention the effects of the economic downturn to which the deficit was contributing. The media, as far as I could tell, provided almost no context for understanding the agreement—why it was necessary, why it was difficult to conclude, why it could not be painless. The picture was, rather, one of victimization and of governmental ineptitude, which greatly reinforced the tendency of members of Congress, especially in an election year, to distance themselves as far as possible from budgetary unpleasantness—in other words, simply to vote no.

I voted for the agreement, although I had substantive objections that were as strong as those of many of my colleagues and could only imagine what my Republican opponent would make of my vote in his campaign ads. I just did not see how I, after having advocated extraordinary efforts to put our fiscal house in order for years, could credibly or in good conscience vote against a plan that, despite its flaws, represented the largest deficit-reduction package in our nation's history. I felt, moreover, that we Democrats would be in a stronger position to shape the final implementing legislation to our liking if we produced our quota of votes for the agreement. This reasoning was reflected in some notes I made the day after the vote:

What a different situation it would be today if the budget agreement had gone down for a lack of Republican votes alone, with some 130 [instead of 108] Democrats recorded "yes." The news stories would be of Republican division and default, and we would have the upper hand in rewriting a budget that more faithfully reflects Democratic priorities. As it is, we share in the public blame for the failure to act, and we seek partisan accommodation with a weaker hand. . . . If, on the other hand, the agreement had gone down for a lack of Democratic votes alone, there would be hell to pay. The fact that both parties defaulted forces the President to moderate the blame-game and in fact helps turn the spotlight back on him and his failure to lead.

The budget vote produced the spectacle of a weekend government shutdown, with hundreds of tourists who had been denied entrance to national museums packing the House and Senate galleries. This was because the president chose to veto the continuing resolution that we passed to keep the government running until October 12. He did this, no doubt, to heighten public awareness of Congress's failure, but the result was to highlight his own failure as well. A subsequent *New York Times-CBS News* poll showed that, at that point, only 27 percent of the American public approved of Congress's handling of its job, down from 42 percent in January. But only 24 percent registered the view that President Bush was likely to do a better job than Congress on the deficit.[14]

Meanwhile, House and Senate leaders—minus the divided House Republicans—frantically sought to get a new budget resolution approved to replace the failed agreement. This was accomplished just before the holiday weekend ended by a 250–164 vote (including only 32 Republican yeas) in the House and a bipartisan 66–33 vote in the Senate. This time, Bush signed the accompanying continuing resolution. Government employees came to work as usual, and our committees proceeded to tackle the final budget reconciliation and appropriations bills for the balance of the fiscal year.

The new budget resolution differed from the rejected agreement mainly in its omission of specific reconciliation proposals. The spending limits and budget process reforms remained largely intact. But controversial revenue and entitlement provisions, most notably the increased Medicare premium and a proposed two-week delay before unemployment compensation payments could begin, were dropped. Having registered a no vote on the first resolution and having (arguably) given the committees added flexibility to write a more equitable reconciliation bill—and recognizing, no doubt, that public outrage at our gridlock was fast surpassing the discontent of specific groups on specific items—over 100 Democrats switched to a yea vote on the second resolution. This left only 28 negative Democratic votes, an impressive change from the earlier picture of disarray and a hopeful sign that the majority party might be able to seize control of the process.

House Democrats, buoyed by indications that our tax fairness message was finally hitting home, regrouped nicely over the next week as the Ways and Means Committee went about its work. On October 16, we passed a reconciliation bill that dropped most of the budget agreement's regressive tax proposals (for example, on gasoline and home heating oil) and substituted (1) an increase in the top marginal rate to 33 percent,[15] (2) a surtax

FIGURE 7.1   The House budget battle as depicted by AUTH in the *Philadelphia Inquirer*, October 1990. AUTH copyright 1990 *Philadelphia Inquirer*. Reprinted with permission of UNIVERSAL PRESS SYNDICATE. All rights reserved.

on millionaires (which, as Elizabeth Drew noted, gave us "small revenue and a big symbol"),[16] and (3) an expansion of the earned-income tax credit for the working poor. The Republicans were reduced to carping at the Democratic plan, for Foley quite rightly refused to make any alternative proposal in order on the House floor unless it hit the overall $500-billion deficit-reduction target. This the Republicans were unable to produce, given their commitment to no new taxes and their inability to agree on spending cuts sufficient to make up the difference (see Fig. 7.1).

Senate approval, however, still depended on maintaining bipartisan support. The Senate consequently passed a reconciliation bill that was much closer to the original budget agreement, setting the stage for a difficult House-Senate conference. During the next few days, the White House considered pulling out of the discussions, and House Democrats considered rejecting the conference agreement they saw shaping up. But both sides feared the political consequences of failure, and in the end, the conference bill—which contained a 31 percent top rate (with a 28 percent maximum rate for capital gains),[17] no surtax, and a complex scheme for reducing deductions and phasing out personal exemptions for the wealthy—was passed with the president's approval. The 228–200 vote finally came on October 27, 1990, with the Democratic margin slipping to 181–74 and

House Republicans still unreconciled (47–126). After the subsequent passage of the last of the thirteen appropriations bills, our work was done, and the 101st Congress wearily adjourned.

FUTURE PROSPECTS

Congress, as a result of the budget agreement, avoided bruising battles over the budget in 1991 and processed most of its appropriations bills without major controversy. The fiscal 1992 budget submitted by the president adhered to the agreement, as did the budget resolution cleared by the House on April 17, although we shifted spending figures within the caps to give additional support to health and education programs for children and to economic development and energy initiatives.

These proposed increases in the president's budget, which the Appropriations subcommittees generally accepted, were offset by decreases in some sixty lower-priority programs. One appropriations bill in particular, reported by the VA, HUD, and Independent Agencies Subcommittee, demonstrated just how constraining the new limits could be. The subcommittee concluded that the spending allocation under which it was laboring required it either to cut out a major item completely or to pare down a number of programs to a degree that would damage their effectiveness. The subcommittee adopted the former strategy, cutting out NASA's space station for fiscal 1992 so that other space, scientific research, housing, and veterans' programs could be funded more adequately. Unfortunately, this decision was later reversed on the House floor. But this only postponed the day of reckoning, and it prefigured funding dilemmas soon to arise in numerous policy areas.

Despite the spending caps and pay-as-you-go rules and the constraints they imposed, the Congressional Budget Office predicted in early 1991 that the deficit for the current fiscal year would exceed $300 billion. House Budget Chairman Leon Panetta spoke for many of us when he exclaimed, "We went through an awful lot of hell to get to $300 billion deficits. I never see the light at the end of the tunnel. Everybody predicts it, but we never get there."[18] These figures reflected the economy's slide into a recession, exacerbated by the Persian Gulf War, with revenues falling off and entitlement claims increasing even as the discretionary spending caps remained inviolate.

In August, CBO lowered its estimate of the fiscal 1991 deficit to $279 billion, mainly because the savings and loan cleanup got started more slowly than anticipated and because of foreign contributions to Operation Desert Storm. But the more long-run projections, based on a range of negative economic indicators and updated revenue and entitlement trends, were far more pessimistic: a $362-billion deficit for fiscal 1992 and $278 billion for 1993, up from earlier projections of $294 billion and $221 billion, respectively. The 1996 deficit was now pegged at $156 billion, compared to a prediction of $66 billion six months earlier. Without the 1990 budget agreement, CBO concluded, the projected deficit figures for 1995 and 1996 would have been almost twice as great. Still, it now appeared "that the main accomplishment of [the agreement] was not to reduce the size of the structural deficit, but rather to prevent it from becoming substantially larger."[19]

It had been clear all along that the budget agreement would have to be revisited after the 1992 elections for it provided only a single cap for the three discretionary spending categories (domestic, defense, and international) in fiscal 1994 and 1995, leaving the relationship among them to be renegotiated. However, the escalating deficit projections made it likely that the reckoning would have to come sooner and placed the adequacy of that overall cap in doubt. "If we wait for a politically convenient post-election moment," Senate Budget Chairman Jim Sasser warned in mid-1991, "we'll limit our opportunities and perhaps destroy our last chance to bring the deficit under control."[20] At the same time, pressures for an early reconsideration of the individual spending caps intensified, as the rapidly changing situation in the Soviet Union raised the possibility of much deeper defense cuts and the lingering recession focused renewed attention on domestic needs. As 1991 drew to a close, the five-year budget plan was looking less and less durable, but it seemed likely that even substantial shifts among the spending caps would leave a major long-term shortfall.

Thus, the protracted budget crisis continues. We continue to bear the consequences of the supply-side mythology that Ronald Reagan brought to the White House and of the policy excesses indulged in under its influence. "That experiment," as economist Lester Thurow wrote, "continues to warp the political process. Its enduring influence explains why Congress and President Bush found it so difficult to reach any budget agreement at all . . . and why the public, nourished on a decade of false promises, seems unwilling to make even modest sacrifices to assure the nation's economic future."[21]

Certainly, the "warp" produced by the budget crisis has extended to the operations of Congress. It has centralized power and devalued the work of the standing committees, discouraged and preempted needed initiatives and investments, and shifted policy debate away from substance and into primarily fiscal terms. The original budget process, of course, aimed to improve the coordination of congressional policymaking and to make certain that the fiscal impact of disparate decisions was duly considered. Those are still legitimate and important objectives, but they assumed a grotesquely distorted form during the 1980s. Budget concerns came to dominate policy debate but in a way that often made a mockery of the analytic standards and fiscal soundness to which the architects of the budget process aspired. And though budget leaders sometimes struggled valiantly, they were saddled with enormous problems with solutions that far exceeded what public opinion and any achievable political consensus would support. The result, all too often, was budget deliberations and decisions that, for all the time and energy they absorbed, became exercises in smoke-and-mirrors accounting and political evasion and only patched things up from year to year.

The 1990 agreement was somewhat better than that, and its reform provisions should make for an improved process in the future. The fixed deficit targets of G-R-H had imposed certain limits on budget resolutions and had forced all parties to the table in order to implement them. But they had prompted at least as much deceptive accounting and pie-in-the-sky forecasting—to minimize both the projected deficits and the tasks confronting budget leaders—as genuine deficit reduction. The alternative mechanisms adopted in 1990, caps on major categories of discretionary spending along with pay-as-you-go requirements on taxes and entitlements, provided more practical and less easily evaded controls.

The 1990 struggle, however, left the future of budget summitry in doubt. Many Democratic House members complained bitterly that the summit process was co-opting our leaders and preempting the role of the majority party; they claimed vindication when, after the initial rejection of the summit agreement, Ways and Means Democrats reported and the House passed a reconciliation bill more consistent with Democratic values. But it is not likely that the normal budget process, without summitry, could have produced anything approximating the final 1990 outcome, given the shakiness of the Democratic majority in the Senate and the realities of divided government. The president's resources included not only a veto pen but also the rhetorical high ground; unless he could be brought into the fray and compelled to offer some genuine solutions, Democrats faced the prospect of becoming the party of sacrifice and pain and of inviting their own political demise. The summit process, for all of its messiness and its blurring of the lines of institutional and party responsibility, did, at least, force a measure of seriousness and realism on the leaders of both branches (with the notable exception of House Republicans) and heighten their incentives to formulate a constructive solution to an intractable national problem.

David Mayhew, in a recent book certain to attract widespread attention and debate, argued that divided party control of Congress and the executive has not been as debilitating as is sometimes thought and that unified party control has not been as invigorating, in terms of national policy output.[22] But in the realm of budget enforcement, where the normal rewards of entrepreneurship are missing and the incentives for supporting serious solutions are frequently negative, divided party control has complicated matters significantly and has made summitry necessary. This is not to say that large-scale budget solutions would be easy to come by under conditions of unified government, if Democrats were to win the presidency or Republicans to assume congressional control. The ruling party would find it difficult to unite around and push unpopular measures, and the opposition would be tempted to carp irresponsibly from the sidelines. But the leaders of each branch would have a greater stake in the other branch's positive performance, as opposed to simply trying to set it up for a fall, and the normal process would probably suffice for executive-congressional negotiation and accommodation.

As long as divided party control continues and massive deficits remain, the temptations for evasion and blame-shifting will be enormous. After 1990, neither side is eager to repeat the summit experience. But it is an open question whether either branch or either party can muster the responsibility and the discipline to make the normal process work—or, indeed, whether public understanding and support would be sufficient to underwrite such efforts. This would require an improved working relationship between the White House and the Congress and a common understanding, not about every budget detail or even about overall spending priorities but about the appropriate exercise of each branch's statutory and constitutional responsibilities for budgeting. The president should submit a fiscally sound and politically realistic budget, based on credible economic assumptions. Although rapidly changing circumstances will call for some flexibility on the discretionary spending caps agreed to in 1990, the president's budget should stay within the overall spending limit and should address the underlying structural deficit as well. Congress should then revise and refine this document in line with its own priorities, but it should neither expect nor be expected to construct a totally new fiscal blueprint. Substantial conflicts would no doubt emerge, to be worked out in conference committees and through normal interbranch channels.

All this is very much worth a try, but budget matters are likely to remain uniquely contentious and difficult. Posturing and nay-saying will remain tempting political alternatives for both individuals and parties. The ideological stakes will be high and often not amenable to compromise. The must-pass quality of budget measures, the dependence of other appropriation and authorization bills on them, and the looming of deadlines and governmental shutdowns will continue to encourage brinkmanship on budget matters and to threaten Congress in particular with procedural and political chaos. We therefore may find ourselves returning to summitry, seeking bipartisan cooperation and "cover," sooner than we think.

What is certain is that budget matters must continue to receive our attention if we are to bring our country back to fiscal health and to make the investments necessary to our future prospects. There is no salvation to be found in new gimmickry: The proposals some peddle, like a presidential line-item veto, would only make the problem worse (see Chapter 10), and others, like a balanced-budget constitutional amendment, have been oversold. We have improved the machinery to some extent, and we can, no doubt, do more. But the main thing we need is sufficient political resolve and responsibility to make our existing machinery work as it was intended. This will require not only statesmanship of a high order but also new levels of public understanding and a willingness on the part of key interest groups to adopt the long view. It is fervently to be hoped that the deceptions, distractions, and dangers of the budget politics of the 1980s can be transcended in the decade ahead. But it will not happen easily, and we are not there yet.

8

Serving the District

This book has mainly focused on the aspects of my job that I share with 434 other members of the House of Representatives in Washington, D.C. It is also evident, I suppose, that there are daily reminders of the fact that I am only *one* of these strong-willed people trying to shape national policy outcomes. But as I often remind constituents in my community meetings, I am the *only* one of the 435 who is responsible for assisting individuals, organizations, and local governments in the Fourth District in their dealings with the federal government. The district-based aspects of the job are fully as important and as demanding as the three days per week that I normally spend in Washington. Like roughly half of my colleagues, I keep my main residence in the district and return there every weekend. I spend as many workdays there as in Washington, in and around the three district offices where half of my staff is based. And even in Washington, much of what I and my staff do is district centered. That is especially true of my work on Appropriations, as I will demonstrate in this chapter. It is also true of the work of my legislative assistants, most of whose time is spent dealing with the policy concerns of local groups and correspondents.

STAYING IN TOUCH

Much of my time in North Carolina is spent traveling the district and maintaining an extensive schedule of public appearances. During my first four years in office, I addressed 44 local civic club or chamber of commerce meetings; spoke at 51 school classes or assemblies and at 9 high school, college, or professional school commencements; held 90 community meetings across the five counties; visited churches and synagogues on some 52 occasions, sometimes delivering the Sunday sermon; and toured 47 district plants and research facilities. Most of these were congressional, rather than campaign, functions. Members of Congress develop a good sense of what is and is not appropriate on such occasions, which we generally approach not as partisans but as representatives of all our

FIGURE 8.1   Talking to constituents after a community meeting in Raleigh, January 15, 1992. Photo by Karen Tam.

constituents. Still, these events are a valuable opportunity for outreach, a chance to become known and to establish relationships beyond one's present circle of friends and supporters. Richard Fenno found that members' "careers" in relating to their constituencies typically proceed from "expansionist" to "protectionist" stages.[1] I doubt that either my own temperament or the nature of my district—rapidly growing, politically volatile—will ever permit me to move completely beyond the expansionist stage. In any event, that is where I am now, and a heavy schedule of public appearances has been an important means of widening my circle of engaged constituents.

The community meetings have been especially important (Fig. 8.1). After some initial experimentation, we settled on a format that seems to work well: Postcards announcing the session are sent to every boxholder in a given area, and then I hold an open meeting on the date announced, giving a brief report on congressional activities and taking any and all questions from the floor. In rural areas, we may schedule several such meetings in a single day, stopping at one country store or community building after the other. The meetings in the larger towns and at the county courthouses last longer, are scheduled for the evening hours, and frequently draw 100 to 200 people. Most of my presentation is about policy matters, but I always have staff members along to assist constituents with individual problems. These meetings are well suited to my personal style and find a receptive audience in my district—with its high levels of education and issue-awareness and its large numbers of retirees and persons involved in government, teaching, and research—and they have proved an invaluable means of outreach during my first three terms.

We have also instituted several annual events aimed at particular groups of constituents. The Farm Breakfast became a Fourth District tradition under my predecessor, Rep. Ike Andrews. I generally invite the chairman of a key committee or subcommittee to speak at these breakfasts, and we attract some 120 farmers and agricultural leaders. My annual senior citizens' luncheon has attracted as many as 300; it is an informal occasion, at which I usually discuss current issues of interest. I also sponsor an annual veterans' breakfast along with two colleagues from neighboring districts, Martin Lancaster and Tim Valentine. On one occasion, we heard from Les Aspin, House Armed Services chairman; on another, from Veterans Affairs Chairman Sonny Montgomery. We also sponsor a small business procurement workshop for the same three districts every eighteen months or so. This grew out of work Lancaster and I did on procurement during our first terms, and it has met an obvious need. The last time this workshop was held, we had booths for 50 federal agencies, military bases, and prime contractors and almost 500 business participants.

I communicate with the district through two or three newsletters per year, which go to every boxholder, and more specialized mailings, which go to people I know are interested in particular issues. At least once each congress, I include a mail-back questionnaire in a newsletter, giving constituents an opportunity to register their views on a number of major issues. Having been skeptical of the way some members asked loaded questions designed to elicit preferred responses, I have tried to word our questions straightforwardly. We usually get a good rate of return—some 5,000 to 6,000 questionnaires mailed back, many with elaborations on the answers written in the margins or in accompanying letters. We spend a great deal of time tabulating and disseminating the results and sending out specific responses when needed. But it is well worth the effort, for this lets us establish a direct communications link with thousands of new people and develop lists of constituents interested in particular issues for future reference.

My staff and I also try to maintain effective contact with the news media in the district. Members of the media, especially television, are often attracted to campaign fireworks, but it takes considerably more effort to interest them in the day-to-day work of the Congress. We send a weekly five-minute radio program, in which I discuss an issue before the Congress, to fifteen stations in the district. We also send radio feeds and, occasionally, satellite television feeds to local stations from Washington, offering commentary about matters of current interest, and we arrange interviews on these topics when I am home. In addition, we provide a steady stream of press releases to newspaper, radio, and television outlets; most of these either offer news about my own initiatives or give some interpretation of major items of congressional business, often relating them to North Carolina. We furnish copies of my statements and speeches and let stations know when they can pick up my floor appearances on C-SPAN. I also do a monthly call-in show on cable television, which is then distributed and rebroadcast on most cable systems in the district.

A different strategy is required to meet the needs of smaller radio stations and weekly newspapers, which will generally cover a member of Congress only when he or she visits their community or announces something that pertains to that locality. We let these outlets know when and why I will be in town, and I often arrange to drop by the radio station or newspaper office while there. The smaller papers are also concerned with human interest items, such as pictures of local school groups that recently visited Washington or of summer interns in my office from that community.

Considerable ingenuity is required to relate the work of the Congress to local concerns in an informative and interesting way, and we have gradually gotten better at doing this. In the midst of the child-care debate in 1990, for example, we arranged a visit to a local day-care center, with reporters present. This encouraged coverage of the pending legislation in terms of what it would mean to local parents and centers like the one we visited. Similarly, when I introduced a revised version of my advanced technical training bill in 1991, we invited the press to accompany me on a tour of a local technical college, where they could see the training already under way and hear from faculty and students about the need for prototype programs of the sort my bill would provide.

As congressional districts become more populous and spill over existing community boundaries and as constituents become more reliant on the media and less on personal and party channels for their political information, members must develop extensive mail and press operations if they are to communicate effectively. Of course, there is still no substitute for moving around the district personally; people like to *see* their representatives. But such forays miss thousands of people, while television and computerized mail offer manifold new possibilities for reaching them. Even those of us who regard ourselves stylistically as "workhorses" still have to pay attention to media and public relations, far more than our predecessors ever did. The political landscape in North Carolina and elsewhere is littered with fallen members who assumed that their work in Washington would speak for itself and who did not fully understand what effective communication under modern conditions requires. At its best, such communication conveys a sense of *partnership*—bringing constituents in on what is happening in Congress and what their representative is thinking and doing; it is a process of explaining and interpreting but also inviting reciprocal communications.

Media and mail operations obviously have the potential to improve a member's political standing, and they have been criticized by some as giving an unfair advantage to incumbents. There is no question that these privileges can be abused; I have seen members' newsletters that I thought went over the line, looking more like campaign brochures. Indeed, the line is hard to draw with precision: It is one thing to limit the *quantity* of mailings (the recently instituted mail-counting system should limit districtwide newsletter mailings to three per year), but it is considerably more difficult to regulate their *content* (one rule limits the number of times one can use *I* or *my* in a newsletter). Nevertheless, members of the House invite public cynicism if we do not enforce the rules seriously and, more importantly, honor the *spirit* of the rules personally.

Our critics have a credibility problem of their own, however, when they interpret our efforts to communicate as nothing more than a crass attempt to gain political advantage. My standard way of handling such charges is to invite the critics to actually examine the newsletter or targeted constituent letter, to see whether it communicates useful information or is mere self-promoting puffery. Fortunately, for every such critic, I seem to have hundreds more who find our mailings informative and useful. Of the various charges that the Congress-bashers bring against us, the attacks on franked mail and our other attempts to communicate seem among the most one-sided and indiscriminate; for that reason, perhaps, they rarely seem to hit home.

CASEWORK

The staff members in my three district offices spend most of their time on what is called casework—assisting individuals and sometimes firms or organizations in their dealings with the federal government. The most common areas of concern are Social Security, Medicare, veterans' benefits, tax problems, immigration and naturalization, and passports. Some of these services are routine, as when we expedite the issuance of passports; others involve convoluted disputes over benefits or entitlements that have been years in the making. Often, on determining that we can or should do nothing to change a situation, we simply aim to ensure that a case is given fair consideration and that the person understands the reasons for the agency's decision.

Sometimes, however, our intervention results in the correction of an agency error or the rectification of an injustice. In one such case, the wife of a serviceman had spent six months trying to get a claim processed for her daughter under CHAMPUS, the armed forces health care program for dependents. Our office contacted the agency that was holding up the claim, and within two months, our constituents received payment amounting to $1,659. Another woman, the wife of a veteran, had applied numerous times for Veterans Administration survivor benefits for her daughter, but because of various bureaucratic snafus, the claim had never been processed. Four days after my staff contacted the VA regional office, the benefits were started, and retroactive payments totaling $2,632 were sent. A third case involved a small business with considerable experience in specialized electronics work for the military. The firm was unable to bid on a particular job because military procurement officials had decided not to open the project to competitive bidding. Our inquiries revealed that the military had no defensible reason for this decision; subsequently, the bidding process was opened, and the local firm was able to pursue the contract.

Among the most difficult of our cases—and the most compelling in human terms—are those involving persons or families who wish to immigrate to the United States. The flow of these cases is highly responsive to world events, as when thousands of Kuwaitis fled their country after the Iraqi invasion. Similarly, conditions of political uncertainty and economic hardship in Eastern Europe and the former Soviet Union, along with the loosening of restrictions there, continue to stimulate emigration requests. My staff and I worked with one particularly resourceful young Soviet Jewish émigré in ultimately successful efforts to bring his immediate family to the United States—efforts that included a well-publicized call from me to his mother in the USSR on International Women's Day 1990, as well as more discreet attempts to get the State Department to place the family on a priority list. We also worked intensively with a Raleigh couple trying to adopt three Romanian children after they heard of the plight of youth in that country following the downfall of the Nicolae Ceausescu government. Under pressure from a number of congressional offices with constituents who were similarly situated, the Immigration and Naturalization Service finally issued exit visas from Romania for these children, despite the fact that they did not meet the normal criteria for such papers.

Congressional offices thus operate a kind of appeals process for bureaucratic decisions, a function that has sometimes been likened to that of the ombudsman in Scandinavian countries. It is not an ideal mechanism, and constituents vary considerably in their ability and inclination to use it. Nonetheless, House members have a strong incentive not only to deal with those constituents who present themselves but also to advertise the availability of their services and then to handle the cases effectively, in ways that will inspire favorable comment. A reputation for good constituent service is an important political asset; party and ideological differences often mean nothing to a constituent who has been helped, just as they mean nothing to us as we perform the service.[2] It is also inherently satisfying to help people in these ways, where the results are frequently more immediate and tangible than in legislative work.

Members are also often asked for help with another sort of agency decision: the approval and funding of projects and programs. Although it is quite common in an appropriations bill to direct that funds be spent on a particular project or in a specified fashion, the ground rules are less clear for projects that are to be funded at the discretion of an executive agency, often after a process of professional review. And precedents and practices vary from program to program. In some instances, when asked by an applicant in whom I have confidence, I have simply dropped a note to the agency, flagging the application as one I hope will be given careful consideration. On other occasions, I and my staff have gotten more extensively involved—helping a church apply for sponsorship of a housing project for the elderly, for example, or helping nudge a county government's application for general aviation airport construction through the Federal Aviation Agency (FAA) approval process. Occasionally, I have intervened when trouble developed in what should have been a routine review and award process—as I did when a local university's grant from the National Science Foundation for an Engineering Research Center got held up in an interagency dispute. Such applications from local groups, institutions, and governments are, of course, far more numerous than requests for direct appropriations, and the procedures for handling them are far more routinized, located in another branch of government. Yet a member of Congress does well to follow them closely and can sometimes intervene with good effect.

APPROPRIATIONS

In his landmark 1973 study of congressional committee operations, Richard Fenno identified two "strategic premises" that governed the work of the House Appropriations Committee. The first was to "reduce executive budget requests," the second "to provide adequate funding for executive programs."[3] The latter premise obviously was in some tension with the first, reflecting the ambivalence of House members as to how they wanted this powerful committee to perform. During the past fifteen years, the second premise has increasingly come to predominate, as the House has vested fiscal control in the budget process and as the Reagan administration's policies cast Congress in the role of defender of governmental programs. Nowadays, the Appropriations Committee frequently finds itself at odds with the Budget Committee and the Office of Management and Budget, chafing under the constraints and the spending caps imposed by the budget process. It is also the primary access point for members who wish to protect or promote specific programs and projects. This is why an Appropriations seat is so valuable: It enables one to influence such decisions directly and also to broker requests from colleagues.

The current division of labor has a good deal to be said for it, despite the conflict it engenders. Appropriations always had serious limitations as a control device: Its spending decisions were made piecemeal, the revenue side of the equation was covered by a different committee, and entitlements and contract obligations removed much spending from discretionary control.[4] It is hard to imagine that the sort of incremental reductions the Appropriations Committee used to make would have much impact on contemporary budget deficits—although, admittedly, one can also speculate that the Reagan administration would have had a harder time decimating the federal revenue base and doubling defense spending had it been operating under the old system, without the tools furnished by the budget process. In any event, we now look to the budget resolution and the annual reconciliation bill, rather than individual appropriations bills, as the major instruments of fiscal control. Each Appropriations subcommittee is assigned a spending cap within the terms of the budget resolution. And each runs the risk of rejection on the House floor and, beyond that, sequestration if that limit is violated.

As the VA-HUD-Independent Agencies example from 1991 illustrates (see Chapter 7), the spending limits imposed by this process can be quite constraining. But *within* these caps, the Appropriations subcommittees still have wide discretion in determining what gets funded and at what level, and members vie intently for their favor. During my first two terms, I did this from outside the Appropriations Committee, and in 1991 I brought a far more extensive and detailed list to the table as a new Appropriations member.

The key contact for any member seeking an appropriation is the relevant subcommittee chairman, for the thirteen subcommittees enjoy a great deal of autonomy. A Republican member would, of course, contact the subcommittee's ranking minority member, and a Democrat would be well advised to do likewise, for the subcommittees operate in a spirit of bipartisan comity. Such contacts should be replicated at the staff level and followed up with a letter making the case for the request more systematically. As a new member not on the committee, I always enlisted the help of Bill Hefner, an Appropriations member from my state who also had the distinct advantage of being a subcommittee chairman, one of the so-called college of cardinals. I also informed the full committee chairman and his staff of any request and enlisted the help of all other committee or subcommittee members who had special knowledge of or interest in the project.

In this fashion, I took a range of Fourth District projects to the Appropriations Committee during my first two terms and was able, in most instances, to secure favorable action: $5 million for the permanent installation of an experimental radar system to increase the capacity of Raleigh-Durham Airport; a $1.7-million planning grant to prepare for construction of a laboratory on the University of North Carolina campus to be leased by the Environmental Protection Agency; a $550,000 federal share for the restoration of a historic building on a predominantly black college campus; and a $750,000 first installment on the federal share for construction of a new building for the North Carolina Biotechnology Center.

I was able to lift my sights considerably as a new Appropriations member in 1991. Drawing on augmented staff resources, I consulted widely in the district and developed and defended a considerably expanded list of projects. I also worked with colleagues from North Carolina and other states in making the case for their proposals. And on my own and other subcommittees, I weighed in on behalf of funding priority for national programs I regarded as especially important.

I concentrated, of course, on my two subcommittee assignments: transportation, and rural development and agriculture. In both cases, I developed a list of funding priorities, which my staff reviewed in detail with the subcommittee staff and I then discussed with the subcommittee chairman. Both subcommittees held extensive hearings through the spring, which I attended regularly. We scheduled three witnesses from the district for the transportation hearings—the Raleigh transportation director, the head of the regional transit authority, and the director of the Raleigh-Durham Airport—to engage them in the process and to make our case publicly. But neither subcommittee held a markup of the sort I had become accustomed to on the Banking and Science committees.

On both of my former committees, the "chairman's mark"—the chairman's draft of a bill—is a document of considerable importance, but it is often only a starting point for a protracted process of revision and amendment. Not so on most Appropriations subcommittees. The chairman and ranking minority member, with their staffs playing a major role, assemble and evaluate myriad member requests and incorporate many of them, in some fashion, in a chairman's mark. This bill is unveiled before the subcommittee at an appropriate time and generally is altered very little in subcommittee or full committee markups. The starting point for this document is the administration's budget request, presented and defended by agency heads in the hearings; members are furnished documents showing how the chairman's draft differs from the administration's request on each item. However, the differences are often substantial, and there is no question that the bill has been reviewed item by item and given the subcommittee's own imprint.

Special consideration is given to requests of subcommittee members; they are generally informed, often through staff channels, of what is in the draft of the chairman's bill and given an opportunity to respond before markup. The vast majority of disagreements and problems are resolved at this stage. The few items that spill over into the formal markup sessions may be resolved when the chairman accepts an amendment or offers an accommodation or when the proponent makes his or her point and then decides to withdraw the proposal. Only occasionally is a matter forced to a recorded vote. This may happen when a matter intrudes that is not amenable to the kind of incremental adjustment found in most appropriations compromises—such as the question of abortion funding on Labor-HHS-Education or District of Columbia appropriations bills. But there are very few such matters involved in transportation and agriculture funding bills, and members evince a high level of satisfaction with the way the decision processes on these subcommittees work for them.

I was pleased with the results of my first session on the committee. In the 1991 transportation appropriations bill, I obtained first-year funding for a three-year, $23-million highway project; $750,000 for the federal share of a $1-million study of long-range transportation needs and possible mass-transit alternatives in the Research Triangle area; a grant to the city of Raleigh to purchase ten vans for an experimental suburban feeder service for the city's bus system; an earmarking of Amtrak funds to support an additional intrastate train for North Carolina; $1 million in research funds to establish a statewide environmental data base for highway planning; $2.5 million to upgrade the instrument landing system at Raleigh-Durham Airport; and a directive to the FAA to permanently install the airport's experimental radar system on schedule. The agriculture bill included the remaining $1.45 million in federal funding for the N.C. Biotechnology Center; additional funding for peanut and other agricultural research, much of it based at N.C. State University; and a $3.5 million contribution toward construction of a nutrition research center at the Bowman Gray School of Medicine of Wake Forest University.

This latter project—one Bill Hefner and I were advocating on behalf of a colleague in a neighboring district—demonstrated the importance of having a "cardinal" on one's side. When Hefner learned that the draft of the chairman's mark contained only $1.5 million for Bowman Gray, he walked to the room where the chairman and his staff were finalizing the mark and prevailed on them to change the figure. The agriculture bill also gave me a chance to follow up on some rural housing interests I had developed on the Banking Committee. Our hearings in Raleigh in early

1990 had pointed up an absence in many rural communities of the kind of expertise needed in order to plan effectively or to take advantage of available federal assistance. As a result, Farmers Home Administration programs were being utilized very sporadically in North Carolina and other states.[5] We therefore wrote into the appropriations bill $2.5 million in program preparation assistance for nonprofit organizations to put together rural housing proposals.

Committee membership also placed me in an improved position to request assistance from other subcommittees. The Labor-HHS-Education Subcommittee earmarked $17.9 million in initial construction funds for the National Institute of Environmental Health Sciences in the Research Triangle Park. The Commerce-Justice-State Subcommittee increased funding for advanced technology development and suggested the funds be awarded to a cooperative textile research program at N.C. State and three other universities. The Energy and Water Development Subcommittee included extra funds for recreational development at a Corps of Engineers lake near Raleigh. The Foreign Operations Subcommittee's report supported Agency for International Development (AID) funding for the MBA Enterprise Corps, a program to send young business school graduates to assist new enterprises in Eastern Europe, initiated at the University of North Carolina and including fifteen other business schools. And the VA-HUD-Independent Agencies Subcommittee acceded in conference to a $5-million planning grant for a new Environmental Protection Agency building in the Research Triangle Park.

I was not the only member supporting many of these projects, of course, and I could no doubt have obtained funding for some of them from outside the committee. The Appropriations Committee, after all, maintains a high level of House support by accommodating large numbers of members. Nevertheless, there is no question that my Appropriations position has opened up many new opportunities for me to obtain support for worthy projects in my district and across North Carolina and also to influence funding levels and program direction across a broad spectrum of federal activity.

This mix of local and national concerns, so evident on the Appropriations Committee, is built into every member's job description. Most of us are constantly attentive to our districts, in proposing legislation and securing funding, in interpreting and explaining what Congress is doing and how we are representing our constituents, in deploying staff and budgeting our own time and attention. Life in Congress is, by definition, a divided existence—living in Washington and in the home district, overseeing staff in both locations, constantly traveling between the two, serving at once as national legislators and local representatives, both shaping the rules and assisting individuals in coping with them. These multiple roles create strains and tensions with which members must learn to deal. But the mix can be enormously challenging and stimulating. At least, that is the way I feel about it. I know of no other job like the one I have, and I feel extraordinarily fortunate to be where I am.

9

Religion and Politics

I had the good fortune to come of age politically in the early years of the modern civil rights movement—the years between the Montgomery, Alabama, bus boycott that first brought Martin Luther King, Jr., to prominence (1955–1956) and the passage of the landmark Civil Rights Act of 1964. I say good fortune because of the particularly challenging and especially positive kind of political experience this movement gave me and thousands like me in my student generation. Had we come along a few years earlier, I often thought, we would have faded into the blandness of the Eisenhower years. And the generation following ours had a far different political experience as the civil rights movement splintered into reformist and radical wings and the Vietnam War brought forth disillusionment, protest, and fierce political conflict. Many lost faith in politics as an instrument of positive change.

This contrasted markedly with the climactic moment of my own early political experience, which occurred on June 19, 1964, during my second summer as a junior staff member in a U.S. Senate office. On that day, I crowded into the Senate gallery to witness the final passage of the Civil Rights Act. It could scarcely have been a more dramatic moment, as the dying Sen. Clair Engle (D.-California) was wheeled into the chamber to cast this momentous vote. It was a moment capable of convincing a young person that the system worked, that enough dedicated people, working together, could right ancient wrongs. All in all, it was a fitting climax to the formative political years that many in my generation experienced.

An important element in this experience for many of us was religion. Our religious backgrounds shaped our response to the civil rights struggle, and our religious outlook was challenged and broadened in turn. Religion had been central to my own upbringing; the Price family had been pillars of the First Christian Church of Erwin, Tennessee, ever since my grandfather's family had moved there in 1901. We were present whenever the church doors were open, including Sunday evening services and Wednesday night prayer meetings. I was particularly influenced by Henry Webb, the minister there during my teenage years who also taught at nearby Milligan College. I went off to Mars Hill intending to be an engineer, as befitted a member of the Sputnik generation, but with Webb's urging that I consider the ministry in the back of my mind.

Mars Hill College was identified with a Baptist regimen considerably stricter than my own upbringing. However, Robert Seymour, the community's young pastor who had trained at Yale Divinity School, helped me and many others move from a primarily individualistic understanding of our faith to appreciate its social and prophetic dimensions. Just before I transferred to the University of North Carolina, Seymour came to Chapel Hill to help found a new kind of Baptist church, which was racially inclusive and affiliated with the American as well as the Southern Baptist Convention.[1] This became my church home in Chapel Hill, as it still is today. And despite my lack of Baptist credentials, I was elected president of the Baptist Student Union at UNC.

On campus, the religious organizations took the lead in protesting discrimination and pressing for change. Many took to heart Martin Luther King's indictment of the church as a "thermometer that records the ideas and principles of popular opinion," rather than a "thermostat that transforms the mores of society."[2] And many of us saw in civil rights a challenge to translate the personal ethic of "love thy neighbor" into social terms.

One who has lived through such an experience is unlikely to make the mistake of assuming that the separation of church and state can or should mean a neat compartmentalizing of religion and politics. Indeed, the ensuing years have seen an increase in religiously oriented political movements. A number of those churches that King criticized for their "completely other-worldly religion [making] a strange, un-Biblical distinction between body and soul, between the sacred and the secular"[3] have been politically mobilized, though frequently in the service of an agenda considerably different from what King had in mind. As a result, the debate over the place of religion in politics has intensified, often generating more heat than light. In the present chapter, I will reflect on how that debate has looked from Capitol Hill and how its terms might be clarified.

RELIGIOUS AGENDAS

If I had not already been sensitive to the problematic relationship between religion and politics by virtue of my own religious background and divinity school training, my first campaign, against an incumbent identified with the religious Right, certainly would have made me so. I have already described his "Dear Christian Friend" letter to prospective supporters, warning that he might be replaced by "someone who is not willing to take a strong stand for the principles outlined in the Word of God"—namely, me. Even before that letter appeared, however, I had scheduled a meeting to air issues related to religion with ministers from across the district; the last half of the present chapter, in fact, had its beginning as a talk prepared for this group. I also visited many churches, particularly in the black community, where introducing candidates in the course of a service is still quite common (although many justifiably look askance at candidates who drop in only on election eve or who do not remain for the entire service). These visits convinced me anew of the vitality and diversity of the churches in the black community and their importance in stimulating and shaping political action.

Since my election, I have received thousands of calls, letters, and visits from religiously motivated organizations and individuals. Black community churches tend to stress social and economic concerns, and we have helped some of them become sponsors of low-income housing projects. Jewish congregations have been concerned with the security of Israel, though by no means totally uncritical of that government's present policies. A number of congregations, mainly Protestant, have coupled local social activism with advocacy on national issues, sometimes in conjunction with organizations like Bread for the World and Habitat for Humanity. And extracongregational groups like Witness for Peace have been forceful advocates on international issues, particularly those pertaining to Central America. In all of these instances, I have been invited into services, classes, and forums: I have benefited from the exchange and been impressed with how the awakening of social concern and activism that I witnessed in the 1960s has continued to characterize American religious life.

My relations with the religious Right have been far less constructive, although I have had enough positive experiences with individuals to convince me that, in many cases, communication and even a meeting of the minds is possible. It is also important not to overgeneralize about the political tendencies of conservative or evangelical Christians. Our polls show that some one-fifth of the white voters of the Fourth District regard themselves as "fundamentalists," but only 46 percent of this group express a favorable view of Rev. Jerry Falwell, the most prominent of the religious Right's political advocates. Many, perhaps most, of the others resist and resent the efforts of such self-styled leaders to mobilize them on behalf of a particular political agenda.

Still, in my district and across the country, the religious Right is a force to be reckoned with. During my first five years in office, 1987–1991, the issue that inspired the most communication and advocacy from within religious communities was, by a good margin, the Civil Rights Restoration Act of 1988—most of it *against* the bill. I found this especially ironic and sad in light of my memories of the passage of the 1964 Civil Rights Act (which the 1988 proposal sought to protect from adverse judicial interpretations). To be sure, the mainline Protestant, Catholic, and Jewish bodies lined up in favor of the bill. But their efforts at grass-roots mobilization were anemic compared to the thousands of letters and calls from the other side that kept the phones in all of my offices tied up for two weeks. "Grove City" (the bill's shorthand designation, taken from the Supreme Court decision it sought to reverse) is still talked about with considerable awe among my staff, and it has become the high-water mark against which all future floods of calls about flag-burning, gun control, congressional pay raises, and the like are to be measured.

Many of the calls were inspired by a widely circulated memorandum from Jerry Falwell, head of the Moral Majority, that described this rather modest bill as "the greatest threat to religious freedom and traditional moral values ever passed." The Civil Rights Restoration Act, he warned, could force churches "to hire a practicing active homosexual drug addict with AIDS to be a teacher or youth pastor."[4] My incredulity that people could ever believe such an absurd statement was overwhelmed by the mass of calls that we received, many from well-meaning and genuinely concerned people. In the end, however, Falwell and his allies did not succeed, and the White House operatives who had hoped the religious Right could help them sustain President Reagan's veto of the bill had reason to doubt the utility of the alliance. In fact, this might well be the textbook case of a lobby overreaching—using such outrageous tactics and such absurd misinformation that it became a point of honor with members not to be swayed. As Bill Hefner said on the House floor,

> I find reprehensible not those thousands of people who have made the phone calls, but . . the people that have instigated this misinformation. . . . If it means that I lose my position in the U.S. House of Representatives [if I do not] cave in . . . and base my vote on what people believe to be true but what I know not to be true, I say to my colleagues this job is not worth that to me.[5]

In the end, the House voted to override the veto by 292–133, displaying remarkably little slippage from the original vote in favor of the bill (315–98).

A new offensive on the part of religious Right organizations was evident in 1990—nowhere more so than in North Carolina, with Sen. Jesse Helms on the ballot—organized mainly around three issues: abortion, pornography, and child care. Abortion, of course, is the touchstone issue for most of these groups. Pornography was revived as an issue by controversies over the funding of some allegedly obscene and sacrilegious works of art by the National Endowment for the Arts (NEA). Congress sent the NEA an unmistakable message in 1988, cutting its appropriation by the amount of the offending works, and set up additional procedures for the review of grants. This was not enough, however, for politicians like Senator Helms and for many of the protesting organizations that had their own reasons for wishing to keep the pornography issue alive.

The most anomalous of this triumvirate of issues—and certainly the strangest protest effort for organizations professing concern for family values—was child care. I gained a greater understanding of some of the angry calls and letters we had been getting on this subject when I happened to tune in to James Dobson's national radio program, "Focus on the Family." Ironically, his preoccupation that day was with distortion—the way the media had deliberately (and conspiratorially, he thought) underestimated the size and enthusiasm of the antiabortion demonstrations recently held in Washington. Dobson then turned to the child-care bill just passed by the House and proceeded to give about as distorted an account of it as I could have imagined!

This was something I knew a good deal about for I had been active in the discussions and compromises undertaken prior to the consideration of the child-care issue on the House floor. It was an important bill—expanding the remarkably successful Head Start program in early childhood education, authorizing school-based "latchkey" programs for young children who otherwise would go home to empty houses each day, and expanding social services block grants to the states for child-care assistance. The critics argued that the bill encouraged mothers not to stay at home with their children—showing remarkable insensitivity to single-parent households or to the economic factors often forcing both parents to work. But it was true that mothers who stayed home often did so at some financial sacrifice, and we agreed to an expansion of the earned-income tax credit for families with young children that could be claimed both by families that purchased child care and by those in which the mother stayed home. We also responded to the critics' claim that the bill discriminated against church-based day care; we agreed that the model of church-state separation applicable to public education was not appropriate here and devised a program of certificates and vouchers that could be utilized at church-run centers.

These compromises—which addressed what the critics had said were their major concerns—had no effect on leaders like James Dobson or on many of their followers, like the angry "stay-at-home moms" who packed my community meetings. They seemed determined to maintain the sense of a great cultural and religious divide between themselves and politicians like me, the sense that their "traditional values" were being conspired against. I finally concluded, admittedly with some difficulty, that I was wasting my breath to discuss what the child-care bill actually contained.

Attacks such as these—which turn on their head the religious values being professed and then often invoke divine sanctions against those who disagree—have led some to regard religion as a dangerous and imperious presence in politics. But that is not a satisfactory conclusion or, indeed, a realistic one, given the inseparability of religious faith and belief from the wellsprings of political motivation. The fact that political applications of religious convictions may be misguided or wrong does not justify dismissing or condemning all such expressions. But it does underscore the importance of thinking carefully about what the relation between religious life and the political order ought to be in a democracy.

THE TWO REALMS

The relation of the sacred and the secular has inspired theological discussion for thousands of years. The Jewish and Christian faiths are distinctive in setting up a problematic relationship, a tension, between the kingdom of God and the kingdom of earth. In some of the earliest Old Testament writings, in the book of Samuel, a great ambivalence is expressed about the very idea of an earthly king in Israel, so that it "may be like all the nations."[6] That ambivalence about the political realm reappears in various forms throughout the scriptures.

Later theologians have related the sacred and the secular, the religious and the political, in a variety of ways. This variety was best analyzed in H. Richard Niebuhr's masterful *Christ and Culture*, where a "series of typical answers" to this "perennial Christian perplexity" were elaborated.[7] Some theologians have seen worldly kingdoms as a vehicle for divine law. Others have seen this world as virtually abandoned by God. Most theologians, however, have tried to keep those two views in tension. God's word has been interpreted as both a call and a guide to social involvement. Yet God's word remains transcendent, always imperfectly embodied in our institutions, always standing in judgment over them. Other religious traditions have been much more single minded, either in renouncing the world or in identifying earthly and Godly rule. Judaism and Christianity, over most of their histories, have maintained the tension and thus have witnessed recurring debates about exactly what the relationship should be. I do not aim to contribute to that debate so much as to reflect on it and its implications for our contemporary American situation. My thoughts fall into six related propositions, the first being that religious faith powerfully and positively shapes our political advocacy and practice.

Our capacity to compartmentalize our lives is often quite remarkable. This was particularly evident as the civil rights movement challenged the southern church in the 1960s; people who were loving and generous in their personal relationships often saw no contradiction in their support of social practices and laws that denied others their humanity. But such compartmentalization is ultimately untenable. Many in my generation found guidance in the writings of Reinhold Niebuhr, whose interpretation of the relation of the religious ethic of love to politics is still helpful today.[8] A love ethic can never be perfectly embodied in politics, he taught, but it nonetheless compels its adherents to seek justice as a proximate public expression of love. To fail to achieve justice in our common life is just as surely a betrayal of the ethic of love as it would be to reject a neighbor's need face to face.

Such applications are not always simple or straightforward. In the years prior to World War II, for example, Niebuhr challenged those who interpreted the love ethic to counsel nonresistance and pacifism. He went so far as to term modern pacificism a heresy that owed more to Enlightenment notions of human perfectibility than to that "Christian realism" that, in taking full account of human sin and the will-to-power, recognized "that justice [could] be achieved only by a certain degree of coercion on the one hand, and by resistance to coercion and tyranny on the other hand."

While such realism warns against oversimplifying the task of "achieving justice in a sinful world," it also recognizes that world for what it is and thus preserves a tension between religious ideas and their historical manifestations. Our basic American political values have readily identifiable religious roots. But our religious traditions also prompt an ongoing critique of our faltering efforts to realize liberty and justice, just as they offer a corrective to the excesses of individualism and materialism in American life.

My second proposition is that in a pluralistic democracy we must seek common ground with those of diverse traditions and those whose values do not have conventional religious roots. I remember discussions in the 1960s among people whose involvement in the civil rights movement stemmed from religious convictions as to whether persons from radically different backgrounds and traditions could work together effectively for the cause. Of course, the answer to that was yes. We bring our deepest convictions and insights to our political advocacy, but at the same time, we recognize the validity of other traditions and the common ethical ground we share. In politics, we debate the issues, not the doctrines. We debate with people whose theological and philosophical perspectives differ, and we can often find a basis for concerted action. This is the happy experience of American democracy.

My third point is that if we cannot find common ground, there may be good reason for stopping short of embodying our moral precepts in civil law. In the absence of a broad consensus, it is often preferable to leave the individual and communal expression of conscience free.

Theologians have long debated the question put by Thomas Aquinas: "Whether an effect of law is to make men good?"[9] Our religious traditions contain law-like moral codes that continue to shape civil law. There are also reciprocal effects, despite often-heard protestations that "you can't legislate morality": The legal order inculcates rudimentary moral standards, and obedience to the law may habituate one to at least the external forms of goodness. But morality is prior to the law, and its imperatives are never exhausted by religious or civil codes. Nor can the legal order compel behavior that is, in the deepest sense, moral. This is partly because of inevitable flaws in human law and partly because law, in its generality, falls short of the individual's moral potential. Most fundamentally, however, it is because the instrumentalities of law cannot compel the good *will*, from which morality springs.

All of this means that, though our religiously inspired judgments as to what is moral and our political judgments as to what can and should be embodied in law are related, they are not the same thing. Their relationship is problematic even in a homogeneous religious setting. And in a country where multiple religious and ethical traditions flourish, we should move cautiously indeed in enshrining in civil law moral precepts that do not have broad consensual support. It is thus perfectly consistent, for example, for one who is deeply convinced that abortion is wrong also to conclude that it is not prudent to embody a prohibition of abortion in civil law. If we have difficulty finding common ground in a pluralistic society, if we run into severe conflict in translating deeply held moral convictions into precepts of civil law, it is often wise to demur and to leave conscience free.

I would also argue that religious toleration and the separation of church and state are essential protections of the freedom of religious expression and practice. In the midst of the controversy over the use of religion in my first congressional campaign, a local minister allied with the incumbent was quoted as saying that my view represented that of a "pluralistic person in a pluralistic society." That statement is worth examining. I would readily acknowledge commitment to a pluralistic society, a society in which the expression of religious conviction is free and unimpeded. However, that does not mean that I am a "pluralistic person." In fact, the genius of a pluralistic society is its ability to combine a strength of conviction, a rootedness in tradition, with a respect for the convictions and traditions of others. And when we stand up for toleration and religious freedom, we're not suggesting that somehow our religious convictions are weak or indecisive. On the contrary, we're standing up for the strength of those convictions and defending our right to express them.

Governor Mario Cuomo of New York, a practicing Catholic, put it this way: "To assure our freedom, we must allow others the same freedom even if occasionally it produces conduct which we hold to be sinful. . . . I protect my right to be a Catholic by preserving your right to believe as a

Jew, a Protestant or a non-believer or anything else you choose."[10] That states a basic truth, I believe, about American democracy.

The first amendment to the U.S. Constitution contains two complementary protections of religious freedom: Government is not to "establish" religion, but neither is it to prohibit "the free exercise thereof." There are to be no state-sponsored religious exercises and no religious tests, formal or informal, for political participation or for election to office. Those precepts protect the freedom of religious expression we all possess. At the same time, the state is not to discriminate *against* religion. For example, the so-called equal access statute at the federal level, ensuring that religiously oriented school organizations will not be discriminated against *because of* their orientation, has recently been upheld by the Supreme Court.[11] After school hours, such clubs can use meeting rooms and school facilities on the same basis as other organizations.

We all have a stake in the defense of religious liberty and toleration through the separation of church and state and the guarantee of religion's free exercise. And we are not somehow saying that we are "pluralistic people" or that we lack strong convictions when we do this. On the contrary, we bear witness to the very strength of these convictions and to our belief that religious expression simply cannot and must not be impeded.

My fifth point is that our religious traditions point up the limitations as well as the possibilities of politics and give us a realistic perspective on political power. These traditions reject cynicism and the placing of arbitrary limits on our aspirations, but they also provide a realistic view of human nature and of the pervasiveness of sin and self-interest in society. We should have no illusions about the evils of which human beings, individually and collectively, are capable. Our task in politics therefore becomes not only to utilize power for the common good but also to check the pervasive and inevitable abuses of power, to make the best of a sinful world. Reinhold Niebuhr's most quoted line is pertinent here: "Man's capacity for justice makes democracy possible; but man's inclination to injustice makes democracy necessary."[12] No policy or program, even the most well-intentioned, can be assumed to be free of the taint of self-interest and self-seeking. Consequently, the task of democracy is not only to realize our positive aspirations but also to provide a check against inevitable miscarriages of justice and abuses of power.

The framers of the Constitution believed that no governmental power could safely go unchecked. They therefore "contriv[ed] the interior structure of the government [so] that its several constituent parts [might], by their mutual relations, be the means of keeping each other in their proper places." James Madison's reflections on these arrangements revealed a persistent streak of Calvinism among these heirs of the Enlightenment:

It may be a reflection on human nature that such devices should be necessary to control the abuses of government. But what is government itself but the greatest of all reflections on human nature? If men were angels, no government would be necessary. If angels were to govern men, neither external nor internal controls on government would be necessary. In framing a government which is to be administered by men over men, the great difficulty lies in this: You must first enable the government to control the governed; and in the next place oblige it to control itself. A dependence on the people is, no doubt, the primary control on the government; but experience has taught mankind the necessity of auxiliary precautions.[13]

Thus do we draw on our religious traditions in recognizing the distortions and dangers to which the exercise of political power is liable and in protecting ourselves against them.

It is important to distinguish this realistic view from the more simplistic antipower ideology that persistently rears its head in American politics. Government is hardly the only realm in which power exists or can be abused; political power can, in fact, be used to counter or control economic or other kinds of power. Realism requires that we not only attend to the dangers of strengthening a given organ of government but also ask what powers and interests might fill the vacuum if it is weakened. And, as I have suggested in Chapters 6 and 7, there is nothing automatically efficacious about checkmated governmental institutions; a simplistic distrust of power is sometimes a poor guide to what is required to make institutions function accountably and effectively. What the realism rooted in our religious traditions offers is, rather, an awareness of the admixture of self-interest and self-seeking in all human endeavors, of the necessity to use power deliberately as we pursue the common good, and also of the need for checks and safeguards as we recognize the vulnerability of such power to distortion and abuse.

A final and related point is this: Our religious traditions warn against absolutizing anyone's political power or program, regarding this as a form of idolatry. The very worst kind of pride is often religious pride: equating our own point of view, our own interest or ideology, with the will of God.

There is a story in the Old Testament that, as far as I know, is unique in the ancient world. King David, at the height of his powers, commits a grievous sin, and the lowly prophet Nathan visits him and calls him to account, pronouncing God's judgment: "Why have you despised the word of the Lord, to do what is evil in his sight?"[14] God's word, then, stands above even David, king of all Israel. That insight—that conviction that no person or institution stands above or is to be identified with God's will— is at the very heart of our religious traditions.

The American statesman who best understood this was Abraham Lincoln. Recall the words of his second inaugural address, all the more remarkable for being uttered after almost four years of civil war:

> Both [sides] read the same Bible, and pray to the same God; and each invokes His aid against the other. It may seem strange that any men should dare to ask a just God's assistance in wringing their bread from the sweat of other men's faces; but let us judge not, that we be not judged. The prayers of both could not be answered—that of neither has been answered fully.[15]

On another occasion, responding to a clergyman who expressed the hope that the Lord was on the side of the Union, Lincoln reportedly responded, "I know that the Lord is always on the side of the right. But it is my constant anxiety and prayer that I and this nation should be on the Lord's side."[16] We are all too quick to claim that God is on our side, to claim divine sanction for the program that we are promoting or the power that we seek. But the important question is the one that Lincoln asked. We ought never to lose that sense of God's transcendence and of the fallibility of all our human efforts, political and otherwise. This is the ultimate reason for rejecting the political pretensions of those who would equate their own program with God's will. Not only does that kind of religious pretension violate the tenets of American pluralism and American democracy, it also violates the deepest insight of our religious traditions themselves. These traditions counsel a kind of religious humility, a sense that our own will, our own efforts, our own striving, are never to be equated with the will of God. We are not to invoke the divine mandate lightly.

The imperatives of faith will continue to inspire political action, and indeed, they must—for the prophetic charge to "let justice roll down like waters"[17] requires not simply fair dealings among individuals but the *collective* implementation of a social standard. The fact that others may claim a religious sanction for seemingly antithetical policies does not make the ethical imperative any less compelling. We must do the best we can. But there are good reasons—rooted not only in democratic experience but also in the theology of divine transcendence and human fallibility—for refusing to identify any particular ideology or political program with the will of God and for rebuking those who presume to do so. "For my thoughts are not your thoughts, neither are your ways my ways, says the Lord."[18]

10

Representation and Responsibility

As a member who came to the Congress in 1987 from a teaching career that included a good deal of work in ethics and public policy, it has seemed strange to me to hear talk of an "ethics craze" in government and to witness a continuing preoccupation with ethical matters, centered around the fall of House Speaker Jim Wright but by no means limited to that episode.

My first assignment on joining the Duke University faculty in 1973 was to devise an ethics course that would be required as a component of the graduate public policy curriculum. Over the ensuing decade, I worked with a growing group of academics and practitioners across the country, holding workshops, writing papers, attending conferences—promoting the study and teaching of ethics while developing its intellectual content and broadening its applications. I thus stepped into the swirling waters of ethical agitation and debate in the House with considerable background in the subject, but that background often seemed to have precious little relevance to what passed for ethical discussion there.

I say that not in criticism of the fields of political ethics and public policy as they have developed. In fact, I am more inclined to be critical of prevailing public and congressional conceptions of ethics, what I will somewhat disparagingly term "ethics committee" ethics. This does not mean that the ethics committees and the congressional code of conduct should appreciably broaden their domain. The point, rather, is that the implications of ethical reflection and analysis for the Congress—for the policies it makes and how its members function—go far beyond what can or should be contained in a code or enforced by a watchdog committee. It is that broader conception of ethics and its relevance to legislative life that I will explore in this chapter.

Numerous colleagues and I had examined the ethical content of the legislator's role and the inherent limitations of ethics committee ethics as part of a major Hastings Center project in the early 1980s.[1] What I encountered in 1987 was an intensifying ethical concern in Congress itself, which culminated on the House side in the appointment of the Bipartisan Task Force on Ethics and the passage of the Government Ethics Reform

Act of 1989 but which failed to produce any significant broadening of the terms of discussion and debate.

A readiness to believe the worst about the motives and the integrity of public officials has characterized American political culture from the beginning. Historians like Bernard Bailyn and James Sterling Young documented the prevalence of a strong antipower ideology in the revolutionary and subsequent generations, a conviction that those with political power would invariably abuse it and that corruption and self-aggrandizement were endemic to government.[2] Young, in fact, attributed the disabilities and demoralization of the early congresses in large measure to the tendency of the members to internalize the dominant public view of "power-holding as essentially a degrading experience. . . . The power-holders did not, in their own outlook, escape a culturally ingrained predisposition to view political power and politics as essentially evil."[3] Such cynicism and the mistrust of officeholders and public institutions have been heightened in recent years by highly publicized scandals and by the capacity and the tendency of the modern mass media to publicize and dramatize the foibles and failings of politicians.

For most of their first two centuries, the House and Senate had no written codes of behavior but dealt sporadically and often inconsistently with discrete acts of wrongdoing.[4] I came across one such instance in researching a brief bicentennial piece on those who preceded me in representing my district in North Carolina. I discovered that one of my predecessors, a Reconstruction congressman named John Deweese, had resigned his seat in 1870 one day before he and two other members were censured for selling appointments to the military academies. Progressive era reform sentiments and various election scandals led to a series of federal campaign practices statutes beginning in 1907. But it was not until after World War II that Congress moved to adopt more general codes of conduct for its members. The first was a government-wide aspirational code, adopted in 1958 in the wake of the Sherman Adams–Bernard Goldfine scandal in the Eisenhower administration. Widely publicized congressional scandals a decade later—involving Sen. Thomas Dodd, Senate Majority Secretary Bobby Baker, and Rep. Adam Clayton Powell— led both chambers to adopt their first formal codes of conduct. These were toughened considerably in 1977 and again in 1989.

The most recent changes, passed after the resignation under fire of Speaker Jim Wright, tightened limits on outside employment and eliminated speaking fees (honoraria), strengthened financial disclosure requirements, enjoined members from converting campaign funds to personal use on retirement, and prohibited lobbying by members and staff for one year after leaving their positions. Most of these provisions were contained in the report of the Bipartisan Task Force on Ethics, accurately described by its cochairman as "the most sweeping reform of congressional ethics in the last decade."[5] But the proposals did not break new ground conceptually and were comprehensive only in relation to the already defined domain of congressional ethics.

Dennis Thompson told of one instance in which a breakthrough did, indeed, occur. In Tennessee during 1977, in the wake of a political scandal, the leaders of the state senate decided they needed a tough code of ethics:

> Senators who did not want the code were reluctant to vote against it in the prevailing climate of reform, but when the code came to the floor, they thought they had found a way out. One senator proposed, as a substitute amendment, the Ten Commandments and the Golden Rule. The leaders knew that in Tennessee no legislator could vote against the Ten Commandments or the Golden Rule, and they scrambled to find a parliamentary compromise that would save the code. The substitute amendment became a regular amendment, and Tennessee became the only state to have a code of ethics that included, along with strong conflict-of-interest provisions, all ten of the commandments. From Article IV with its detailed procedural rules, the document jumped immediately to Article V, which read in its entirety: "Thou shalt have no other gods before me."[6]

But even Tennessee has now fallen into line; when the code was revised in 1985, Thompson reported, the Ten Commandments quietly disappeared!

The 1985 Hastings report acknowledged that a code of official conduct should only be "one element in a well-rounded effort to inspire the conduct of legislators as well as to engender trust on the part of the public in those legislators." Nonetheless, it still was critical of the limits of existing codes: "They are generally narrow in scope, short on aspirational statements, and fail to deal with the full range of representative or legislative functions."[7] The report proposed three touchstones for legislative ethics: *autonomy* (the "obligation to deliberate and decide, free from improper influence"), *accountability* (the "obligation to provide constituents with the information and understanding they require in order to exercise responsible democratic citizenship"), and *responsibility* (the "obligation to contribute to the effective institutional functioning of the democratic legislative process").[8] Existing codes address the first two principles in their conflict-of-interest and public disclosure provisions, but they still construe "autonomy" and "accountability" quite narrowly and barely deal with "responsibility" at all.

The Hastings authors suggested that a more adequate code of legislative ethics might, like the former code of professional conduct of the American Bar Association, contain aspirational elements and espoused ideals as well as precisely defined rules of conduct.[9] They probably underestimated the difficulty of reaching consensus on aspirational maxims and did not suggest what kind of enforcement mechanisms, if any, might be appropriate in this realm. But they were correct in noting the severe limitations of ethics committee ethics. Using that as my point of departure, I want to proceed not to precisely delineate what might or might not be codified but to look beyond personal and official probity and ask what further ethical dilemmas and challenges confront legislators as they define and carry out their jobs.

ETHICS AND POLICY

Members of Congress and other legislative assemblies continually make policy choices, not just in hundreds of roll-call votes each year but in crafting legislation for introduction, refining bills in committee, and engaging in debate at each stage of the process. These policy choices are, among other things, choices of value. Legislators, like most citizens, value human liberty, feel that policies should be just and fair, argue for taking the public interest or the common good into account, and may speak of furthering human solidarity and community. They have varying degrees of awareness, of course, of the historical, philosophical, and theological grounding of such concepts, of how they might complement or contradict one another, and of the implications they might hold for specific questions of policy. But such concepts do describe valued social states and help shape, however loosely, the process of deliberation and debate.[10] For years, I taught a course called Ethics and Public Policy that was based on the assumption that policymakers and the policy process would benefit from more careful and critical reflection on our inherited notions of human well-being and the public good, coupled with more explicit efforts to discern the implications of these ideas for particular policies and institutions. Much of what I have experienced during two terms in the U.S. House has strengthened that assumption.

This is not to say, of course, that the ethical assessment of policy among practicing legislators generally takes the same form that it does in the academy—or, indeed, that it should. Dennis Thompson argued persuasively that the demands of the role of the legislator, in particular the *ethical* demands, may conflict with the "generic requirements of ethics." "Ethics demands a general perspective, but legislators are also obligated to look after their own particular constituents. Ethics requires autonomous judgment, but legislators are also expected to defer to electoral decision." Moreover, if these legislators are to give effect to their values and intentions, they must collaborate with and defer to colleagues whose values and goals they only partially share. Lawmakers normally do not operate from a universalistic perspective; on the contrary, they occupy *particular* positions within the legislative system, and their roles may be partial or one-sided, depending on the opportunities they have and their expectations about what others will do. "The duties of any single representative depend on what other representatives do or fail to do, and thus the proper role of a representative cannot be determined without reference to the state of the legislative system."[11]

Still, as members develop, articulate, and justify their own positions, their notions of social value come into play. And one element in the viability of a legislative proposal—or in the credibility of a critique of executive or administrative policy—is its resonance with widely held notions of justice or the public good.

One of the few books that attempted to describe and characterize the process of valuation as it takes place among policymakers is *A Strategy of Decision* by David Braybrooke and C. E. Lindblom. This is a book that has held up remarkably well in its account of how public officials cope with their environment, and my service in the House has led me to appreciate it anew. Braybrooke and Lindblom showed that the process of social evaluation does not normally conform to the conventional (or, one might say, stereotypical) "rational-deductive" or "synoptic" ideal. Various features of legislative and other policymaking settings—the multiplicity of values and interests and the conflicts among them; shortages of time, information, and analytic capabilities; the multiplicity of decision points; the dominance of margin-dependent choices and of remedial orientations—all render synoptic decisionmaking impractical.[12] But this is not to say that normal practice—what Braybrooke and Lindblom described as the strategy of "disjointed incrementalism"—is value free. Rather, they suggested that existing practice comports remarkably well with utilitarianism, that "family of theories" that "allows meliorative and distributive considerations a decisive role in confirming all moral judgments that are open to dispute, and . . . supposes that, among these meliorative and distributive considerations, social welfare and group happiness justify supporting an action or policy, while their opposites do not."[13]

It is no secret that distributive considerations loom large in congressional policymaking and that distribution is often conceived in terms of the benefits or breaks sought by organized, active interest groups. But aggregative notions of utility—the sort of value we are getting at when we speak of "the public interest"[14]—are also frequently considered, and they may serve as a standard against which narrower professions of interest are measured.

Life on the Banking Committee could be considered the supreme test of this, I suppose, for the committee's environment is replete with organized interests, and policy deliberations sometimes seem little more than a pulling and hauling among them. But even the legislative battle that best exemplified this in the 100th Congress—the attempt to repeal the Glass-Steagall Act, to expand bank powers, and to rationalize banking regulation—also demonstrated something more. On one level, the episode displayed familiar group conflicts: banks versus securities firms, banks versus insurance firms, money-center banks versus independent banks, and so forth. But persuasive public interest arguments were also developed and utilized. Proponents of Glass-Steagall reform were therefore not simply responding to the interests of major American banks; they were also attempting to increase the availability and lower the cost of capital in many regions of the country, bolster American banks' slipping competitive position internationally, and move toward a rationalized system of regulation. The story did not end happily: Interest-group conflicts, plus a major turf battle between the Banking and Energy and Commerce committees, eventually killed the bill. But the broader economic considerations that gained currency both in Congress and in the executive helped move reform proposals considerably beyond the points they had earlier reached.[15]

In the Banking Committee's second major area of jurisdiction—housing—competing concepts of social value often arise with unusual clarity. How, for example, should community development block grants be targeted? I used this issue as a textbook case in my class on ethics and public policy, and it is still debated from time to time on the Banking Committee. One's sense of justice, reinforced in the case of my class with a reading of John Rawls's *A Theory of Justice*,[16] might lead one to give priority to the poorest neighborhoods, to those most in need. But the sort of utilitarian calculations described by Braybrooke and Lindblom might lead one to a different—and in my view, more defensible—conclusion, at least as long as total community development (CD) funding does not go far beyond its present level. CD funding, which is mainly used to rehabilitate dilapidated housing and to provide local infrastructure improvements, is quite modest. Yet it can be quite effective in halting deterioration and in turning a *marginal* neighborhood around, providing benefits that extend far beyond those persons directly assisted. In the poorest neighborhoods, by contrast, such funds might likely sink without a trace. Other types of housing programs are needed in the poorest areas, of course, but it would be a mistake to target CD funds too narrowly in this direction; the money should be used where it can be effective and can do the most good for the most people.

A related dilemma in the area of public housing was explored at a Raleigh field hearing of the Banking Committee's Subcommittee on Housing and Community Development as we prepared to write the 1990 housing bill. Ever-tightening federal preference rules in public housing have required that priority be given to those who pay more than 50 percent of their income in rent, who are involuntarily displaced, or who are living in substandard housing. "At face value," the director of the Greensboro Housing Authority testified, "these rules suggest fairness, providing that scarce housing resources go to the most needy."[17] But she went on to describe how the rules were requiring the authority to replace working families who left public housing with multiproblem families and individuals who could not function independently. These were people who frequently placed a great strain on the inadequate network of community services (such as budget counseling, job training, and tutoring) and aggravated community drug and security problems. What was being lost was the socioeconomic *mix* that had given public housing projects some stability and had provided indigenous role models and leadership. The obligation to assist the most destitute obviously stood in some tension with the need to promote the well-being of those already in the project, to ensure the viability of the project as a whole, and to enable it to function as a community.

These are difficult dilemmas, but it is often possible to devise solutions that address the competing values effectively. In the 1990 housing bill, for example, I successfully pushed an amendment to allow up to 30 percent of the slots in public and assisted housing to go to persons who met the income eligibility requirements but fell outside the federal preference criteria. Another type of solution—more difficult to come by, unfortunately, in these tight budget times—is to "expand the pie" or otherwise alter the policy so that the trade-offs are less painful. In this case, that would mean increasing federal support for public and assisted housing so that the waiting lists were not as long and the unmet needs not as desperate. My point here is simply to stress that policy choices are value choices and that to initiate or to support a policy is to affirm a certain notion of social value. Legislators will make such choices one way or another, but I believe they will be better choices—more ethically responsible choices—if they are made in explicit awareness of the social values being pursued and with a conscientious and thoughtful effort to relate those values to the problem at hand.

"RESPONSIBILITY" IN CONTEXT

I now want to look at the legislator's responsibility from a different perspective, moving beyond the ethics of policy choice to the *role* he or she assumes as a member of an ongoing institution. Legislators must define themselves in relation to forces impinging on them from outside and from within the legislature and in terms of their responsibility for the institution's collective performance. Dilemmas of role definition and institutional responsibility will depend, in the specific form they take, on the character of the legislative system and the possibilities it offers its members. I will therefore highlight some critical features of the U.S. Congress as it currently operates before focusing on specific dilemmas of role and responsibility that arise in this setting.[18]

An examination of the portrayals by leading congressional scholars of members in their institutional environment reveals a significant shift over the past three decades: from an emphasis on members' *adaptation* to well-defined norms and procedures to a portrayal of them as purposive *agents* in a fluid organizational setting. In the former category, one thinks of Richard Fenno's landmark studies of the Appropriations committees and Donald Matthews's 1960 study of the Senate centering on the "folkways" of the institution, "its unwritten rules of the game, its norms of conduct, its approved manner of behavior"—just like, as one senator put it, "living in a small town."[19] Consider, by contrast, the premise of David Mayhew's influential 1974 work, *Congress: The Electoral Connection.* "I have become convinced," Mayhew wrote, "that scrutiny of purposive behavior [of individuals] offers the best route to an understanding of legislatures—or at least of the United States Congress."[20] Mayhew therefore posited the assumption that members of Congress were "single-minded seekers of reelection" and found a close fit between the behavior such an assumption led one to predict and actual congressional performance.

Although this shift reflects changing fashions in social service research—from the use of functionalist or "sociological" models to assumptions more characteristic of the economist[21]—it also owes much to changes in the institution being studied: A number of developments have made an individualistic portrayal of Congress an increasingly plausible one. Many observers have chronicled changes in House and Senate folkways and a decline in their influence on member behavior. Particularly significant has been the fading of the expectation that one would serve an extended period of apprenticeship before taking an active role in committee or on the floor. Members still value subject-matter specialization and expertise, but they have become less hesitant to get involved in areas beyond their committee assignments. The introduction of bills and issuing of pronouncements on a wide variety of subjects, formerly the hallmark of a few mavericks, have become widely engaged in and tolerated, and members are less concerned to maintain a facade of committee or party unity as they take their causes or their amendments to the floor.

These changes are rooted, to a considerable extent, in the altered context in which members are elected and seek reelection. I have already outlined these changes in Chapter 6: the decline of party as a determinant of public perceptions or assessments of politicians; reduced party control over the means of communicating with and mobilizing voters; and the rise of television, direct mail, and other technologies that promise unmediated contact with voters but also offer opponents the same possibility. Members, in other words, are increasingly on their own electorally, and the incentives for party regularity and for adherence to institutional folkways have been weakened as a result.

Members have responded to these conditions in a variety of ways. Mayhew stressed the prevalence of three strategies: *position taking* (making speeches, introducing bills and amendments, assuming postures designed for maximum electoral appeal), *advertising* (building name familiarity and a favorable image through newsletters, media reports to the district, and targeted mail), and *credit claiming* (performing favors for constituents and helping secure projects for the district).[22] What these strategies have in common is their entrepreneurial character; they are more readily understandable in terms of the profit-and-loss calculations of individual political agents than in terms of the established norms of the legislative institution.

Anxious to gain visibility and leverage earlier in their congressional careers, members have also pressed for reforms that have dispersed authority and resources more widely within the institution. The most visible result of this has been a proliferation of subcommittees—senators are currently spread among 87 subcommittees and House members among 148—and a series of rules changes, mainly in the House Democratic Caucus, mandating a high degree of subcommittee autonomy. At the same time, there has been some democratization and expansion of the functions of the party caucuses and whip organizations, making them more promising as vehicles of participation, and informal groups and caucuses have proliferated.

Many members have found this reduction in the power of full committee chairs and the spreading around of legislative resources quite serviceable in terms of their desire for a piece of policy turf and enhanced visibility. But organizational fragmentation has posed certain problems for Congress as an institution. It has heightened the tendency toward particularism, the servicing of narrowly based interests with limited regard for broader considerations, as members have gravitated toward subcommittees in whose jurisdictions they and their districts have a particular stake. It has complicated congressional policymaking by making mobilization of the chamber more difficult and by providing numerous checkpoints for those who wish to oppose new departures in policy. It has, as I demonstrated in Chapters 6 and 7, helped prompt other sorts of congressional reforms—the centralized budget process, for example, and the increased powers over committee assignments, bill referrals, and the scheduling and structuring of floor debate granted to the party leadership—that represent a partial corrective to those changes that have dispersed power. However, the net effect of congressional reform has been to put more resources in the hands of individual members and to complicate the task of managing and mobilizing the institution.

WHAT SORT OF MEMBER SHALL I BE?

Thus, a survey of members in their legislative and electoral settings reveals an organizationally fragmented Congress with many of the norms and structures that formerly ordered behavior in a weakened state; particularistic pulls from constituency and other interest groups, often unmediated by party; increased opportunities for electoral and policy entrepreneurship but in a volatile environment that requires constant attention and offers few reliable mechanisms of support; and weakened inducements to committee or party solidarity or to institutional patriotism. Now I return to the question of what sorts of ethical dilemmas—decisions as to role and responsibility—the legislator in this setting faces.

In posing these questions, I assume that members cannot eschew the profit-and-loss calculations related to maintaining their electoral viability and preserving their power base within the institution. I also assume, however, that a broad range of legislative strategies and involvements are compatible with and, indeed, can be supportive of self-interest in these senses. Most members of Congress, most of the time, have a great deal of latitude as to how they define their roles and what kind of job they wish to do. If they do not have the latitude, they can often create it, for they have a great deal of control over how their actions are perceived and interpreted. Consequently, I conceive of these ethical dilemmas as choices a politician makes within the bounds of political "necessity."

1. *To what range of values and interests should I be responsive?* It is tempting to believe that one is being properly representative and responsive if one gives a respectful hearing to those groups that present themselves on a given issue and then reaches a reasonable accommodation among them. Such an assumption finds support within the pluralist school of political science. Braybrooke and Lindblom, for example, expect those most intensely interested and directly affected to make their voices heard on a given policy question: "Normally, people are not slow to protest when a policy looks like worsening their condition."[23] Public officials, such analysts conclude, will generally feel constrained to be attentive to these groups and to strike some sort of balance among them. Perhaps that is an acceptable operationalization of representative government under contemporary conditions.

But perhaps not. A number of analysts have argued persuasively that the politically active organizations or constituencies prepared to press their views on a given question are likely to be a highly selective sample of all those whose interests and values are affected.[24] Furthermore, one cannot assume that all affected interests will find ready access to the political arena. Some lack the organizational or other resources to make their voices heard. Others may be frozen out by virtue of the ties that exist between dominant groups and clientele-oriented committees and agencies. And broader and more diffuse interests will generally have more difficulty mobilizing their constituencies and developing effective organizational structures than will those more narrowly based interests whose stakes are more immediate and tangible.

A responsible legislator will take the initiative in looking to those poorly organized or nontraditional interests that the system might exclude and to broad, shared public interests and values that are inadequately mirrored in the "pressure system." Many of the developments I have surveyed promote an uncritical particularism: the fragmentation and clientele orientations of subcommittees, the increased campaign role of organized interests, the decline of parties as institutions mediating between those interests and public officeholders. But taking a broader view of one's representative role need not be seen as self-sacrificial behavior, at least most of the time. In fact, legislators often find it politically profitable to cultivate new constituencies or to appeal over the heads of contending groups to a broader public concerned with one issue or another. Such strategies do not succeed automatically: Legislators must *work* at increasing the salience and attractiveness of their policy stances. To transcend the brokering role and to make such moves politically viable and attractive to their colleagues, members must shore up supportive groups, cultivate the media, and otherwise attempt to "broaden the *scope* of conflict."[25]

Responsible representation does not require a dark view of any and all collaboration with "the interests." But neither does it permit a sanguine view of representation as a mere balancing of pressures or an expectation that competition among the interests that are organized and active in a given area will ensure an equitable outcome. It is important to take account of the biases and exclusions of the group system and of the full range of values and interests a policy question entails.

2. *To what extent and in what fashion will I contribute to the work of the legislature?* It is often said, by observers and by members themselves, that we legislators are very thinly spread. However, such complaints may miss the mark in accounting for institutional performance. The real problem is the erosion of the inducements to engage seriously in the *work* of Congress. Pulling one's weight in committee and developing a substantial area of expertise are still serviceable strategies for members who would gain the esteem of the colleagues. But the weakening of the norms of apprenticeship and specialization, together with the pressures for self-promotion created by the new electoral environment, have made showhorse behavior more profitable and less costly than it was in the past. Members today have

stronger incentives to latch onto a piece of policy turf, to gain control of a subcommittee, and to cultivate an image of policy leadership. At the same time, though, their incentives to engage in the painstaking work of legislative craftsmanship, coalition-building, and mobilization may actually be weaker. Such activities are more difficult under conditions of organizational fragmentation, and the pressures to do one's homework are less compelling. Moreover, as Mayhew stressed, the electoral payoffs for merely taking a position or introducing a bill may be just as great as those that reward more extensive or conscientious efforts: "Would Senators Hatfield and McGovern," he asked, "have been any the more esteemed by their followers if their [anti–Vietnam War] amendment had won rather than lost?"[26]

In stressing the importance of serious legislative work, I do not mean to denigrate the nonlegislative aspects of the job. I believe that constituent communication and service are worthwhile in their own right and, moreover, can support the member's legislative efforts in important ways— enhancing the two-way, representative relationship and giving the member the kind of leeway he or she needs for flexible and cooperative legislative involvement.[27] But alterations in both the electoral environment and the congressional ethos have made it thinkable, perhaps even profitable, for a number of members to engage almost exclusively in constituency-cultivation activities to the detriment of Congress's legislative and oversight tasks. And even when members do turn their attention to policy, their involvement is too often superficial and fleeting.

This sort of position-taking can be just as deceptive and manipulative as other forms of self-promotion. "Appearing to do something about policy without a serious intention of, or demonstrable capacity for, doing so," as Richard Fenno stressed, "is a corruption of the representative relationship."[28] And of course, such behavior robs the legislative institution of the energy and persistence needed to make it work, at precisely the time when the tasks of coalition-building and mobilization have become appreciably more difficult. Congress still contains many skilled and persistent legislators—more, I think, than Mayhew's model would lead one to predict—and some have managed to make their legislative power and productivity a substantial electoral asset. Indeed, the institution still depends on members' assuming such roles and adopting such priorities, but this behavior is currently more dependent on the choices and proclivities of the members themselves and less on institutional pressures and constraints than it was in the past.

3. *What responsibilities do I bear for the functioning of the committee and party systems?* "Public duty," wrote Edmund Burke, "demands and requires that what is right should not only be made known, but made prevalent; that what is evil should not only be detected, but defeated. When a public

man omits to put himself in a situation of doing his duty *with effect*, it is an omission that frustrates the purposes of his trust almost as much as if he had formally betrayed it." Such a demand for seriousness of purpose speaks directly, of course, to the superficial and symbolic gestures that too often pass for policymaking in the contemporary Congress. But what Burke specifically had in mind was the need for members of parliament to associate, to cooperate under the standard of a party:

> No man, who is not inflamed by vain-glory into enthusiasm, can flatter himself that his single, unsupported, desultory, unsystematic endeavors, are of power to defeat the subtle designs and united cabals of ambitious citizens. When bad men combine, the good must associate; else they will fall, one by one, an unpitied sacrifice in a contemptible struggle.[29]

Public duty, Burke argued, gives powerful ethical support to party fidelity. He was profoundly skeptical of the tendency of politicians to tout their own independence or to portray themselves as motivated by conscience; too often, he suspected, this was a cover for the pursuit of private advantage. Party operations, Burke believed, could and should leave room for occasional dissent, but the desire for concord and for effectiveness would properly nudge fellow partisans toward agreement:

> When the question is in its nature doubtful, or not very material, the modesty which becomes an individual and that partiality which becomes a well-chosen friendship, will frequently bring on an acquiescence in the general sentiment. Thus the disagreement will naturally be rare; it will be only enough to indulge freedom, without violating concord, or disturbing arrangement.[30]

Such a view, of course, squares imperfectly with the individualistic notions of moral autonomy to which Americans typically repair—what has sometimes been termed our "Lone Ranger" ethical bias. The late Sen. Jacob Javits no doubt anticipated his readers' applause as he declared: "In this clash of loyalties—loyalty to constituents, loyalty to party, and loyalty to myself—my constituents and I had to prevail."[31] But we should be wary of imputing ethical superiority to the loner. If the committees and the parties play a legitimate and necessary role in developing and refining measures, in aggregating interests, in mobilizing the chamber, should not there be a burden of proof on the member who would violate the comity and the discipline necessary to their successful functioning? This is neither to endorse mindless party regularity nor to deny that members should sometimes resolve conflicts with their party or committee in favor of personal convictions regarding constituency interests or the public good. But such choices should be difficult and not arrived at lightly.

Party voting in Congress has displayed a long-term decline over the course of this century, although it has increased substantially, especially among House Democrats, in the last twenty years.[32] For this, the renewed role of the parties in recruiting and supporting candidates bears some responsibility, as do various measures that have enhanced the role and extended the reach of the House leadership. Yet neither constituency nor chamber pressures compel most members to support or work within the party; to what extent they do so depends to a considerable degree on individual choice. The same is increasingly true of work on committees, most of which have seen their ability to maintain a united front on the floor and to command the deference of the parent chamber decline. Although many members may welcome the reduced hold that these systems now have on them, they also have reason to reflect on the price the *institution* has paid in its reduced capacity to act in an orderly and concerted fashion. It will not do to simply revel in one's status as a free agent; an adequate ethic will give substantial weight to the need to maintain mechanisms of *collective* action and responsibility.

4. *How should I present myself in relation to the legislature's practices and performance?* Former Congressman Bob Eckhardt (D.-Texas) suggested that every member of Congress performs three functions: lawmaker, ombudsman, and educator.[33] This last function, as I have shown, may be closely related to the first: Lawmakers who wish to do more than simply defer to the strongest and best-organized interests on a certain matter must give some attention to explaining their actions and educating their constituents, helping them place the issue in broader perspective or perhaps activating alternative bases of support. And the extent to which a member is willing and able to undertake such explanations is ethically as well as politically significant.[34]

Here, I turn to another facet of the legislators' educative role: their portrayal of Congress itself. On traveling with House members around their districts, Richard Fenno noted that the greatest surprise for him was the extent to which each one "polished his or her individual reputation at the expense of the institutional reputation of Congress":

In explaining what he was doing in Washington, every one of the eighteen House members took the opportunity to picture himself as different from, and better than, most of his fellow members in Congress. No one availed himself of the opportunity to educate his constituents about Congress as an institution—not in any way that would "hurt a little." To the contrary, the members' process of differentiating themselves from the Congress as a whole only served, directly or indirectly, to downgrade the Congress.

This was in the mid-1970s, and every indication is that such tactics have become even more prevalent as Congress-bashing by advocacy groups and in the media has intensified. "We have to differentiate me from the rest of those bandits down there in Congress," Fenno heard a member say to a campaign strategy group. "'They are awful, but our guy is wonderful'—that's the message we have to get across."[35]

So much for the traditional norm of institutional patriotism! Opinion polls regularly reveal that public officials in general and Congress in particular rank low in public esteem, an evaluation reinforced by the recent spate of ethics charges in both houses but rooted much more deeply in our country's history and political culture. Every indication is that we members reinforce such an assessment by distancing ourselves from any responsibility for the institution's functioning. And we are phenomenally successful at it, matching a 30 percent approval rate for Congress with a 95+ percent reelection rate for ourselves.

My point is not that a member should defend Congress, right or wrong. I understand very well the disadvantages of being put on the defensive about Congress's ethical problems—pointing out that only a small number of members are involved, for example, or that Ethics Committee proceedings are generally bipartisan and fair—although I believe many of these defenses have merit. Rather, I am speaking of a more general tendency to trash the institution. It is often tempting—but, I believe, also deceptive and irresponsible—to pose as the quintessential outsider, carping at accommodations that have been reached on a given issue as though problems could simply be ignored, cost-free solutions devised, or the painful necessities of compromise avoided. Responsible legislators will communicate to their constituencies not only the assembly's failings but also what it is fair and reasonable to expect, what accommodations they would be well advised to accept, and so forth. In the past, institutional patriotism has too often taken an uncritical form, assuming that whatever the process produces must be acceptable. But self-righteous, anti-institutional posturing is no better. The moral quixotism to which reelection-minded legislators are increasingly prone too often serves to rationalize their own nonproductive legislative roles and to perpetuate public misperceptions of the criteria one can reasonably apply to legislative performance.

Therefore, although it may be politically profitable to "run *for* Congress by running *against* Congress," the implications for the institution's effectiveness and legitimacy are ominous. As Fenno concluded, "The strategy is ubiquitous, addictive, cost-free, and foolproof. . . . In the short run, everybody plays and nearly everybody wins. Yet the institution bleeds from 435 separate cuts. In the long run, therefore, somebody may lose. . . . Congress may lack public support at the very time when the public needs Congress the most."[36]

LEGISLATIVE STRUCTURES
AND LEGISLATIVE ETHICS

Although the American founders regarded civic virtue—a willingness to forego private advantage for the sake of the commonweal—as essential to the health of the new republic, they were unwilling to trust human nature to its own devices. On the contrary: They believed government must be *structured* in a way that not only anticipates self-serving behavior but turns it to good account. "Ambition must be made to counteract ambition," wrote James Madison in "The Federalist" (no. 51):

> This policy of supplying, by opposite and rival interests, the defect of better motives [is] particularly displayed in all the subordinate distributions of power, where the constant aim is to divide and arrange the several offices in such a manner as that each may be a check on the other—that the private interest of every individual may be a sentinel over the public rights.[37]

It can be argued, analogously, that certain of Congress's organizational features have structured the pursuit of political advantage and turned it to the institution's account. The committee system, for example, accommodates the aspirations of disparate members but also represents a corrective of sorts to congressional individualism—a means of bringing expertise and attention to bear on the legislature's tasks in a more concerted fashion than the free enterprise of individual members could accomplish. The committee system channels members' desires for leverage and status into activity that serves the institution's needs and builds its policymaking capacities.

Such an institutional maintenance function is even more obvious in the case of Congress's powerful "control committees"—Appropriations, Ways and Means, Rules, and now, Budget—and in the party leadership. Mayhew argued that the willingness of members to defer to these control mechanisms and to reward those who operate them with power and prestige can be understood as the "purchase" of a collective good—the preservation of the institution against the consequences to which unchecked individualism and particularism could otherwise lead.[38] But members do not make these calculations in a vacuum; they come into an institution where these structures and the norms, patterns of authority, and powers to reward and punish that support them are already in place. If members are to function effectively, they must, to a significant degree, honor these norms and direct their own initiatives through approved channels.

It is important to subject such institutional structures and norms to ethical scrutiny. Despite Madison's expectation that the checking and balancing of power would protect the public interest, we know that, in fact, the constitutional system has historically given advantages to certain types of interests at the expense of others. Similarly, the norms and structures that gave inordinate power to Congress's committee chairs in the 1950s had a distinctive policy impact, inhibiting overdue changes in civil rights and other areas. As Roger Davidson contended, that period's folkways were promulgated by and served the interests of the conservative coalition that ran both chambers during the 1950s.[39] And there were powerful ethical arguments for modifying this particular pattern of institutional maintenance.

I do not mean to suggest that the directions in which Congress has moved and the policies it has adopted in the ensuing years represent some sort of ethical decline. Indeed, the contrary case could convincingly be made. What I do want to suggest, however, is that congressional behavior has become less structurally and normatively constrained in the past thirty years and that this loosening, rooted mainly in the electoral incentives facing individual members, poses serious problems for the functioning of Congress as an institution. Both its capacity to produce coherent policy and the quality of its policy product are at stake.

These dilemmas demand renewed attention to congressional organization and structure. Of particular importance are efforts to strengthen party organs—to bolster the caucuses as forums for policy debate, to increase the leadership's capacity to overcome committee fragmentation and parochialism in bringing proposals to the floor, and to maintain strong vote-gathering operations. And though our budget difficulties are more political than structural, it is still important to strengthen and streamline the budget process.

Strengthening the structures and norms by which the Congress supplies "the defect of better motives" and protects its institutional capacities, however, will not dispense with the need for a heightened sense of individual responsibility. In today's Congress, members are often essentially on their own—in dealing with the entreaties of interested groups, in deciding what kind of contribution they will make to the work of the legislature, in making the party and committee systems work, and in shaping citizen perceptions and evaluations of the institution. Such dilemmas will continue to be central to legislative life, posing questions of value that members cannot help addressing in one way or another. How we deal with them will decisively shape the capacity of Congress for leadership and the quality of its performance.

11

Concluding Reflections

Critical challenges confront Congress and other American political institutions. Although I have enjoyed five productive and stimulating years in the House of Representatives, my satisfaction is tempered by the conviction that Congress's collective response has often been inadequate to our country's needs. We are faced with a stubborn recession and the need to ease the pain it has caused and promote economic recovery. The long-term challenges are even more daunting: to lay the groundwork for improved economic performance and an enhanced quality of life by investing in research, education and training, rebuilding and extending our infrastructure, broadening access to adequate health care, stimulating savings and investment, and achieving budgetary accountability and control.

There are important signs of progress, such as approval of a six-year highway and transit program in 1991 and of major energy and higher education initiatives in 1992. On many fronts, however, Congress has found it difficult to act, and the president has offered little beyond occasional vetoes of Democratic initiatives. Assessments from both inside and outside Congress often stress the ascendance of symbolic gestures over substantive solutions. "Rose Garden ceremonies at the White House and 30-second ads by members of Congress have replaced real action and accomplishment," noted Rep. Pat Williams (D.-Montana). Referring to the president's much touted promotion of voluntary activity, he added, "What we have is a thousand points of light and no batteries."[1]

The most obvious immediate barrier to effective governmental action is the federal budget deficit. The failure to correct the problem in the 1980s, when the economy was healthier and could have more easily withstood austerity measures, has left Congress and the president with equally unpromising alternatives: either rely on symbolic, hortatory, and largely ineffectual actions to counter economic adversity or fund more serious recovery measures at the expense of a dangerous deepening of the deficit. Additional disabilities are political: Divided government discourages concerted action and encourages evasion and the shifting of blame. The prevalence of negative campaigning and symbolic politics breeds risk-averse behavior among politicians and discourages serious or controversial policy initiatives. Public opinion remains divided and contradictory, demanding action but rejecting any imposition of costs. And our political parties are frequently unable to pull contending forces together or to enforce any sort of accountability for collective governmental success or failure.[2]

A realistic program to address the nation's needs must, therefore, go beyond specific policy initiatives—some of which (such as a national program of health insurance) would be difficult enough to pass under favorable economic and political circumstances—to a much broader effort to address the *conditions* of effective action. Favorable political changes, such as electing a president and a congressional majority of the same party, might come with shifts in the public mood and the emergence of inspired leadership. Certainly, I would welcome the unique experience of serving in the House with a Democratic president. But our difficulties run much more deeply than such a prescription suggests, and they require, I believe, major alterations in the way we conceive of—and practice—citizenship and leadership.

Some critics have found an answer in far-reaching constitutional and institutional changes. Political gridlock in the midst of unmet needs has naturally stimulated widespread cries for reform, particularly in the operations of Congress. In earlier chapters, I have touched on needed changes in campaign financing, the budget process, and committee and party operations. I have also stressed the importance of how members define their roles and responsibilities, suggesting that legislative norms and structures can only go so far in supplying "the defect of better motives." I will revisit the topic here, not simply to embellish my own reform agenda but also to suggest that congressional reform is in danger both of being oversold and of taking some harmful turns. It would be ironic and unfortunate, indeed, if, in responding to Congress's failings, we were to render the institution weaker and even less capable of meeting the nation's policy needs.

Institutional reform, I believe, is not an end in itself but must be part of a larger effort to revitalize American politics, to repair the frayed linkage between the needs and aspirations of the American people and the actions of their government. Mere institutional tinkering or reform schemes that offer a quick fix are not the answer. Rather, we need to find a renewed sense of common purpose in our communities and our country, better ways of articulating a vision of the common good and of acting on its behalf. Reform efforts are likely to fall short, and they may even make matters worse, unless they are placed in this broader framework.

During my years of teaching and writing about the ethical foundations of public policy, I became convinced that the idea (and the experience) of *community* contributed a unique and critically important perspective to policy debate. Clearly, ideas such as distributive justice and the public interest may capture our imagination and influence our thinking. But they are apt to assume a rather abstract, irrelevant quality or to become distorted and limited amid the clamorings of self-interest unless they are underwritten by a personal identification with the community and a sense of responsibility for its well-being.[3] My years in public office have brought this theorizing down to earth and have convinced me of its practical significance. I do not believe that we will be able to solve our problems— or to get beyond the defensive maneuvering and unproductive standoffs that increasingly characterize our politics—until we recapture a sense of common purpose, locally and nationally, and begin to act more consistently as a community.

If this sounds hopelessly ambitious or even utopian, that is the measure of the challenge to both leadership and citizenship that we face. Obviously, I cannot do justice to these matters here. But neither can I adequately convey the congressional experience without reference to this bigger picture. Accordingly, I will conclude with a discussion of two urgent needs facing our body politic. One concerns the quality of our public dialogue, which I will address in terms of the dangerous gap that has developed between our political campaigns and the decisions and demands of governance. The second concerns the necessity, wherever we find ourselves within the political system, of acting on the imperatives of citizenship.

REFORM AGENDAS

I decided at an early point not to call this book *A Political Scientist Goes to Washington.* In some ways, it would have been an apt title, for my training and work as a political scientist have helped shape my perceptions of my congressional experience and certainly my recounting of it here. But I did not like the connotations. "Political scientist" was only one of several identities I brought to Washington, and my primary purpose in coming was certainly not to study. Moreover, in bringing to mind *Mr. Smith Goes to Washington,* Frank Capra's famous film, such a title might have suggested that I wished to perpetuate a stereotype of Washington as a den of conspiracy and corruption or that my academic background had prepared me poorly for the harsh realities I encountered. Neither was, in fact, the case.

Being cast as a kind of academic Mr. Smith, however, is something I have occasionally had to endure. "I'll bet you're discovering it's not like they say in the textbooks!" people sometimes say, or they ask, "How are you finding things in the *real* world?" To such remarks, I often think but seldom respond: "If you think academe is never-never land, you should try politics for a while!" The fact is that the congressional studies of my generation, on which I was trained and to which I made a modest contribution, were based on close and sympathetic observation of the institution and provided an accurate picture of its workings—a view that went beyond the personality-centered and episodic accounts often rendered by journalists and members themselves. To be sure, being a member is a very different experience, in terms of what one learns and how one feels, from being an academic observer, no matter how intimate and careful that observation has been. But for an orientation to the place, I could have done far worse.

As a young political scientist, however, it seemed to me that the hands-on style of contemporary congressional research, often based on member interviews, along with the functionalist framework into which scholarly analysis was often cast, threatened a loss of critical distance from the institution.[4] The policy frustrations and failures of the early 1960s suggested the need for a performance-based critique of Congress—a need that was lessened but not removed by the post-1964 spate of congressional productivity. Books with titles like *Obstacle Course on Capitol Hill* and *House Out of Order* underscored the point.[5] It was therefore with a great deal of anticipation that I, along with a dozen other young academics, agreed to spend the summer of 1972 with Ralph Nader's Congress Project in Washington. As the scholarly arm of the enterprise, our goal was to combine solid research on the workings of congressional committees with a critical assessment of institutional performance and specific suggestions for reform. To some extent, we realized this goal, although I have never experienced as many frustrations and difficulties with a publishing project before or since.[6] What we received in the meantime, however, was an introduction to the kind of Congress-bashing that was to come full flower in the 1980s.

Nader apparently decided in midsummer that our studies were not moving fast enough and were not likely to attract sufficient attention. As a result, he put three of his in-house writers to work on a volume that, despite our protests to the contrary, presumed to anticipate and summarize our findings.[7] *Who Runs Congress?* dealt with Congress's policy failings only incidentally, highlighting, instead, such topics as "Who Owns Congress?" and "Lawmakers as Lawbreakers." Some attention was given to the distribution of power within Congress, but the idea was mainly to highlight instances of arbitrariness and abuse rather than to try to distinguish dysfunctional concentrations of power from those that might enhance congressional performance. In one area—portraying Congress as "overwhelmed by the vastly greater forces of the presidency"[8]—the Nader critique differed from what was to come; in fact, it has often seemed that such a subservient state was precisely what the Congress-bashers of the

Reagan era, often highly partisan, had in mind. But in most respects, *Who Runs Congress?* anticipated the themes of modern congressional criticism and represented an unfortunate departure from the older but still important performance-based critique.

The high (or low) point of the progression was reached in a 1989 *Newsweek* piece that Rep. David Obey (D.-Wisconsin) dubbed "the worst example of institution trashing that I have seen in my twenty years here."[9] (As I read the article, I could not help wondering who had taught these people political science!) In the space of six pages, readers were informed, without benefit of documentation, that most congressional staff members were employed "to enhance re-election"; that it was now "theoretically possible for a lawmaker to spend virtually his entire working day on the air" (although admittedly no one had done it!); that "trading votes for money or pleasure is just another day at the office"; and that campaign money "allows members to live a virtually expense-free existence" (my wife and I were especially intrigued by that one).[10] The article managed simultaneously to condemn Congress as a "fortress of unreality, its drawbridges only barely connected to life beyond the moat" and to take members to task for "commuting home for four-day weekends!"[11] As for the legislative process, the *Newsweek* writer stated: "When a member of Congress works on an issue, aides collect business cards from lobbyists with an interest. Later, the aides telephone the lobbyists to request a political-action committee (PAC) contribution." Obey's retort to that statement seems appropriate: "As we see the press posing for more holy pictures on ethics, they ought to at least think about the ethical standards that allow them to smear an entire institution for the conduct of a few of our members."[12]

All of this helps explain, even if it does not justify, the increasing tendency of members to run for Congress by running against Congress. The current mode of criticism, with its withering cynicism about all things congressional, encourages a defensive detachment from the institution on the part of members, an exposé mentality on the part of the press, and increasing public distrust and alienation. What tends to get crowded out is any serious attempt to understand how Congress actually works, as well as the sorts of proposals for change that could improve institutional performance. Indeed, much current Congress-bashing actually helps prevent positive change. We need to consider what distributions and concentrations of power will make the institution work effectively, but current criticism tends to stigmatize *all* exertions of power as personal aggrandizement. Similarly, we need to consider what sorts of support services Congress needs to function efficiently, but this criticism often regards such accoutrements indiscriminately as "perks." And though we need to strengthen the members' incentives to contribute to the work of the institution, the critics often view legislative dealings with a jaundiced eye and encourage a righteous aloofness. All of this fuels one's suspicion that many contemporary congressional critics are aiming—some deliberately, some inadvertently—not for a more assertive, competent institution but, rather, for the opposite.

The excesses of Congress-bashing do not gainsay the need, as I have stressed in previous chapters, to mitigate the endless scramble for campaign funds, to prevent abuse of the resources of incumbency, and to eliminate members' dependence on interest groups for their personal incomes. Similarly, to recognize the limitations of ethics committee ethics is not to deny the importance of maintaining high standards of probity and accountability. Therefore, recent measures to ensure that public officials are compensated from public funds (banning honoraria and restricting other outside income), to prohibit the conversion of campaign funds to personal use, to control the frequency and the content of franked mailings, and to clarify the limits of appropriate advocacy on behalf of constituents before regulatory bodies all represent moves in the right direction, in some cases considerably overdue.

The management of Congress must also be placed on a more professional and businesslike footing. Recent management lapses in the House post office and abuses of the banking services of the House payroll office underscore the need to administer the House in a manner befitting a complex enterprise with some 12,800 employees and a budget of almost $700 million. A professional House administrator, appointed by the Speaker in consultation with the majority and minority leaders, should be empowered to plan, coordinate, oversee, and audit the support operations of the House. Until such management reforms are made, the House will continue to pay a heavy price in efficiency and public esteem for its antiquated and sometimes unaccountable administrative practices.

It is equally important, however, to remember the earlier reform agenda aimed at a stronger Congress turning out an improved policy product. This strain of reform helped produce numerous positive changes: the reining in of the House Rules Committee; strengthened leadership control over committee assignments, bill referrals, and floor operations; a measure of accountability by committee chairmen to the party caucus; and Congress's improved budget machinery. These efforts have not met with unqualified success, and much remains to be done. In the meantime, the scene has been complicated by the emergence of a quite different reform agenda, based on contrary premises. Proposals such as the line-item veto and term limitations, emanating from the most vociferous contemporary critics of Congress and masquerading as congressional reform, have gained wide currency, as I often learn in my community meetings. Consequently, it is important to highlight the flaws of such proposals, as well as to stress the directions that more positive change might take.

The line-item veto has more to do with institutional power than with budgeting. By giving the president the authority to veto individual items in appropriations bills, it would shift the constitutional balance of power radically. It would reduce the capacities of individual members to influence governmental priorities, but it would also reduce their incentives to work together in crafting a legislative product; all that would matter would be the acquiescence of the president, item by item.[13] This would, of course, give the president enormous leverage over members, for whom making a deal with the White House would become far more important than working with and accommodating one another.

Those professing unconcern about such a shift in the constitutional balance of power might nonetheless find it prudent to contemplate how desirable such control would be in the hands of a president they disagreed with. As Rep. Mickey Edwards (R.-Oklahoma) noted, Republican support for such a measure requires "a bold gamble that no Republican nominee for president will ever lose to some future Michael Dukakis or Walter Mondale."[14]

But would the line-item veto reduce government spending? That, after all, is the main argument its proponents made for it, usually playing down its checks-and-balances implications. Presidents who wish to reduce spending, it is claimed, often are frustrated when faced with take-it-or-leave-it decisions on massive spending bills; an item veto would let them eliminate wasteful projects one by one, trimming such bills to acceptable dimensions. All of this, however, overlooks the fact that presidents generally ask for *more* money than Congress is willing to appropriate, Ronald Reagan's rhetoric notwithstanding (recall that this was the president who, having condemned Jimmy Carter's deficits, proceeded to quadruple them). In fact, during the Reagan and Bush presidencies (budget years 1981–1991), presidential requests exceeded congressional appropriations by over $12 billion.[15] And even when the overall amounts requested are similar, the spending priorities often differ. This means that members frequently find themselves voting for less than the president requested for one item or another. It is not hard to imagine the pressures a member might feel to vote for the full requested amount (for the Strategic Defense Initiative, the B-2 bomber, or aid to El Salvador, to name some recent examples) if the president had the power to single out an item of particular importance to that member in one or another appropriations bill. It seems likely that presidents would use this leverage and that, in the end, such a system would produce more, not less, government spending.

The proposal to limit congressional terms of service to twelve (some say eight) years has seemed fairly superfluous in North Carolina. After all, my district elected three different congressmen within six years, a neighboring district chose four different individuals within eight years, and our westernmost district reelected its representative only once during a twelve-year span! I realize, of course, that the term-limitation proposal is presented as an antidote to 96 percent reelection rates nationwide and to the considerable advantages of incumbents. I noted in Chapter 2 that turnover in the House is greater than this one statistic would suggest and that Republicans would, in fact, control the House today if they had held the seats they won on at least one occasion during the 1980s. But I understand very well the obstacles facing challengers and have made various suggestions as to how the playing field might be made more level and electoral competition increased. The imposition of term limitations is not on the list.

This is because congressional turnover is not a goal to be sought monomaniacally, disregarding the kind of job members are doing and the wishes of their constituents. And like the line-item veto, term limitations would leave Congress in a greatly weakened state vis-à-vis other elements of the political system.

Term-limit proponents often seem to think that serving in Congress requires no particular experience or expertise, that an assembly composed solely of amateurs could function quite satisfactorily. Perhaps I have said enough in this book to indicate otherwise. I have heard members of the Intelligence Committee say that they were there four years before they even knew how to ask the right questions of career people who were accustomed to revealing only what they wished to, and I confess that I sometimes felt the same way on the Banking Committee. To do the job effectively and knowledgeably requires a long-term investment by the member and, in a sense, by his or her constituents. It is, of course, possible to abuse the knowledge and the status that extended tenure brings, expending them for unworthy ends, but for critics to assume that this usually or invariably occurs says more about their cynical turn of mind than their knowledge of what the institution needs to function effectively.[16] New blood, which infuses the House at about a 10 to 20 percent rate every two years, is important to the institution, but so are the knowledge and confidence that extended service brings.

Term limitations would certainly shake up the internal distribution of power in Congress but not in very helpful ways. The rules changes that modified the seniority system and gave the caucus the power to disapprove sitting chairmen have resulted in the replacement of several infirm and unresponsive leaders—most recently the chairmen of the Public Works and House Administration committees, disapproved at the beginning of the 102nd Congress—and have made the others more accountable. The extension of these reforms, perhaps to permit an initial balloting among several of the most senior members of a committee or to empower the Speaker to nominate committee chairs, is worth considering. However, to limit terms would essentially eliminate both seniority *and* the member's reputation, built up over the years, as bases for choice. The predictable result would be the domination of the selection process by the largest state delegations or perhaps by strong regional blocs.

As a whole, Congress would lose power. In particular, *members* of Congress—the one set of actors in the federal system who regard themselves as representatives of local communities and ordinary citizens—would become less knowledgeable, less seasoned, less confident, and hence more dependent on staff, lobbyists, and bureaucrats for information and advice. Collectively, there would be a slippage in institutional memory, stature, and staying power and a resultant transfer of power to the executive establishment. It is an amazing sign of the times and of shifting political currents that self-styled conservatives—the erstwhile critics of bureaucracy and of concentrated presidential power—should endorse such measures as congressional term limitations and the line-item veto. But it is surely imprudent for them or for anyone else to base such far-reaching institutional changes on short-term political advantage. Those who seek to delegitimize and weaken Congress today could be in for some sober second thoughts later on if a strong and resilient institution is not there when they need it.

In seeking a more positive formula for change, it is sometimes tempting to look back with nostalgia on what Roger Davidson called the "era of the strong committee chairmen." The storied ability of a committee like Ways and Means to mobilize the chamber and to command deference on the floor undoubtedly helped the House check its centrifugal tendencies.[17] But such power also often checked the majority will and quashed important policy initiatives. Subsequent changes in congressional rules and procedures, particularly in the mid-1970s, were a necessary adaptation to the changing needs and desires of members, rooted in their electoral situations; to a considerable extent, they energized the institution, opening up policy entrepreneurship and other productive roles for large numbers of subcommittees, caucuses, and individual members. The speakership and party caucuses were also strengthened, at first to break up the power of the committee oligarchs and then to fill the vacuum left by the weakened "control" committees and to contain the excesses of congressional individualism.

This balance continues to evolve, and from time to time, it needs deliberate adjustment. I stressed in Chapter 6, for example, the importance of further strengthening the leadership's capacity to develop and promote a policy agenda and to intervene earlier in committee decisionmaking. This is necessary if bills are to be brought to the floor in a form that most

Democratic members can support; last-minute scrambling by the whip organization is hardly the way to work out needed adjustments. It is also necessary if scattered initiatives in critical areas—energy, health care, and economic growth and competitiveness, for instance—are to be assembled and promoted as major party measures.

We also need to revisit what proved to be the most difficult and least successful reform effort of the 1970s: the simplification and rationalization of committee jurisdictions.[18] There would be a price to pay in terms of internal conflict; numerous feuds still linger from the last serious effort at committee reorganization in 1974. Defenders of the present system sometimes argue that its former defects have been addressed by the Speaker's enhanced referral and scheduling powers and that jurisdictional fragmentation has its virtues—getting more members engaged on key issues, providing alternative ways of developing measures when problems arise, and so forth. But even conceding such advantages, the present system's scattering of jurisdiction over key policy areas (particularly those, such as energy and the environment, that have come into prominence since the jurisdictional lines last were drawn), its generating of overlapping and competing claims, and its provision of multiple checkpoints for obstruction and delay have gone far past the point of diminishing returns.

Jurisdictional anomalies do have policy consequences. Strong banking reform measures might well have passed in 1988 and 1991, for example, had the House Banking Committee's jurisdiction matched that of its Senate counterpart. But in the House, securities regulation is under the jurisdiction of Energy and Commerce; this permits that committee to take a decisive swipe at any bill that would let bank subsidiaries enter the securities business. Because of the Energy and Commerce chairman's resistance to altering the Depression-era statute that still governs banking and because committee members are neither focused on banking issues nor inclined to challenge the chairman on this matter, congressional action on banking reform has frequently been stymied. To be sure, the House's inability to deal competently and effectively with this issue is not solely attributable to its being divided between two committees. Still, if the bifurcation had not been present, reform legislation might have passed long ago, and Congress might have retained a leadership role that it now has, in effect, forfeited to the regulatory agencies and the courts.

The key litmus test for reorganization measures, as for any congressional reform, is whether they would leave the Congress stronger and make it a more competent and effective institution able to produce better policy. This suggests a couple of caveats, drawing on themes developed in Chapters 9 and 10. The first is to abjure a simplistic distrust of power. ("They just have too much power," a woman once said to me in explaining why senior members' terms of service should be limited.) Congressional reform has reduced and should reduce the power attached to certain persons or positions when it is abused or when it hinders institutional performance. But one cannot scatter power and resources around and leave it at that; effective congressional reform will attend to the need for effective (albeit accountable) concentrations of power. The second caveat is to be wary of the Lone Ranger ethical bias, the tendency to idealize independence and autonomy. Congressional effectiveness requires strengthening the means of *collective* action and instilling in members a sense of responsibility not only for their own integrity but for the performance of the institution.

It is important, finally, to recognize the limits of reform. This is a critical lesson from Chapter 7—budget breakdowns were far less indicative of flawed procedures or machinery than of an absence of political will and public consensus. Budget reforms, Gramm-Rudman-Hollings mandates, and the convening of summits were no match for the political realities. Most realms of congressional activity, fortunately, are less constrained and more promising than this one, but the fact remains: The main concern of those who would move the institution forward should not be endless tinkering with rules and structures but, rather, the mustering of the leadership, the discipline, the energy, and the initiative to take advantage of the opportunities the system already offers.

GOVERNANCE AND CITIZENSHIP

My job keeps me very busy and flying, as they say, "close to the ground"—attending to myriad details in dealing with constituents, tracking appropriations, and all the rest. I sometimes feel that I had a better overview of the current state of American politics and even of certain broad policy questions before I was elected than I do now. I have, however, been in a position to observe some alarming trends in our politics and to develop strong convictions about our need to reverse them. I will therefore conclude with a few thoughts on the ominous gap that has opened up between campaigning and governing and on the need for a renewed dedication to the commonweal on the part of both citizens and their representatives.

Campaigning and governing are, of course, not the same thing; I have discussed in Chapter 3 the transitions from one to the other that any successful candidate must make. However, a more radical discontinuity has developed in recent years. It is in the nature of political campaigns to polarize and to oversimplify, but the negative attacks and distortions have increased markedly. And the link between what candidates say in their campaign advertisements and the decisions they make once in office has become more and more tenuous. George Bush's 1988 campaign, focused on furloughed murderer Willie Horton and the pledge of allegiance to the flag, demonstrated that successful presidential campaigns could subsist on the manipulation of symbols, with scarcely a word about the major decisions the new president would confront. (Bush's "no new taxes" theme was only a partial exception, for it offered no clue as to how he would reduce the deficit or what revenue proposals he would ultimately make.) This suggests that the modern campaign style, which we witnessed early in North Carolina courtesy of Jesse Helms and other candidates of the National Congressional Club, has become the national norm.

This trend has been reinforced by the new technology of campaign advertising and fund-raising; thirty-second television ads and direct mail financial solicitations, for example, put a premium on hard-hitting, over-simplified appeals and the pushing of symbolic hot buttons. The trend has also been both cause and effect of the modern emergence of cultural and value questions, like abortion, race, patriotism, and alternative life-styles, that lend themselves to symbolic appeals. Republican candidates in particular have found in these issues a promising means of diverting voters' attention from economic and quality-of-life concerns and of driving divisive wedges in the Democratic coalition.

The growing gap between campaigning and governing also bespeaks a certain public alienation and cynicism. Voters complain about the nasti-ness and irrelevance of campaign advertising, and my campaigns have demonstrated that such tactics can effectively be turned against an op-ponent. But voters who find little to encourage or inspire them in politics are nonetheless tempted to vote in anger or in protest, inclinations that modern campaign advertising exploits very effectively. As E. J. Dionne suggested, the decline of the "politics of remedy"—that is, politics that attempts "to solve problems and resolve disputes"—seems to have created a vicious cycle:

> Campaigns have become negative in large part because of a sharp decline in popular faith in government. To appeal to an increasingly alienated electorate, candidates and their political consultants have adopted a cynical stance which, they believe with good reason, plays into popular cynicism about politics and thus wins them votes. But cynical campaigns do not resolve issues. They do not lead to "remedies." Therefore, problems get worse, the electorate becomes *more* cynical—and so does the advertising.[19]

If modern campaigns reveal a dangerous decline in democratic account-ability, so does modern governance—but not always in the way one might think. Ironically, the result of the campaigning-governance gap often is not governance in disregard of the popular will but a *failure* of governance, based on an exaggerated sensitivity to the anticipated campaign use of difficult policy decisions. The debates over the budget agreement and the crime bill in the weeks prior to the 1990 election illustrate what I mean. It struck me at the time that the barbs of the journalists and pundits were largely misdirected. They were skewering Congress for the budget "debacle," when, in fact, members deserved considerable credit for making some tough decisions of governance under difficult circumstances. But the pundits said hardly a word about the more glaring failure of governance— the handling of the omnibus anticrime package.

The House Judiciary Committee, dominated by Democratic liberals, brought a bill to the floor that fell considerably short of what most members wanted to support, as demonstrated by the 166–258 vote (including 84 Democratic nays) against a rule that would have disallowed most floor amendments. Therefore, Rep. William Hughes (D.-New Jersey), the moderate chairman of the Judiciary Subcommittee on Crime, offered well-crafted floor amendments on the expansion of the federal death penalty and on reform of habeas corpus procedures that would have let members who wanted to strengthen those provisions do so without compromising basic constitutional safeguards. Nonetheless, members who feared being cast as supporters of anything less than the toughest possible measures joined with liberals to defeat both amendments. The House then proceeded to pass far more extreme amendments authored by Henry Hyde (R.-Illinois) and George Gekas (R.-Pennsylvania) that seriously undermined the right of indigents and other defendants to competent counsel. One problem was that the leadership, preoccupied with the budget battle and overly deferential to the Judiciary Committee, did not whip the amendments effectively. But the main problem was members' memory of Willie Horton and a widespread fear of political attacks. "I hope we never, ever bring up a crime bill again a month before an election," Hughes declared.[20]

Such defensive voting—recall Trent Lott's admonition that "you do not ever get into trouble for those budgets which you vote against"—is part of the price we pay for the deterioration of campaign dialogue and its disengagement from the actual issues of governance. The main electoral pressures perceived by members today do not push them to be active and productive in areas of positive concern as much as to avoid difficult tasks or votes that might serve as the basis for an opponent's attack. This development does not bode well for responsible governance.

Responsibility for our descent into attack politics, increasingly divorced from the major problems faced by the American people, is widely shared— by journalists, interest groups, campaign consultants, and the viewing, voting public. Members of Congress are hardly helpless—or blameless— before these trends. For one thing, our defensiveness in the face of tough votes is often exaggerated; members frequently underestimate their ability to deflect attacks or to deal effectively with hostile charges. All of us feel occasionally that "I'd rather vote against this than to have to explain it," but we should worry if we find ourselves taking this way out too often or on matters of genuine consequence. It is our *job* to interpret and explain difficult decisions, and with sufficient effort, we can usually do so successfully.

We also have some choices about the kind of campaigns we run. By making campaign tactics themselves an issue, we can heighten public awareness of and resistance to distorted and manipulative appeals. Above all, we can tighten the link between what we say in our own campaigns and what we have done and intend to do in office. This is not a plea for dull campaigns; on the contrary, it is our duty to arouse people's concern and anger about areas of neglect, to convince them that we can do better, to inspire them to contribute to the solution. Most people believe that politics and politicians ought to have something constructive to offer in the realms of education, housing, health care, economic development, environmental protection, and other areas of tangible concern. Our task is to get to work on these major challenges in both campaigning *and* governing in a credible way that inspires confidence and enthusiasm. As that happens, hot-button attack politics will increasingly be seen as the sham that it is.

Finally, a word about citizenship. In politics, we expect people and groups to express their wants and interests vigorously, and public officials expect to be judged on how effectively they respond. But in a democracy we require something more. Joseph Tussman's account of the dual roles citizens are called on to play is suggestive:

> Each citizen is a member, a subject, a private person free within the common limits to pursue his own ends. But each is also an agent of the body politic, a ruler, a manner of the sovereign tribunal with all of the duties, obligations, and responsibilities that go with that role. . . .
> The citizen, in his political capacity . . . is asked public, not private questions: "Do we need more public schools?" not "Would I like to pay more taxes?" He must, in this capacity, be concerned with the public interest, not with his private goods. His communication must be collegial, not manipulative. He must deliberate, not bargain.[21]

Although some may regard such notions as unrealistic, they actually remind us of the centrality of civic virtue—the ability and the willingness to make the common good one's own—to democracy. Unless we can strike a better balance between private and public interests in our politics and until citizens and officials alike assume greater responsibility for the common good, I believe that our problems will continue to defy solution and our politics will continue to breed cynicism and disillusionment.

This need was underscored by one of the unhappiest episodes of my first five years in the House, the passage and subsequent repeal of the bill to add major medical, or "catastrophic," coverage to Medicare. This measure, enacted in 1988, inspired indiscriminate attacks on the "seniors-only surtax" by the National Committee to Preserve Social Security and other groups and a firestorm of protest among senior citizens. I received some 3,000 letters opposing the bill, and the topic dominated my community meetings during most of 1989. On one occasion, after hearing an especially long litany of complaints—some quite legitimate but others based on wildly inaccurate notions of the insurance value of Medicare or of what the new provisions would require—I turned to one particularly angry questioner. Most people seemed to agree the added benefits were needed, I observed, but they objected strenuously to the supplemental premium that would be imposed to cover the cost. As far as I knew, I told my constituent, there were three alternatives—and only three—to choose from. Would he have us impose an even greater payroll tax on younger workers, which was already the way we were paying for Part A of Medicare (hospital coverage)? Would he have us turn to the already depleted U.S. Treasury, which was already the way we were paying for most of Part B (doctors' coverage)? Or should we ask the beneficiaries, especially better-off beneficiaries, to bear more of the cost themselves?[22] Instead of giving an answer, the man bristled in anger: "You have no right to ask me that! That's *your* job!"

Though I obviously erred tactically in this instance, I believe my constituent was profoundly wrong: I was justified in asking him how he would solve the problem and, even if he owed no answer to me personally, he had an obligation to think about the issue in terms that went beyond his personal desire not to pay. But this larger obligation of citizenship escaped him entirely. My 1989 Senior Citizens' Luncheon, held a few weeks later, offered a more encouraging example. After a series of largely negative questions and comments on the catastrophic coverage issue, one man arose to announce that he was tiring of the complaints. What we really ought to be considering, he declared eloquently, was why we, as a nation, were spending so much more on older people than we were on the needs of the children who represented our future. The room fell into an embarrassed silence, and the tone of the meeting was totally transformed thereafter. I was quite relieved, of course, but also genuinely moved, for I had witnessed the kind of civic virtue—the assumption of responsibility for the commonweal—that is all too rare in our politics nowadays.

The narrow perspectives that citizens, groups, and leaders often bring to politics result in unproductive standoffs and stand in the way of genuine solutions. The coming debate over health care reform, which many groups and interests will find profoundly threatening, seems certain to provoke defensive maneuvers and attempts at obstruction—and then much hand-wringing about how the system does not work. But the status quo is also threatening and is simply not going to be dealt with effectively unless those concerned are able to transcend the politics of self-protection. This is not a plea, I hasten to add, for removing all conflict from politics: Good citizens still find plenty to debate about. But our country needs a broader and more visionary debate about how *all* of our people are faring and about how to secure our common future. We are unlikely to frame that debate satisfactorily or to meet our challenges decisively unless and until we recapture a strong sense of citizenship.

This need is especially acute for public officials. A central part of my job is to become aware of the interests of my variegated constituents and to respond in appropriate ways. These wants and interests are especially apt to gain my attention and respect when they are formulated with a due regard for the good of the whole. But whether they are or not, that is the context into which I am obligated to place them.

The member of Congress is not entirely on his or her own in seeking and promoting this broader view. The various checkpoints through which a measure must pass may temper its biases and oversights; certainly, a major benefit of strengthened party leadership should be the transcending of interest group or industry "wish lists" and an increased capacity to draft and pass legislation in the public interest. However, just as members have a wide latitude in how they define their jobs, so are we ultimately responsible for how we define and how vigorously we pursue the good of the community. The job has many satisfactions and challenges but none greater than the opportunity it daily affords to act on the imperatives of citizenship.

Notes

CHAPTER 1

1. See David E. Price, "Roll Call: A Congressman Looks Back at Those Who Went Before," Raleigh *News and Observer*, July 30, 1989, p. 1D.

2. David E. Price, "The House of Representatives: A Report from the Field," in Lawrence C. Dodd and Bruce I. Oppenheimer, eds., *Congress Reconsidered*, 4th ed. (Washington, D.C.: Congressional Quarterly Press, 1989), chapter 17.

3. For a historical perspective on this "ancient but now slightly shopworn American custom," see Nelson W. Polsby, "Congress-Bashing for Beginners," *The Public Interest* 100 (Summer 1990), pp. 15–23: "Congress-bashing [in the early 1960s, mainly by liberals] was what people did when they controlled the presidency but didn't control Congress. And that, in part, is what Congress-bashing [mainly by Republicans and conservatives] is about now" (p. 17).

4. Thomas P. O'Neill, *Man of the House* (New York: Random House, 1987), chapter 1: "You can be the most important congressman in the country, but you had better not forget the people back home. I wish I had a dime for every politician I've known who had to learn that lesson the hard way. I've seen so many good people come to Washington, where they get so worked up over important national issues that they lose the connection to their own constituents. Before they know it, some new guy comes along and sends them packing" (p. 26).

CHAPTER 2

1. My experiences in Tennessee led to an effort to measure the electoral effect of voter-contact activities and a conviction that such activities should be an integral part of state and county party operations. See David E. Price, "Volunteers for Gore: The Evolution of a Campaign," *Soundings* 44 (Spring 1971), pp. 57–72, and David E. Price and Michael Lupfer, "Volunteers for Gore: The Impact of a Precinct-level Canvass in Three Tennessee Cities," *The Journal of Politics* 35 (May 1973), pp. 410–438.

2. *Report* of the Commission on Presidential Nomination (Washington, D.C.: Democratic National Committee, 1982), p. 1. For an account of the commission's efforts and rationale, see David E. Price, *Bringing Back the Parties* (Washington, D.C.: Congressional Quarterly Press, 1984), chapters 6–7.

3. Quoted in William D. Snider, *Helms and Hunt: The North Carolina Senate Race, 1984* (Chapel Hill: University of North Carolina Press, 1985), p. 203.

4. My first reference here was to my amendment, initially added to the Financial Crimes Prosecution and Recovery Act of 1990 in the Banking Committee and eventually included in the Crime Control Act of 1990, to authorize regulators to disallow extravagant severance payments ("golden parachutes") to the executives of failing financial institutions. The second reference was to the Savings Association Law Enforcement Improvement Act of 1990, an effort to step up prosecution of S & L fraud.

5. Van Denton, "Carrington Bombards Airwaves Hoping to Oust Price," Raleigh *News and Observer*, October 23, 1990, p. 1A.

6. *Congressional Quarterly Almanac*, 46 (1990), p. 903.

7. Gary Jacobson, "Running Scared: Elections and Congressional Politics in the 1980's," in Matthew McCubbins and Terry Sullivan, eds., *Congress: Structure and Policy* (New York: Cambridge University Press, 1987), pp. 61–65.

8. *Congressional Quarterly Almanac*.

9. Republicans won at least once in 230 districts over the decade. Rhodes Cook, "Self-Inflicted Wounds Cost GOP Majority in 80s," *Congressional Quarterly Weekly Report*, March 3, 1990, pp. 687–691. For an analysis of continuing Democratic control of the House in the face of Republican presidential victories, see Gary Jacobson, "The Persistence of Democratic House Majorities," in Gary W. Cox and Samuel Kernell, eds., *The Politics of Divided Government* (Boulder, Colo.: Westview Press, 1991), chapter 4. Jacobson concluded that political factors (quality of candidates, their policy positions, and voters' reactions to them) are far more important than structural factors (incumbency advantages, gerrymandered districts, biases of the campaign finance system) in producing this partisan result.

CHAPTER 3

1. Richard F. Fenno, Jr., "Adjusting to the U.S. Senate," in Gerald C. Wright, Jr., Leroy N. Rieselbach, and Lawrence C. Dodd, eds., *Congress and Policy Change* (New York: Agathon Press, 1986), p. 142.

2. Ibid., p. 123.

3. A 1990 survey found that some 54 House members and 14 senators had earlier served on congressional staffs. "One Out of Eight Sitting Members Was Once a Staffer, Survey by Roll Call Finds," *Roll Call*, May 28, 1990, p. 3.

4. Fenno, "Adjusting to the Senate," p. 126.

5. On this point, Fenno's ex-professor seems to agree: "You need to establish a set of priorities. . . . Don't let yourself be a piece of cloth pulled at from every side. Don't let yourself unravel." Ibid., p. 128.

6. Presumably, it would not suit journalist Fred Barnes, who, in a profile of John Hiler (R.-Indiana), concluded that "the daily routine of House members is mindlessly hectic and stupefyingly dull." See his "The Unbearable Lightness of Being a Congressman," *The New Republic*, February 15, 1988, p. 19. Barnes provided an enlightening account of Hiler's schedule in Washington and at home, but it was apparently beyond his comprehension that a member could find visiting a local nursing home or addressing Jaycees interesting or worthwhile. Barnes is not alone in this attitude among Washington-based journalists; his amazement is

shared, for example, by George Will in his account of the retirement of Don Pease (D.-Ohio): "A Good Job Gone," *Washington Post* (national weekly edition), November 25, 1991, p. 29.

7. For an attempt to operationalize the showhorse-workhorse typologies and to discuss the conditions of their occurrence, see James L. Payne, "Show Horses and Work Horses in the United States House of Representatives," *Polity* 12 (Spring 1980), pp. 428–456. Payne found that the orientations are indeed distinctive, with few members ranking high on both "legislative work" and "publicity" indices. He also found evidence that "being a show horse pays off electorally" and is far less costly than it once was in terms of advancement within the House.

8. One of Fenno's senators, for example, was having a great deal of trouble settling down to work in Washington. Having stressed in his campaign that his opponent had lost touch with home, he now lived in mortal fear that the same would be said about him. Therefore, he continued "immersing himself in his home state and avoiding the work of the Senate." See Fenno's "Adjusting to the Senate," pp. 130–131.

CHAPTER 4

1. David E. Price et al., *The Commerce Committees* (New York: Grossman, 1975), and David E. Price, "The Impact of Reform: The House Commerce Subcommittee on Oversight and Investigations," in Leroy N. Rieselbach, ed., *Legislative Reform* (Lexington, Mass.: Lexington Books, 1978).

2. See the discussion and listing in Roger H. Davidson and Walter J. Oleszek, *Congress and Its Members*, 3d ed. (Washington, D.C.: Congressional Quarterly Press, 1990), pp. 294–299; also see Susan Webb Hammond, "Congressional Caucuses in the Policy Process," in Lawrence C. Dodd and Bruce I. Oppenheimer, eds., *Congress Reconsidered*, 4th ed. (Washington, D.C.: Congressional Quarterly Press, 1989), chapter 14.

3. Davidson and Oleszek, *Congress and Its Members*, p. 294.

4. Richard A. Mendel, *Workforce Literacy in the South*, A report for the Sunbelt Institute, study cochaired by representatives David Price and Hal Rogers (Chapel Hill, N.C.: MDC, 1988).

5. Data taken from relevant numbers of the *Congressional Quarterly Almanac*. A member's party-support score indicates on what percentage of the votes that divided majorities of the two parties he or she voted with the majority of his or her own party. The average party-support score for all House Democrats in 1989–1990 was 82. On general trends in party voting, see Chapter 6.

CHAPTER 5

1. Robert A. Dahl, *Pluralist Democracy in the United States: Conflict and Consent* (Chicago, Ill.: Rand McNally, 1967), p. 136. Dahl qualified this view considerably in later editions. See, for example, *Democracy in the United States: Promise and Performance*, 4th ed. (Boston, Mass.: Houghton Mifflin, 1981), pp. 135–138.

2. See especially Richard Fenno, *The Power of the Purse: Appropriations Politics in Congress* (Boston, Mass.: Little, Brown, 1966), and the essays collected in Ralph Huitt and Robert L. Peabody, eds., *Congress: Two Decades of Analysis* (New York: Harper & Row, 1969).

3. David E. Price, *Who Makes the Laws?* (Cambridge, Mass.: Schenkman, 1972).

4. For a summary and update of these findings, see David E. Price, "Congressional Committees in the Policy Process," in Lawrence C. Dodd and Bruce I. Oppenheimer, eds., *Congress Reconsidered*, 3d ed. (Washington, D.C.: Congressional Quarterly Press, 1985), chapter 7.

5. See David E. Price, "Professionals and 'Entrepreneurs': Staff Orientations and Policy Making on Three Senate Committees," *Journal of Politics* 31 (May 1971): pp. 316–336.

6. Roger H. Davidson and Carol Hardy, "Indicators of House of Representatives Workload and Activity," Congressional Research Service Report 87–4925, June 8, 1987, pp. 13, 32, 63, and Ilona B. Nickels, "The Legislative Workload of the Congress: Numbers are Misleading," *CRS Review*, July/August 1988, pp. 23–24. These articles also point up a number of difficulties in using such data as a precise indicator of the falloff in legislative initiative. Data on numbers of bills introduced are especially problematic because of changes in the rules of cosponsorship in the House. The increasing tendency to bundle complex budget and other measures together has resulted in fewer—but also longer—bills; at the same time, the growing popularity of commemorative bills and resolutions has kept the overall number of enactments deceptively high. For a survey that, overall, discerns "a sudden and striking contraction" in congressional workload indicators during the 1980s, see Roger H. Davidson, "The New Centralization on Capitol Hill," *Review of Politics* 50 (Summer 1988), pp. 352–355.

7. On the incentives to policy entrepreneurship provided by "environmental factors," especially perceived levels of public salience and conflict, see David E. Price, *Policymaking in Congressional Committees: The Impact of "Environmental" Factors* (Tucson: University of Arizona Press, 1979).

8. On the place of "interested outsiders" in committee affairs, see Richard Fenno, *Congressmen in Committees* (Boston, Mass.: Little, Brown, 1973), p. 15 and passim.

9. *Congressional Quarterly Almanac* 45 (1989), p. 655.

10. National Housing Task Force, *A Decent Place to Live* (Washington, D.C.: National Housing Task Force, 1988), pp. 18–25.

11. Testimony of Chapel Hill Mayor Jonathan B. Howes, *Affordable Housing*, field hearing before the Subcommittee on Housing and Community Development, Committee on Banking, Finance, and Urban Affairs, U.S. House of Representatives, 101st Congress, January 26, 1990 (serial no. 101–75), pp. 14, 153. See also the exchanges on pp. 33–40.

12. Testimony of Floyd T. Carter, ibid., p. 124.

CHAPTER 6

1. Richard Fenno, *Home Style: House Members in Their Districts* (Boston, Mass.: Little, Brown, 1978), p. 244.

2. For useful accounts that root strengthened party operations in the profit-and-loss calculations of individual members (especially liberal Democrats), see Barbara Sinclair, "Strong Party Leadership in a Weak Party Era—The Evolution of Party Leadership in the Modern House," paper prepared for delivery at the Carl Albert Center, University of Oklahoma, April 12, 1990, and David W. Rohde, *Parties and Leaders in the Postreform House* (Chicago, Ill.: University of Chicago Press, 1991).

3. Roger Davidson, "The New Centralization on Capitol Hill," *Review of Politics* 50 (Summer 1988), pp. 350–351.

4. "Three important goals for the Democrats are to enhance the authority of the Speaker; make sure that Democratic membership on legislative committees is representative; and to increase the individual responsibility of each Democrat toward his leaders." Richard Bolling, *House Out of Order* (New York: E.P. Dutton, 1965), pp. 236–238.

5. Sidney Waldman, "Majority Leadership in the House of Representatives," *Political Science Quarterly* 95 (Fall 1980), pp. 383–385.

6. Steven S. Smith and Christopher J. Deering, *Committees in Congress*, 2d ed. (Washington, D.C.: Congressional Quarterly Press, 1990), pp. 179–189.

7. Davidson, "New Centralization," p. 355.

8. For a survey of postreform Democratic factions and an account of the "considerable increase in Democratic unity and cohesion," see Rohde, *Parties and Leaders*, pp. 45–58.

9. Davidson, "New Centralization," p. 358.

10. Lawrence C. Dodd and Bruce I. Oppenheimer, "Consolidating Power in the House: The Rise of a New Oligarchy," in Lawrence C. Dodd and Bruce I. Oppenheimer, eds., *Congress Reconsidered*, 4th ed. (Washington, D.C.: Congressional Quarterly Press, 1989), p. 60.

11. Sinclair, "Strong Party Leadership," p. 46. Rohde aptly termed this system "conditional party government," reflective both of the goals of congressional reformers and of modern electoral realities: "Unlike in parliamentary systems, party would not be the dominant influence across all issues, and the leadership would not make policy decisions which would receive automatic support from the rank and file. Rather, the direction of influence would be reversed and there would be party responsibility *only* if there were widespread policy agreement among House Democrats. When agreement was present on a matter that was important to party members, the leadership would be expected to use the tools at their disposal to advance the cause." *Parties and Leaders*, p. 31; see also p. 166.

12. For an inventory of possible changes ranging from state law to presidential nomination rules, see David E. Price, *Bringing Back the Parties* (Washington, D.C.: Congressional Quarterly Press, 1984), chapters 5–8. For a list of party-strengthening campaign finance reforms more ambitious than the ones outlined here, see ibid., pp. 254–260.

13. This is not to say that limits on party contributions or expenditures should be lifted entirely. Not only would such a change heavily favor well-financed Republican organizations, it could also put parties more completely under candidate control, encouraging their use as mere conduits for funds generated elsewhere. See ibid., p. 258.

14. "Soft money" is money given to parties outside the prohibitions and limitations of federal law. It is most commonly given to state parties under state law, which is generally less restrictive than federal law and in some cases permits direct corporate and union contributions. These funds have often been used, sometimes quite liberally, to benefit federal (especially presidential) candidates.

15. These are essentially the suggestions I made in testimony before the Task Force on Campaign Finance Reform of the Committee on House Administration; see the hearings on *Campaign Finance Reform*, April 30, 1991, pp. 168–183.

16. See Price, *Bringing Back the Parties*, pp. 280–282.

17. Ibid., p. 55, and relevant numbers of the *Congressional Quarterly Almanac*.

18. One glaring example is an amendment my colleague Martin Lancaster (D.-North Carolina) proposed but was not allowed to offer to the Americans with Disabilities Act in 1990. The amendment, which the disabilities lobby opposed but felt would be difficult to defeat, would have required a disabled individual to inform the owner of a public facility of his or her disability and to make suggestions for accommodations before bringing suit, thus encouraging the resolution of problems short of litigation.

19. See Rohde, *Parties and Leaders*, pp. 47, 78–81. On the particularly instructive case of Rep. (now Sen.) Phil Gramm, who was able to convince his constituents that his richly deserved party discipline was a badge of honor, see Price, *Bringing Back the Parties*, p. 67.

20. See the episodes recounted in John M. Barry, *The Ambition and the Power* (New York: Viking, 1989), pp. 393, 542–543.

21. Edmund Burke, "Thoughts on the Cause of the Present Discontents," in his *Works*, 3d ed., vol. 1 (Boston, Mass.: Little, Brown, 1871), p. 526.

CHAPTER 7

1. The exact numbers were 122 Republicans and 20 Democrats. See votes no. 49–52, *Congressional Quarterly Almanac*, 43 (1987), pp. 18H–19H.

2. Allen Schick, *Congress and Money* (Washington, D.C.: Urban Institute, 1980), p. 361.

3. David A. Stockman, *The Triumph of Politics* (New York: Avon Books, 1987), p. 409.

4. *Congressional Quarterly Weekly Report*, April 11, 1987, p. 659.

5. On this point and for an excellent account of executive and congressional roles in the deficit-making of the early 1980s, see Paul E. Peterson, "The New Politics of Deficits," in John E. Chubb and Paul E. Peterson, eds., *The New Direction in American Politics* (Washington, D.C.: Brookings Institution, 1985), chapter 13.

6. *Congressional Quarterly Almanac*, 45 (1989), p. 85.

7. Richard G. Darman, "Beyond the Deficit Problem: 'Me-Now-ism' and 'The New Balance'," address to the National Press Club, Washington, D.C., July 20, 1989, pp. 5, 7.

8. Alan Murray and John Young, "Lingering Animosity from Capital-Gains Fight Threatens Bipartisan Efforts on Cutting Deficit," *Wall Street Journal*, October 5, 1989, p. A30. For a slightly different interpretation of Darman's machinations,

see Jeffrey Bell, "The Bush Administration's Budgetary Monte Hall," *Washington Post* (national weekly edition), September 25, 1989, p. 23.

9. Bush's budgets were thereafter subjected to annual votes on the House floor. The results were invariably embarrassing to the administration: an 89–325 defeat on April 17, 1991, and a 42–370 defeat on March 4, 1992.

10. *Congressional Quarterly Almanac*, 46 (1990), p. 130.

11. Ibid., p. 131.

12. "Now for the House Republicans," *Washington Post*, October 3, 1990, p. A22.

13. Quoted in Helen Dewar and Tom Kenworthy, "Conservative Republicans Assail Budget Pact; Democrats Sceptical," *Washington Post*, October 1, 1990, p. A8.

14. Robin Toner, "Sour View of Congress Emerges from Survey," *New York Times*, October 12, 1990, p. A21.

15. This was viewed not merely as a rate increase but as the correction of an apparent anomaly in the 1986 budget reform legislation, whereby the effective marginal rate was 33 percent for joint filers earning between $78,400 and $185,760 (the so-called bubble) but reverted to 28 percent for those earning more.

16. Elizabeth Drew, "Letter from Washington," *The New Yorker*, November 12, 1990, p. 116.

17. This provision, had it stood alone, would have provided a modest reduction for those in the bubble, as well as an increase for those earning more than $185,760. The net revenue gain for this provision, along with an increase in the alternative minimum tax from 21 to 24 percent, was estimated to be $11.2 billion over five years.

18. Quoted in John Yang, "The One-for-You, Two-for-Me School of Budgeting," *Washington Post* (national weekly edition), February 11, 1991, p. 8.

19. Projections of the underlying standardized-employment deficit, with the business cycle's effects on federal revenues and outlays removed and with Desert Storm contributions and deposit insurance expenditures and receipts excluded, were relatively constant, in the $164- to $188-billion range from 1991–1996. "In relation to the size of the economy, such deficits are no better than those of the late 1980s and considerably worse than the average of the 1960s and 1970s." Congressional Budget Office, "The Economic and Budget Outlook: An Update," A Report to the Senate and House Committees on the Budget, August 1991, pp. XI, XIII, and 16.

20. Jim Sasser, "The Budget Follies Have to Stop," *New York Times*, July 29, 1991, p. A15. Sasser also suggested where he thought the cutting should start: the space station, the superconducting supercollider, and various big-ticket weapons systems.

21. Lester C. Thurow, "The Budget Catastrophe and the Big Lie Behind It," *Washington Post* (national weekly edition), October 15, 1990, p. 23.

22. David R. Mayhew, *Divided We Govern: Party Control, Lawmaking, and Investigations, 1946–1990* (New Haven, Conn.: Yale University Press, 1991). On the weakness of the relationship, over time, between unified party control and "budgetary coherence," see pp. 185–191.

CHAPTER 8

1. Richard Fenno, *Home Style: House Members in Their Districts* (Boston, Mass.: Little, Brown, 1978), p. 172.

2. For a sophisticated analysis of the relation of constituency services to electoral success, see Douglas Rivers and Morris P. Fiorina, "Constituency Service, Reputation, and the Incumbency Advantage," in Morris P. Fiorina and David W. Rohde, eds., *Home Style and Washington Work* (Ann Arbor: University of Michigan Press, 1989), pp. 17–45.

3. Richard Fenno, *Congressmen in Committees* (Boston, Mass.: Little, Brown, 1973), pp. 48–49.

4. See the fuller discussion in David E. Price, "Congressional Committees in the Policy Process," in Lawrence C. Dodd and Bruce I. Oppenheimer, eds., *Congress Reconsidered*, 3d ed. (Washington, D.C.: Congressional Quarterly Press, 1985), pp. 171–173.

5. See *Affordable Housing*, field hearing before the Subcommittee on Housing and Community Development, Committee on Banking, Finance, and Urban Affairs, U.S. House of Representatives, 101st Congress, January 26, 1990 (serial no. 101–75), pp. 60–61, 65–67.

CHAPTER 9

1. Seymour has given an account of his ministry, particularly as it concerned the struggle for racial justice, in *"Whites Only": A Pastor's Retrospective on Signs of the New South* (Valley Forge, Pa.: Judson Press, 1991).

2. Martin Luther King, Jr., "Letter from Birmingham Jail," in Herbert J. Storing, ed., *What Country Have I? Political Writings by Black Americans* (New York: St. Martin's Press, 1970), p. 128.

3. Ibid., p. 127.

4. Rev. Jerry Falwell, "Special Memorandum to Pastors," March 7, 1988.

5. *Congressional Record* (daily edition), March 22, 1988, p. H-1041.

6. I Sam. 8:20.

7. H. Richard Niebuhr, *Christ and Culture* (New York: Harper and Brothers, 1956), p. 2.

8. See Harry R. Davis and Robert C. Good, eds., *Reinhold Niebuhr on Politics* (New York: Charles Scribner's Sons, 1960), chapters 12–14. Quotations are from p. 148.

9. Thomas Aquinas, *Summa Theologica*, Question 92, article 1. Reprinted in D. Bigongiari, ed., *The Political Ideas of St. Thomas Aquinas* (New York: Hafner, 1953), pp. 24–26.

10. Gov. Mario Cuomo, "Religious Belief and Public Morality: A Catholic Governor's Perspective." Paper prepared for delivery at the University of Notre Dame, Notre Dame, Indiana, September 13, 1984, pp. 4–5.

11. *Westside Community Board of Education v. Mergens*, 110 S. Ct. 2356 (June 4, 1990).

12. Davis and Good, eds., *Niebuhr on Politics*, p. 186.

13. James Madison, "The Federalist," no. 51, in Clinton Rossiter, ed., *The Federalist Papers* (New York: Mentor Books, 1961), p. 322.

14. II Sam. 12:9.

15. Philip Stern, ed., *The Life and Writings of Abraham Lincoln* (New York: Modern Library, 1940), p. 841.

16. Francis B. Carpenter, *Six Months at the White House with Abraham Lincoln* (New York: Herd and Houghton, 1867), p. 282.

17. Amos 5:24.

18. Isa. 55:8.

CHAPTER 10

1. Bruce Jennings and Daniel Callahan, eds., *Representation and Responsibility: Exploring Legislative Ethics* (New York: Plenum Press, 1985), and Daniel Callahan and Bruce Jennings, *The Ethics of Legislative Life* (Hastings-on-Hudson, N.Y.: Hastings Center, 1980).

2. Bernard Bailyn, *The Ideological Origins of the American Revolution* (Cambridge, Mass.: Belknap Press, 1967), chapter 3, and James Sterling Young, *The Washington Community, 1800–1828* (New York: Harcourt, Brace, and World, 1966), chapter 3.

3. Young, *Washington Community*, pp. 56, 59.

4. A useful overview is provided in Richard Allan Baker, "The History of Congressional Ethics," in Jennings and Callahan, eds., *Representation and Responsibility*, chapter 1.

5. Rep. Vic Fazio, in *Congressional Record* (daily edition), November 16, 1989, p. H-8745.

6. Dennis F. Thompson, *Political Ethics and Public Office* (Cambridge, Mass.: Harvard University Press, 1987), p. 10.

7. Callahan and Jennings, *Ethics of Legislative Life*, pp. 53, 55.

8. Ibid., pp. 34–42. This framework was first developed by Amy Gutmann and Dennis Thompson in "The Theory of Legislative Ethics," in Jennings and Callahan, eds., *Representation and Responsibility*, chapter 9.

9. Callahan and Jennings, *Ethics of Legislative Life*, p. 55. Note the aspirational character of most of their suggested "next steps," pp. 60–62. For a more cautious view, see John D. Saxon, "The Scope of Legislative Ethics," in Jennings and Callahan, eds., *Representation and Responsibility*, chapter 10.

10. See David E. Price, "Assessing Policy," in Joel L. Fleishman et al., eds., *Public Duties: The Moral Obligations of Public Officials* (Cambridge, Mass.: Harvard University Press, 1981), chapter 6.

11. Thompson, *Political Ethics*, pp. 96, 101.

12. David Braybrooke and Charles E. Lindblom, *A Strategy of Decision* (New York: Free Press, 1963), chapters 3 and 5 and passim.

13. Ibid., p. 206. The authors also claimed that the strategy conveniently compensates for some of the defects commonly attributed to utilitarianism (pp. 212–223).

14. See Brian Barry, *Political Argument* (London: Routledge and Kegan Paul, 1965), chapters 10–11.

15. Studies influential in the 1988 debate included Gerald Corrigan, *Financial Market Structure: A Longer View* (Federal Reserve Bank of New York, 1987); Federal Deposit Insurance Corporation, *Mandate for Change* (Washington, D.C.: Federal Deposit Insurance Corporation, 1987); and Committee on Government Operations, U.S. House of Representatives, *Modernization of the Financial Service Industry* (1988). The Bush administration proposed a similar reform plan in 1991, and the House Banking Committee reported a broad-gauged bill. But advocates failed to articulate a compelling public interest rationale, and the effort fell victim to the same forces that had proven fatal in 1988.

16. Rawls's theory of justice places a burden of proof on social and economic arrangements: Do they maximize the well-being of the "least advantaged" members of society? This might not always require giving first priority to those most in need, but assistance to other groups would depend on whether it improved the lot of those who were worst off in the long run. John Rawls, *A Theory of Justice* (Cambridge, Mass.: Harvard University Press, 1971), chapter 13 and passim.

17. Testimony of Elaine T. Ostrowski, *Affordable Housing*, field hearing before the Subcommittee on Housing and Community Development, Committee on Banking, Finance, and Urban Affairs, U.S. House of Representatives, 101st Congress, January 26, 1990 (serial no. 101–75), p. 97.

18. An earlier but more detailed version of what follows may be found in David E. Price, "Legislative Ethics in the New Congress," in Jennings and Callahan, eds., *Representation and Responsibility*, chapter 7.

19. Donald R. Matthews, *U.S. Senators and Their World* (New York: Vintage Books, 1960), p. 92. Fenno likewise drew heavily on concepts from functionalist social science—role, function, integration, and adaptation—terms that suggested that members conformed to the institutional environment more than they shaped it. See Richard Fenno, "The House Appropriations Committee as a Political System: The Problem of Integration," *American Political Science Review* 56 (June 1962), pp. 310–324, and *The Power of the Purse: Appropriations Politics in Congress* (Boston, Mass.: Little, Brown, 1966).

20. David R. Mayhew, *Congress: The Electoral Connection* (New Haven, Conn.: Yale University Press, 1974), p. 5.

21. See Brian Barry's exposition of "sociological" and "economic" modes of social analysis in *Sociologists, Economists, and Democracy* (London: Collier-Macmillan, 1970.)

22. Mayhew, *Electoral Connection*, pp. 49–77.

23. Braybrooke and Lindblom, *Strategy of Decision*, pp. 185–86. In chapter 10, these analysts proceeded to treat "disjointed incrementalism" as a tolerable substitute for—and in some ways an improvement on—utilitarianism's felicific calculus.

24. See, for example, E. E. Schattschneider, *The Semi-Sovereign People* (New York: Holt, Rinehart and Winston, 1960), chapter 2; Theodore J. Lowi, *The End of Liberalism*, 2d ed. (New York: W. W. Norton, 1979), chapter 3; Robert Paul Wolff, *The Poverty of Liberalism* (Boston, Mass.: Beacon Press, 1968), chapter 4; and

Mancur Olson, Jr., *The Logic of Collective Action* (New York: Schocken Books, 1968), chapter 5.

25. The phrase is Schattschneider's; see *Semi-Sovereign People*, chapters 1–2.

26. Mayhew, *Electoral Connection*, p. 117.

27. On this latter point, see Richard F. Fenno, Jr., *Home Style: House Members in Their Districts* (Boston, Mass.: Little, Brown, 1978), pp. 240–244.

28. Ibid., p. 243.

29. Edmund Burke, "Thoughts on the Cause of the Present Discontents," in his *Works*, 3d ed., vol. 1 (Boston, Mass.: Little, Brown, 1871), p. 526; emphasis added.

30. Ibid., p. 533.

31. Jacob K. Javits, *Javits: The Autobiography of a Public Man* (Boston, Mass.: Houghton Mifflin, 1981), p. 134.

32. See Chapter 6 and David E. Price, *Bringing Back the Parties* (Washington, D.C.: Congressional Quarterly Press, 1984), pp. 51–57.

33. Norman J. Ornstein, ed., *The Role of the Legislature in Western Democracies* (Washington, D.C.: American Enterprise Institute, 1981), pp. 96–97.

34. For discussions of various techniques—and difficulties—of "explanation," see John W. Kingdon, *Congressmen's Voting Decisions*, 2d ed. (New York: Harper & Row, 1981), pp. 47–54, and Fenno, *Home Style*, chapter 5.

35. Ibid., pp. 164, 166.

36. Ibid., pp. 168, 246.

37. James Madison, "The Federalist," no. 51, in Clinton Rossiter, ed., *The Federalist Papers* (New York: Mentor Books, 1961), p. 322.

38. Mayhew, *Electoral Connection*, pp. 141–158; see also David E. Price, "Congressional Committees in the Policy Process," in Lawrence C. Dodd and Bruce I. Oppenheimer, eds., *Congress Reconsidered*, 3d ed. (Washington, D.C.: Congressional Quarterly Press, 1985), pp. 168–175.

39. "Socialization and Ethics in Congress," in Jennings and Callahan, eds., *Representation and Responsibility*, pp. 110–116.

CHAPTER 11

1. Quoted in Helen Dewar, "It's Better to Look Good Than to Do Good," *Washington Post* (national weekly edition), December 2, 1991, p. 12.

2. On this latter point, see Lester C. Thurow, *The Zero-Sum Society* (New York: Basic Books, 1980), pp. 212–214.

3. "The policies we implement in the name of justice, and the deliberations we undertake as to what the common good or the public interest requires, should be (and for most people, I believe, are) underwritten by a sense of social interdependence, of mutual sympathy and shared purpose, and of responsibility for one another's and the collectivity's well-being." David E. Price, "Assessing Policy: Conceptual Points of Departure," in Joel L. Fleishman et al., eds., *Public Duties: The Moral Obligations of Public Officials* (Cambridge, Mass.: Harvard University Press, 1981), pp. 166–167. Complementary pieces include my "Community and Control: Critical Democratic Theory in the Progressive Period," *American Political*

Science Review 68 (December 1974), pp. 1663–1678, and "Community, 'Mediating Structures,' and Public Policy," *Soundings* 62 (Winter 1979), pp. 369–394. I drew particularly on Robert Paul Wolff's notion of "rational community" in *The Poverty of Liberalism* (Boston, Mass.: Beacon Press, 1968), chapter 5, and on John Dewey's concept of the democratic public, as developed in his *The Public and Its Problems* (New York: Henry Holt, 1927).

4. I expressed some of this in an otherwise appreciative review of Richard Fenno's *Congressmen in Committees*, which appeared in *American Political Science Review* 71 (June 1977), pp. 701–704.

5. Robert Bendiner's *Obstacle Course on Capitol Hill* (New York: McGraw-Hill, 1964) was an account of frustrated efforts to pass aid-to-education legislation; Richard Bolling's *House Out of Order* (New York: E. P. Dutton, 1965) was a brief for reform by a prominent House member. See also Morris K. Udall's newsletters from the 1960s, reprinted in *Education of a Congressman*, edited by Robert L. Peabody (New York: Bobbs-Merrill, 1972), especially chapters 19–22.

6. The study that I directed, *The Commerce Committees* (New York: Grossman, 1975), although completed within a few months, was published almost three years later as one of a set of six volumes.

7. Mark J. Green, James M. Fallows, and David R. Zwick, *Who Runs Congress? The President, Big Business, or You?* (New York: Bantam Books, 1972).

8. Ibid., p. 94.

9. Jonathan Alter et al., "The World of Congress," *Newsweek*, April 24, 1989, pp. 28–34. Obey's comments were made in an address to the Center for National Policy (CNP) on May 10, 1989, p. 5. For a later elaboration of many of these themes, see Obey's extended comments on the House floor: *Congressional Record* (daily edition), November 5, 1991, pp. H-9377–H-9383.

10. Alter et al., "World of Congress," pp. 29–30, 32. Concerning staff, Obey responded, "I receive 50,000 letters from home each year. And you know, people who write those letters have the quaint notion that the votes I cast should be well thought out and they expect me to answer their letters. Occasionally, they even expect a thoughtful response. If staff is a perk rather than a business necessity, then why can't *Time* and *Newsweek* put out their magazines without benefit of the helping hands from their Washington reporters?" Obey, CNP address, p. 9.

11. Alter et al., "World of Congress," pp. 28–29.

12. Ibid., p. 31; Obey, CNP address, p. 10.

13. See Nelson Polsby's argument in "Congress-Bashing for Beginners," *The Public Interest* 100 (Summer 1990), p. 18–19. "The item veto," he concluded, "is a truly radical idea. . . . To espouse it requires a readiness to give up entirely on the separation of powers and on the constitutional design of the American government."

14. Mickey Edwards, "A Conservative Defense of Congress," *The Public Interest* 100 (Summer 1990), p. 83.

15. From data prepared by the staff of the House Appropriations Committee. Figures include all discretionary spending, plus those entitlements that are incorporated in annual appropriations bills.

16. A more justified cynicism might, in fact, attend the imposition of term limits. If we assume that qualified people would line up to "take their fling" at

congressional office and would thus gain expertise, what, Nelson Polsby asked, would we expect them to do on leaving office? "Make money, I suppose. Just about the time that their constituents and the American people at large could begin to expect a payoff because of the knowledge and experience that these able members had acquired at our expense, off they would go to some Washington law firm." Polsby, "Congress-Bashing," p. 21.

17. See Roger Davidson, "The New Centralization on Capitol Hill," *Review of Politics* 50 (Summer 1988), pp. 349–350, and David E. Price, "Congressional Committees in the Policy Process," in Lawrence C. Dodd and Bruce I. Oppenheimer, eds., *Congress Reconsidered*, 3d ed. (Washington, D.C.: Congressional Quarterly Press, 1985), pp. 168–175.

18. See David E. Price, "The Ambivalence of Congressional Reform," *Public Administration Review* 34, (November–December 1974), pp. 601–608, and Roger H. Davidson and Walter J. Oleszek, *Congress Against Itself* (Bloomington: Indiana University Press, 1977).

19. E. J. Dionne, Jr., *Why Americans Hate Politics* (New York: Simon and Schuster, 1991), pp. 16–17. Dionne borrowed the concept of democratic politics at its best as "the search for remedy" from Arthur Schlesinger, Jr.

20. *Congressional Quarterly Weekly Report*, October 6, 1990, p. 3224. Only a few relatively noncontroversial provisions of the crime bill—including my amendment disallowing extravagant golden parachutes for the executives of failing financial institutions—finally emerged from conference. The House improved considerably on its 1990 performance, however, when it took up a similar crime bill in 1991. The Judiciary Committee reported a better-balanced measure, and the Democratic leadership whipped the bill effectively, keeping it largely intact on the floor. Speaker Foley's personal efforts made the difference as the House approved the conference report on the bill on November 27, 1991, by a vote of 205–203. Senate Republican filibusterers and President Bush persisted in labeling the bill "pro-crime," but the Democrats' performance placed on the Republicans the onus of choosing to perpetuate an issue rather than helping devise a solution.

21. Joseph Tussman, *Obligation and the Body Politic* (New York: Oxford University Press, 1960), pp. 108, 118.

22. The supplemental premium would have been paid only by the 40 percent of beneficiaries who owed more than $150 a year in federal income tax. The maximum amount, $800, would have been paid by only the wealthiest 5.6 percent of beneficiaries. Faced with massive protests, even on the part of those who would have paid a minimal supplemental premium or nothing at all, and finding no supportive constituency, I said that I might be persuaded to repeal the program but never to shift the costs to the younger workforce. That, in effect, is what the House did on October 4, 1989.

•   •   •   •

About the Book
and Author

Everyone blames Congress; no one *explains* it. Congressman David Price, noted scholar and former professor of political science, is uniquely qualified to guide us through the labyrinth of rules, roles, and representatives that is Congress and to show us how the institution can and does function to solve some of the most pressing social problems on the national political agenda today. In an election year filled with name-calling, teeth-gnashing, and Congress-bashing, it is refreshing to hear Price discuss what it means to simultaneously serve his constituency, his country, and his strong personal convictions about good government.

As students of the political process, we are instructed in campaign strategy and finance, the advantages and disadvantages of incumbency, how to get a legislative project off the ground, the intricate House committee and subcommittee system, the tortuous route a bill travels to become law, and the strong role of parties in Congress. As voters and constituents, we are treated to firsthand accounts of election campaigns fraught with negative ads, town meetings on Medicare, fierce budget battles on the floor of the House, and persistent efforts on behalf of individual North Carolinians.

And as citizen-philosophers, we are drawn into an extended consideration of the complex interrelationships among politics, religion, and ethics. In this context, David Price looks at a variety of issues—the conscientious allocation of housing funds, the correlation between legislative structure and the quality of legislative policy, the confrontation between the public interest and special interests, and the maneuvering of the religious Right—through an introspective lens of moral concern.

Congressman David Price shares invaluable insights into debates on such topics as campaign finance reform, congressional term limits, and controlling the federal deficit. At the same time, he imparts a personal glimpse into life "on the Hill" and its impacts on family, friends, and constituents. Congress, as Price is quick to point out, is certainly not without flaws, but the system will be better served by informed voters, committed representatives, and measured reforms than by ill-considered proposals that would weaken the institution.

The Congressional Experience combines an engaging, enlightening narrative with photos, figures, maps, and tables to tell the story of David Price's odyssey from the ivory tower of Duke University to the citadel of Capitol Hill. Along the way, we get a clear sense of the challenge, disappointment, elation, and deep concern implicit in serving as a member of Congress—especially the kind of member David Price has chosen to be.

A former professor of political science at Duke University, David E. Price has represented North Carolina's Fourth Congressional District since 1987. He is an at-large Democratic Whip and a member of the Appropriations Committee. His previous publications include *Who Makes the Laws?* and *Bringing Back the Parties.*

Index

AARP. *See* American Association of
    Retired Persons
Abortion, 122, 128, 129, 132, 166
Accountability, 40, 139, 156, 160, 162,
    166
Activism/activists, 39, 58, 75, 79, 82, 127
Adams, Sherman, 138
Agenda, party, 76, 77–78, 163–164
Akaka, Daniel, 49
Amendment process, 39, 66, 76, 87–88
American Airlines, 34
American Association of Retired Persons
    (AARP), 63, 69, 71
American Bankers Association, 63
American Bar Association, 139
American Enterprise Institute, 32
Americans with Disabilities Act, 78,
    176(n18)
Andrews, Ike, 9, 11, 115
Annunzio, Frank, 60, 63
Antipower ideology, 134, 138, 164–165
Aquinas, Thomas, 131
Arms Control and Foreign Policy Caucus,
    52–53
Army Research Office, 55
Asheboro, North Carolina, 8, 35
Aspin, Les, 33, 34, 115
Atkins, Chester, 79

Bailyn, Bernard, 138
Baker, Bobby, 138
Banking reform, 61, 64, 142, 164,
    180(n15)
Baptist Student Union at UNC, 7, 126
Barnard, Doug, 70
Barnes, Fred, 172(n6)
Bartlett, E. L. ("Bob"), 3, 34, 44, 58

Bartlett, Steve, 66, 69, 70, 71
Bennett, Charles, 33
Benson, Cliff, 17(fig.)
Bentsen, Lloyd, 99
Black Caucus, Congressional, 90
Blacks, 2, 13, 75, 127
Boland, Edward, 48
Bolling, Richard, 76, 175(n4)
Bonior, David, 85
Bosworth, Barry, 55
Bowman Gray School of Medicine, 122
Braybrooke, David, 141, 142, 146
Bread for the World, 127
Brookings Institution, 32
Broyhill, James, 44
Budget and Impoundment Control Act of
    1974, 92, 93, 94
Budget issues, 48, 55, 58, 76, 78, 89, 91–
    112, 119, 120, 153, 160, 165, 167
    continuing resolutions, 96, 99, 103, 106
    deficits, 92, 93–94, 95, 102, 108–109,
        120, 155, 161, 177(n19)
    media coverage, 105
    presidential requests, 93, 94, 97, 100,
        108, 161, 177(n9)
    reconciliation process, 93, 95, 96, 99,
        106–107, 110, 120
    summitry, 92, 97–98, 99–108, 110, 111,
        165
Budget Study Group, Democratic, 37, 54,
    98, 101
Burke, Edmund, 90, 148–149
Bush, George, 21, 78, 97, 99, 101, 102,
    103, 106, 155, 165–166, 177(n9),
    183(n20)
    administration, 65, 161